ON BLACK *BANDES DESSINÉES* AND
TRANSCOLONIAL POWER

STUDIES IN COMICS AND CARTOONS
Charles Hatfield and Rebecca Wanzo, Series Editors

ON BLACK *BANDES DESSINÉES* AND TRANSCOLONIAL POWER

Michelle Bumatay

THE OHIO STATE UNIVERSITY PRESS
COLUMBUS

Copyright © 2025 by The Ohio State University.
All rights reserved.

Library of Congress Cataloging-in-Publication Data
Names: Bumatay, Michelle, author.
Title: On Black bandes dessinées and transcolonial power / Michelle Bumatay.
Other titles: Studies in comics and cartoons.
Description: Columbus : The Ohio State University Press, 2025. | Series: Studies in comics and cartoons | Includes bibliographical references and index. | Summary: "Examines the diversity of Black francophone cartoonists' aesthetic and material responses to the colonially inherited medium of bandes dessinées. Considers twentieth- and twenty-first-century comics by artists such as Pahé, Marguerite Abouet, Barly Baruti, and Papa Mfumu'Eto, among other creators from nations including the Democratic Republic of the Congo, Ivory Coast, Cameroon, and Gabon"—Provided by publisher.
Identifiers: LCCN 2024044525 | ISBN 9780814215821 (hardback) | ISBN 9780814284049 (ebook)
Subjects: LCSH: Comic books, strips, etc.—Africa, French-speaking—History and criticism. | Postcolonialism—Africa, French-speaking.
Classification: LCC PN6710 .B86 2025 | DDC 741.5/960917541—dc23/eng/20241031
LC record available at https://lccn.loc.gov/2024044525

Other identifiers: ISBN 9780814259375 (paperback)

Cover design by Sarah Flood-Baumann
Text composition by Stuart Rodriguez
Type set in Palatino Linotype

CONTENTS

List of Illustrations		vii
Acknowledgments		ix
INTRODUCTION		1
CHAPTER 1	A Tale of Two Kinshasas, or The Plurality of Everyday Postcolonialism	20
CHAPTER 2	The AYA Effect, or Marguerite Abouet's Timely and Timeless Interventions	41
CHAPTER 3	Reframing Migration in the Twenty-First Century	72
CHAPTER 4	Black *Bandes Dessinées* and Decolonial Ecocriticism	104
CODA	Black *Bandes Dessinées* and Beyond	128
Works Cited		133
Index		145

ILLUSTRATIONS

FIGURE 1.1.	Barly Baruti's celebration of Papa Wemba as King of La Sape	27
FIGURE 1.2.	Last page of *Papa Wemba*	28
FIGURE 1.3.	Papa Wemba struggles to compose a song	29
FIGURE 2.1.	Vignette title page about the pandemic lockdown in *Akissi*	59
FIGURE 2.2.	Conversation between Kouamé and Gor in *Commissaire Kouamé*	63
FIGURE 2.3.	A cameo of Abouet next to Innocent in *Aya de Yopougon*	66
FIGURE 3.1.	Gawa's static life at the edge in *An Eternity in Tangiers*	83
FIGURE 3.2.	Spectral migrants entering a detention zone in "Entre la vie et la mort"	86
FIGURE 3.3.	Borderization's human and more-than-human agents in "Si la Mer Méditerranée pouvait parler . . ."	88
FIGURE 3.4.	Didier Viodé exposes the racism of borderization in "Visa rejeté"	90
FIGURE 3.5.	Bouna's final moments in a plane's landing gear in "Le voyage de Bouna"	94
FIGURE 3.6.	Left-hand page depicting two figures' dissolving personhood in *Alpha*	100

FIGURE 3.7.	Right-hand page highlighting a White tourist in *Alpha*	101
FIGURE 4.1.	A singular splash page exalting nature in *Objectif terre!*	110
FIGURE 4.2.	The African spirit's amorphous approach in *Cargaison mortelle à Abidjan*	116
FIGURE 4.3.	The African spirit's final warning in *Cargaison mortelle à Abidjan*	118
FIGURE 4.4.	Stylized phone conversation in *Cargaison mortelle à Abidjan*	122
FIGURE 4.5.	Phone call that initiates the plot in *Aya de Yopougon*	126

ACKNOWLEDGMENTS

To say that the completion of this book has been circuitous would be an understatement. Working on Black *bandes dessinées* as they have developed and changed in real time, trying to track down rare and often ephemeral texts, changing jobs with varying levels of institutional support multiple times—all of this has meant that this project has mutated over the years. Along the way, several organizations and individuals have been instrumental in helping me conduct research and develop it into this book; without their support, *On Black* Bandes Dessinées *and Transcolonial Power* would not exist. I am grateful for the faculty development funds at Beloit College that helped me conduct research. I am equally thankful for the grant I received from FSU's Council on Research and Creativity as well as financial support from FSU's College of Arts and Sciences and I am honored to have been selected as the 2024 recipient of the Stephen Risley Family Fellowship, all of which has given me the time to finish writing and revising this book.

I consider myself very fortunate to have found generous and encouraging mentors early in my research trajectory. I am eternally grateful to Dominic Thomas for his unflinching endorsement of my research interests from the very start, even when comics studies was just burgeoning and few French and francophone studies scholars considered researching or teaching comics. For the generosity of their informal mentoring and engagement with my work over the years, I am indebted to Mark McKinney, Fabrice Leroy, Peter J. Bloom, Ann Miller, Maggie Flinn, Nancy Rose Hunt, Catherine Labio, Michelle Bloom, Billy Grove, and Joe Sutliff Sanders. I would also like thank all those who invited me to share portions of this book as I was developing it: in addition to many listed above, Hélène Blondeau at the France-Florida Research Institute at the University of Florida; Paulina Barrios and Uchechi Okereke-Beshel and the Department of African, Middle Eastern, and South Asian Languages and Literatures at Rutgers University; Frederick Luis Aldama at the University of Texas, Austin; and Peter Russella and the Department of French and Italian at the University of Wisconsin, Madison. Likewise, I am grateful to my mentors and colleagues at FSU including Martin Munro, Joseph Hellweg, Reinier Leushuis, and Irene Zanini-Cordi.

Several individuals who have fortified my writing and thinking (both directly and indirectly) have my sincere appreciation and admiration. For reading and commenting on early versions of my chapters, I thank George MacLeod and especially Katelyn E. Knox and Allison Van Deventer, whose boot camp and now book are simultaneously rigorous and accessible. *On Black* Bandes Dessinées *and Transcolonial Power* is all the richer and more cohesive thanks to Katelyn's and Allison's meticulously thoughtful prompts, questions, and feedback. Likewise, I am grateful to the professional assistance of developmental editor Julia Boss, whose discerning read of key sections helped me clarify the book's main contributions and weave together the central threads. Writing, thinking, and discussing with others (as well as laughing and dancing) have been a crucial lifeline throughout this long, meandering adventure; for all that they are and all that they do, my thanks go to Kirk Sides, Kristen Stern, Michaela Hulstyn, Alex Milsom (especially for starting a writing group at precisely the right moment), Jeannine Murray-Román, Vincent Joos, Lucy Swanson, Philippe Brand, Beth Coggeshall, and Matthew Goldmark.

My deepest gratitude goes to my family—Lynn, Andy, and Monica—for teaching me the ever urgent value of a life full of passion and predicated on compassion and to my partner, Marc, for laughing, dancing, singing, and learning with me, for always asking more questions with me, and for reminding me who I am, especially when I get lost. This book is dedicated to them.

INTRODUCTION

In December 2010, Gabonese cartoonist Patrick Essono, known as Pahé, posted a single-panel cartoon on his blog that was a sardonic snapshot of a specific moment from the Premier Salon des Auteurs Africains de Bande Dessinée (First Salon of African Comics Authors), held in Paris just steps from the Panthéon and the Sorbonne (Pahé, "Missié").[1] The cartoon features two figures drawn in Pahé's deft and deceptively simple style. On the left sits a White moderator wearing glasses and holding a microphone, while on the right sits a caricature of Pahé himself, who, in stark contrast, is drawn with all-black skin and oversized red lips.[2] This unmistakable allusion to racist Western stereotypes stands out because of Pahé's restraint and is a direct function of the commentary of the cartoon. In response to the moderator's question "Faut-il interdire Tintin au Congo?"[3] Pahé jokingly replies, "Oui au Congo! Pas au Gabon."[4] The lack of any visible difference in the lettering of the moderator's speech, such as italics or underlining, renders

---

1. All translations are mine unless otherwise indicated. Portions of this discussion of Pahé's blog post first appeared in *Research in African Literatures*; see Bumatay, "African Bande Dessinée Festivals."
2. I capitalize the term "White" to emphasize how the artists analyzed in this book visibly signal the constructedness of an identity derived from the (equally constructed) concept of whiteness.
3. "Should we ban Tintin in the Congo?"
4. "Yes, in the Congo! Not in Gabon."

his question ambiguous. Is he asking if Tintin, a fictional character, should be banned from going to the Congo, or is he asking if Hergé's 1931 album *Tintin au Congo* should be banned altogether? Pahé's retort responds to the first possible question while flippantly sidestepping the second. Pahé, whose nom de plume derives from his initials in the fashion of famous French and Belgian cartoonists, was a key guest at the Salon since, by that time, he had already gained regional fame in central Africa for his political cartoons, as well as international success thanks to his two-volume autobiographical *bande dessinée* series *La Vie de Pahé* (Pahé's life) published by Swiss-based Éditions Paquet. In addition to doing signings and interviews, he participated in a panel on the decolonization of African *bandes dessinées* organized around legal efforts in Belgium and France to censor Hergé's *Tintin au Congo* or, at least, mandate that the publisher Casterman add an insert to contextualize the colonial and paternalist ideologies espoused within. The public debate sparked by these efforts and taken up by the panel point to the polarization associated with cancel culture, especially around racist Western popular culture from the late nineteenth and early twentieth centuries. Rather than weigh in on the debate (at least in the cartoon snapshot), Pahé cheekily relies on what Richard J. Powell describes as "satiracy" in the US American context—a culturally informed reading-between-the-lines of Black satire—to illustrate the dehumanization of racist caricatures such as those amplified by Hergé in *Tintin au Congo*, through the juxtaposing styles of the moderator and his own caricatural self-portrait (69).[5] At the same time, he destabilizes, to borrow from Rebecca Wanzo, the "visual imperialism" of mainstream French and Belgian *bandes dessinées* (4). Pahé's cartoon is but one example of how Black francophone artists, that is francophone artists from Africa and of African descent, respond to the embedded racialization at work in Western visual imperialism broadly and French and Belgian popular visual culture more specifically. *On Black* Bandes Dessinées *and Transcolonial Power* exposes the diversity of Black francophone artists' and authors' aesthetic, narrative, and material uses of the colonially inherited medium of *bandes dessinées* and argues that what they do constitutes important reparative work that combats racist stereotypes while exposing and challenging transcolonial power imbalances.

The Salon, which took place at the beginning of December 2010 in Paris at the town hall in the fifth arrondissement, marked an important turning point for *bandes dessinées* by African artists, but its list of participants and how it was framed by organizers and state sponsors highlight the problems

---

5. For more on Pahé's strategic deployment of "satiracy" in his autobiographical work, see Mehta, "Visualizing"; Boukala, "Autoreprésentation"; Bumatay, "Humor."

of categorization on the one hand and the transcolonial relationship between France and other francophone regions on the other. Curated primarily by French librarian, editor, and African *bande dessinée* specialist Christophe Cassiau-Haurie, this first (and only) Salon brought together approximately thirty artists from throughout francophone Africa and the Indian Ocean as well as artists from Belgium. Yet Marguerite Abouet, author of easily the most recognized Black *bande dessinée* series *Aya de Yopougon* as well as her publisher Gallimard were absent. Given that Abouet is repeatedly marketed as African and that by 2010, the stellar international success of the first six volumes of *Aya de Yopougon* had subsequently allowed her to branch out to other series (*Bienvenue* and *Akissi*), her omission seems strange. Perhaps she was omitted for the reason that she produced her work in collaboration with a French illustrator, or that her work was published in France by a French publisher, or that she had been living in France for some time at that point. However, if any of these were the criteria for her omission, then plenty of the other participants should have been excluded as well. For example, Congolese artist Barly Baruti had already been working with Frank Giroud on the mainstream series *Éva K* (published by Éditions Soleil from 1995–98) and *Mandrill* (published by Glénat from 1998–2007). Pahé had already published two volumes of his autobiographical series *La Vie de Pahé* (Éditions Paquet 2006, 2008) and started working with the French cartoonist Sti on their series *Dipoula* about the daily life of a boy with albinism in Gabon (also with Éditions Paquet 2008, 2012), and portions of his autobiographical series had been adapted into an animated television series, *Le Monde de Pahé*, for the channel French 3, which aired in France, Belgium, and Switzerland (but not in Gabon) (Mehta, "Visualizing" 112). Likewise, many participants had been living in Europe for some time (Congolese Pat Masioni, Chadian Adjim Danngar, and Congolese Willy Zekid for instance) or had spent long stretches living in Europe. Moreover, the inclusion of a select group of Belgian artists (Jean-Philippe Stassen, Éric Warnauts, Guy Raives, Seraphine, and Jean Dufaux) but no French artists is equally puzzling especially given that the Salon was planned as part of France's yearlong series of events commemorating the fiftieth anniversary of African independences and therefore received funding from the French government; the Salon was even presided over by Jacques Toubon, who had been appointed the previous year by French President Nicolas Sarkozy as the general secretary of the series.[6]

---

6. For more detail on the Salon, its symbolic staging steps from the 1956 Premier Congrès des écrivains et artistes noirs, and the role of *bande dessinée* festivals for the promotion, circulation, and development of Black *bandes dessinées*, see Bumatay, "African Bande Dessinée Festivals."

Indeed, the elasticity or rather ambiguity of key terms and concepts such as "Africa," "Europe," "France," and even *"bande dessinée"* expose tensions derived from the unevenness of French and Belgian colonialisms and postcolonialisms on the one hand and anxieties around continued imperial power and sociolinguistic and cultural hegemony on the other.[7] These tensions and anxieties characterize much of the efforts of institutions, cultural gatekeepers, and scholars in the Global North (here defined as Europe and the Anglo-American contexts) working with and on *bandes dessinées* by artists and authors of African origin or descent. Primarily under the guise of a certain understanding of geography carried over from European colonialism and through nationalist lenses, scholars have painted a portrait of Black *bandes dessinées* that artificially cordons artists and authors off from each other and other contexts to avoid discussing the construct of race, the processes of racialization, or the changing nature of the constructions of Blackness and anti-Black racism.[8]

On Black Bandes Dessinées *and Transcolonial Power* is the first book-length study in English about Black francophone artists and their work. As a concept, Black *bandes dessinées* does not describe a cultural field, nor is it meant to delineate a subgenre of what has come to be known in French as the Ninth Art. Rather, it is a concept to help us think through the work of Black artists and authors producing *bandes dessinées* and their material, textual, narrative, and artistic strategies on the one hand and the changing imperial formations of the mainstream field of Franco-Belgian *bandes dessinées* on the other. Part of this approach, of course, involves interrogating the term "Black," but it also throws into question the terms *"bande dessinée"* and "Ninth Art" as well. Exploring the range of material objects, collaborative practices, cultural influences, audiences, and reception alongside close analysis of artists' and authors' practices exposes the limitations of existing approaches ostensibly organized according to geography and political borders. Categorization based on continental, national, and regional locales attempts to sidestep the question of race by refusing to acknowledge that this sociocultural and political construct, continually reconfigured since the sixteenth century, is a crucial tool for shaping Europeanness, whiteness, and Modernity. But why choose the term "Black" and not "sub-Saharan African" or even *"noir"* in French? Though "Black" might be seen as a contentious term, it instantly captures the difficulty of categorization along national lines

---

7. For more on how examining the changing historical definitions of "Black" necessarily involves investigating the constructed nature of related terms such as "Europe" and "Africa," see Hine et al.

8. See, for example, Wynter; S. Browne; Mbembe, *Critique*.

as well as the plurality of identity and belonging. As with writers, artists, musicians, and filmmakers from Africa and of African descent, *bande dessinée* artists and authors are mobile and often either leave their birthplace or split their time amongst various cities, countries, and continents. Furthermore, the choice of the English word "Black" rather than the French word *"noir"* is influenced by the broader social history in France whereby visible minorities appropriate American cultural signifiers as an alternative to the stunted discourse available to them in the ostensibly colorblind French Republic.[9]

This is also why I eschew the English terms "comics" or "graphic novels," since understanding the French term—*"bande dessinée"*—and the many specific cultural objects to which it can refer is crucial for critical analysis of such texts. Indeed, even the terms "comics" and "graphic novels," though sometimes used interchangeably, can refer to distinctly different cultural objects. In the French-speaking world, *bandes dessinées* constitute a veritable cultural force. The term—translated as "drawn strip"—is much more technical than "comics" and lacks the same kind of demeaning connotations associated with comics and funnies in North America. Since the 1960s, *bandes dessinées* have been known as the Ninth Art, a term coined to legitimize them by placing them alongside film and literature. Resulting from this more technical terminology and the physical likeness to books rather than disposable magazines or newspapers, *bandes dessinées* have held a more privileged position in mainstream French and Belgian cultures. Yet, this is not to say that anxiety around the sociocultural status of *bandes dessinées* is no longer an issue. In the wake of the *Charlie Hebdo* attack on January 7, 2015, when French brothers Saïd and Chérif Kouachi forced their way into the satirical magazine's building and murdered twelve people and injured almost a dozen more, the city of Angoulême, during the annual International Comics Festival held just weeks later, unveiled the naming of "Place Charlie" in honor of the victims and as an official gesture toward the defense of the freedom of expression, with many national and international leaders in attendance. During the festival's closing ceremonies, Fleur Pellerin, the French Minister of Culture and Communications, speaking on behalf of President François Hollande, reiterated the important cultural status of *bandes dessinées* and described them as an asset for France's radiance in the world (in French, *rayonnement*) ("Festival d'Angoulême"). It is not difficult to hear in her words the continued investment in French cultural hegemony,

---

9. For more on how a discourse of racial politics has developed in France, see Keaton et al., *Black France*. And for a discussion of the difficulty of translating terms derived from racialization, see Dubois, "Translator's."

more specifically, the use of *bandes dessinées* to radiate France's greatness and French universalism, an important practice started during the colonial era.

Rather than generate a set of criteria for work by Black francophone artists and authors, the notion of Black *bandes dessinées* sheds light on their practices, taking into account the specific contexts within which they produce, which subsequently allows us to understand the sociopolitical and cultural stakes of their work as well as its reception. The title's juxtaposition of the English word "Black" and the French term *"bandes dessinées"* announces both the central topic, Black artists' work challenging the status quo, and the deep history of their works' materiality. Like Ann Miller's *Reading Bandes Dessinées*, this book insists on the sociocultural specificity of Franco-Belgian *bandes dessinées*, though here, the term, when brought together with the qualifier "Black," foregrounds the postcolonial dimension of work by Black artists working in French. Indeed, the English word "Black" eschews a national or geographically delineated approach to the production and reception of *bandes dessinées* by Black artists to expose both the ubiquity of colonial-era visual culture and the ongoing influence of colonially established infrastructures that perpetuate drastic imbalances between the Global North and the Global South. When we privilege the mechanism of racialization rather than geography, we see Black artists throughout the francophone world advancing a range of narratives and countervisualities, to use Nicholas Mirzoeff's concept, that not only challenge Western visual imperialism but also critique the necropolitics of the postcolony and of neocolonialism, advance correctives to Western epistemologies, and offer decolonial ways of seeing and being in the world (5).

Currently, there are no books in English exclusively dedicated to the work of Black francophone artists in a comprehensive manner. *Africa Comics* (2006), edited by Samir Patel and published by the Studio Museum in Harlem as the catalog for the museum's exhibition of the same title, offers an impressive multilingual survey of work by cartoonists in Africa and provides a general description of comics production on the continent at the time, through short essays by cultural anthropologists and African art historians. While the curators and contributing authors highlight the increasing vibrancy of comics throughout Africa, not just in francophone regions, much has changed since then thanks to the zeitgeist of production captured by the exhibition and the catalog, what contributor Massimo Repetti has referred to as an "African wave." With the sole exception of this catalog, books in English about comics from Africa focus on political and editorial cartoons and typically dedicate only a small fraction of their content to work in francophone countries.[10] Nor is there a directly competing title in French. Although foundational for this book and further research on Black *bandes dessinées*, scholarly publications, primarily the work of Christophe Cassiau-Haurie, Hilaire Mbiye Lumbala, Alain Brezault, and Sandra Federici, have employed national or continental frameworks and have been oriented toward cataloging publications and interviewing artists rather than analyzing the range of their restorative aesthetic, narrative, and material practices.[11]

Foregoing geographic delineations as an organizing principle for analyzing the work of Black francophone artists and authors actually expands both our cartography and chronology of Black *bandes dessinées*. For example, though other scholars point to the international trajectories and collaborative networks of many artists, their overemphasis on movement from Africa to Europe runs the risk of obscuring other important trajectories and hubs of activity. A good example is that of Willy Zekid, penname of Willy Mouélé. Though he eventually moved to France, he initially left the Republic of Congo for the Ivory Coast, where he was a key contributor to the magazine *Gbich!*, working on star characters including his own Papou as well as Lassane Zohoré's iconic Cauphy Gombo. Another important example is Serge Diantantu. Originally from the Democratic Republic of the Congo, Diantantu also emigrated to France, but his work and where it is published contribute to a global notion of Blackness beyond the continent of Africa. In particular, his historical series on slavery (the five volumes of *Mémoire de l'esclavage*) and his album-sized volumes on important Black men and women throughout history are all published by Caraïbéditions, based in the French Antilles (Guadeloupe and Martinique) and focused on the French overseas departments. In fact, Diantantu's project on international Black figures echoes the work of former professional French footballer Lilian Thuram, who has become an important anti-racist activist in France. As part of his endeavor to combat racism through education, Thuram, originally from the French overseas department of Guadeloupe in the Caribbean, cowrote a two-volume autobiographical *bande dessinée* entitled *Notre Histoire* that drew from his cowritten book *Mes étoiles noires: De Lucy à Barack Obama* and wove in stories about important Black francophone figures who fought for

---

10. See, for example, Lent, *Cartooning*; and Limb and Olaniyan, *Taking*.
11. See, for example, Cassiau-Haurie, *La Caricature*; *Histoire*; *Comment peut-on faire de la BD en Afrique?*; *Quand la BD d'Afrique s'invite*; *Dictionnaire*; Federici, *L'Entrance*; *'Je'*; and Lumbala, *Cases*.

equality in their respective historical periods.[12] Because Thuram is French, he is absent from work on so-called African *bandes dessinées* even though artists working in Réunion, a French overseas department in the Indian Ocean, are included. Though the closer proximity of islands in the Indian Ocean to the continent of Africa might justify this discrepancy, it nevertheless highlights the ambiguity of key terms such as "African" and "French." Furthermore, the hesitancy to include Black artists from the French Caribbean while unflinchingly accepting artists from the Indian Ocean demonstrates the refusal to consider race and racialization as important factors. In *Quand la BD d'Afrique s'invite en Europe* (When comics from Africa show up in Europe; 2012), Christophe Cassiau-Haurie's brief and awkward mention of the French overseas departments performs the French Republic's color-blind discourse: "Curiously, these five departments are home to populations predominantly of African origin. Can we see in those places a resulting solidarity among artists of the same geographic origin? Perhaps . . ." (19).[13] The passive construction of the first sentence, explaining that the overseas departments are home to populations predominantly of African origin, completely silences France's centuries-long involvement with the slave trade and implementation of plantation slavery in both the Caribbean and the Indian Ocean. Refusing to acknowledge that King Louis XIV signed the Code Noir in 1685 or that Napoléon Bonaparte reinstated slavery in 1802 after the First French Republic abolished it in 1794, and that sugar production in the Caribbean and the Indian Ocean not only enriched France but also brutally institutionalized racial hierarchy, allows Cassiau-Haurie to unironically find the demographics of the overseas departments curious and speculate at the potentially shared solidarity among Black French citizens descended from enslaved people in these locations with Black Africans descended from colonial subjects. Thus, shifting our attention to the mechanisms of racialization, especially those derived from European visual imperialism, helps us map new geographies for Black *bandes dessinées*, which opens up important comparative analyses instead of speculation.

Relatedly, realigning our priorities away from geographic delineations, without ignoring them, and focusing on artists' practices offers a different chronology of Black *bandes dessinées* and throws into question nomenclatures predicated on Western imperialism. For example, the Réunion-based *bande*

---

12. For more on Thuram's antiracism activism and how *Notre Histoire* claims Black francophone history as French history, see Bumatay, "*Notre Histoire*."

13. "Curieusement, ces cinq départements abritent des populations majoritairement d'origine africaine. Peut-on y voir la conséquence d'une solidarité entre artistes de même origine géographique ? Peut-être . . ." Ellipsis in original.

dessinée magazine *Le Cri du Margouillat*, founded in 1986, is often categorized as African in spite of the island's status as a French overseas department since 1946. Indeed, that the European Union's geography stops at Turkey yet extends to the Caribbean, South America, and the Indian Ocean due to contemporary France's geography exposes the constructed and historically changing nature of the notion of Europe. Considering *Le Cri du Margouillat*, to which an ethnically diverse group of artists contribute, as a French publication and at the same time part of the history of Black *bandes dessinées* challenges narratives that proclaim the ostensible entrance of African artists into the European *bande dessinée* market. African artists who also happen to be French (through their nationality) were already publishing their work in France. Similarly, we should think of the independent Paris-based publisher Amok, founded in 1994 by French artists Olivier Marboeuf (originally from the French overseas department of Guadeloupe) and Yvan Alagbé (born to a French mother and a Beninois father) as part of the history of Black *bandes dessinées*. This inclusion allows us to see how Black artists participated in and contributed to the small press movement of the 1990s, foundational to the transformation of mainstream Franco-Belgian *bandes dessinées* long before Gallimard's publication of *Aya de Yopougon*.

Beyond contributing to work focused on cartooning and the production of *bandes dessinées* on the African continent, *On Black* Bandes Dessinées *and Transcolonial Power* complements and expands existing work both on postcolonial *bandes dessinées* in Europe and on Black comics worldwide. Mark McKinney's *Redrawing French Empire in Comics* (2013) analyzes *bandes dessinées* produced in France about French Indochina and Algeria, whereas his book *Postcolonialism and Migration in French Comics* (2021) once again uses a postcolonial lens, through which to examine work by French artists who are also ethnic minorities. Though McKinney includes Black francophone artists in his most recent book, his work prioritizes a national framework and therefore focuses exclusively on artists' sociopolitical and cultural commentary in France as French citizens. *On Black* Bandes Dessinées *and Transcolonial Power* serves as a robust companion piece that reads artists' practices as not limited to only writing and drawing back to empire. Instead, by focusing on how Black francophone artists challenge racialization at work in Western popular culture, *On Black* Bandes Dessinées *and Transcolonial Power* examines questions similar to those posed by scholars working on Black comics primarily in the US American context.

From taking stock of racialized stereotypes to tracking resistance and highlighting artists' range of restorative strategies, scholarship on Black comics worldwide provides a generative comparative model for Black *bandes dessinées*. In *Black Images in the Comics: A Visual History* (2003), Fredrick Strömberg compiles an overview of representations of Black people in comics from around the world, beginning with the very first comics and *bandes dessinées* and continuing until the start of the twenty-first century. Similarly, Jan Nederveen Pieterse has outlined in *White on Black: Images of Africa and Blacks in Western Popular Culture* (1992) the ways in which Western popular culture has changed over the course of the twentieth century to try and maintain a discourse of dominance over Africa and Africans, arguing that imagery and ideologies developed during colonialism persist, transform, and have been perpetuated through the period of decolonization and into postcolonialism. Focusing on the representation of Black Americans in comics as well as on comics by Black Americans, many scholars have significantly reshaped how we understand the dynamic network of sociocultural, political, and material factors informing artists' practices; how we view the history of resistance through the creation of specific strips, publications, and publishing companies; and our understanding of the mobilization of genre-specific tropes and gendered approaches to Black comics studies.[14] Likewise, the interdisciplinary anthologies *Black Comics: Politics of Race and Representation* (2013), edited by Sheena C. Howard and Ronald L. Jackson II, and *The Blacker the Ink: Constructions of Black Identity in Comics and Sequential Art* (2015), edited by Frances Gateward and John Jennings, demonstrate the wide diversity of artists' strategies and of our analytical tools for unpacking the important restorative work being created. As alluded to in the opening of this introduction, the works of Rebecca Wanzo and Richard J. Powell are particularly poignant for thinking through the francophone context of Black *bandes dessinées*. In *The Content of Our Caricature: African American Comic Art and Political Belonging* (2020), Wanzo posits nineteenth- and early twentieth-century caricatures of racialized bodies in the United States as a form of "visual imperialism" that not only justified colonialism and discrimination but also informed cartoonists' practices. Through a rich cultural studies approach that examines a diverse range of material objects, Wanzo demonstrates how cartoonists and their work expose and undermine the implicit racism of mainstream US American visual imperialism, thereby articulating new definitions of national belonging and history. In *Going There: Black Visual Satire* (2020), Powell examines how Black American artists, including cartoonists from the twentieth and twenty-first centuries, employ satire as a self-reflexive mode of sociopolitical critique. Like Wanzo, Powell assembles

---

14. See Brown, *Black Superheroes*; Whitted, *EC Comics*; Nama, *Super Black*; Whaley, *Black Women*.

a diverse corpus to illustrate the range of responses to the history of racist stereotypes in the United States.

Though *On Black* Bandes Dessinées *and Transcolonial Power* is not limited to one geographic location, the hegemony of Western racist stereotypes prevalent in visual and print culture of the late nineteenth century and first half of the twentieth century, including early mainstream Franco-Belgian *bandes dessinées*, constitutes a similarly centralized visual imperialism in the francophone world. Since their inception in the second half of the nineteenth century, French and Belgian *bandes dessinées* have participated in and contributed to a visual culture that was mobilized in the métropole to garner popular support and legitimize colonial expansion.[15] Examples include travel postcards and posters; colonial expositions; children's books, toys, and games; and advertisements for exotic goods such as Banania.[16] In addition, both France and Belgium exported *bandes dessinées* to their colonial territories in tandem with their respective civilizing missions. As Mark McKinney convincingly demonstrates, early and influential artists Alain Saint-Ogan and Hergé not only mimicked the ideology of their historical moments but also engaged in generating, defining, and codifying a visual iconography of France's and Belgium's respective colonial territories and their peoples, thereby encoding, in a sense, certain visual stereotypes into the very makeup of *bandes dessinées* (McKinney, *The Colonial Heritage*).[17] While I am

---

15. French historians Pascal Blanchard and Nicolas Bancel have conducted extensive research into French and European colonial visual cultures and their lasting legacies. Subsequently, they have written and edited a number of key texts that present and analyze a rich archive of visual artifacts. Moreover, they spearhead the ACHAC research group (Association pour la Connaissance de l'Histoire de l'Afrique Contemporaine [Association for the Understanding of Contemporary Africa]), established in 1989. See Blanchard et al., *Images*; Blanchard et al., *Human Zoos*; Blanchard et al., *Culture postcoloniale*; Lemaire et al., *Colonisation*; Blanchard and Boëtsch, *Le Racisme*. See also Peabody et al., *Visualizing*; and Landau and Kaspin, *Images*.

16. The ongoing ubiquity of the Banania logo and its critiques exemplify both the power of popular visual culture and its detrimental psychological and social effects. The logo features an adult *tirailleur sénégalais*, or French colonial soldier, with an exaggerated smile paired with a slogan in pidgin French. The soldier's uniform, grin, and informal French coalesce into a powerful stereotype that simultaneously aims to authenticate the supposedly exotic product (a chocolate and banana drink mix) and the so-called civilizing mission. Both Léopold Senghor and Frantz Fanon famously critiqued this logo in particular for the prevalent and long-lasting damage it caused. For more on this logo and its legacy in France, see Donadey, "'Y' a bon Banania'"; and Achille, "A l'approche."

17. According to many *bande dessinée* historians, the founding fathers of this medium in the French-language context, Alain Saint-Ogan (creator of *Zig et Puce*) and Hergé (creator of *Tintin*), were deeply involved with newspapers. That Hergé's star character, Tintin, is a reporter is not coincidental; starting in 1929, the Belgian journal *Le XXe Siècle* began publishing Hergé's Tintin series in the spin-off *Le Petit Vingtième* as a supplement to attract young readers.

not trying to suggest that these early artists are solely responsible for creating a visual language of racism, and nor do I want to deny the rich history of caricature as a fundamental predecessor to *bandes dessinées*, I agree that the emergence of *bandes dessinées* is caught up with a modernist European epistemology and an imperialist culture, and though many *bandes dessinées* historians dismiss the paternalistic images of Hergé's *Tintin au Congo* as little more than representative of its historical moment, as others have argued, through simplification and amplification Hergé and other key artists at the time succeeded in fixing certain clichés and cultural stereotypes.[18]

Like Black francophone authors, Black francophone artists adopt, adapt, and modify imperially imported modes of representation, all while facing financial, logistical, and political realities that impact their decisions. Prioritizing a diachronic approach, *On Black* Bandes Dessinées *and Transcolonial Power* illustrates the vast range of artists' practices and argues that their decisions are overdetermined not only by cultural, political, economic, and material factors but also by targeted audiences and sociocultural and logistical shifts in marketability. Some artists, especially those producing serialized *bande dessinée* strips and magazines, like Senegalese T. T. Fons, and collaborative endeavors, such as the magazine *Jeunes pour jeunes* in the Democratic Republic of the Congo, uncritically imitate existing European styles to tell localized stories from their point of view. As Massimo Repetti has documented, most often they take inspiration from the simplicity of the *ligne claire* aesthetic popularized by Hergé in the Tintin series, the comedic and expressive Charleroi School exemplified by Jijé and André Franquin in series like *Spirou* and *Gaston*, and from other mainstream styles championed by key artists, titles, and genres such as Jijé's more realistic work.[19] Others, like the Congolese artists Barly Baruti and Pat Masioni, particularly interested in valorizing Black cultures, traditions, history, and humanity, while informed by existing styles, counteract the reductive visual economy of European styles through highly detailed verisimilitude and a marked emphasis on environment, be it urban centers or different natural terrains. Some, like Pahé, trained as political cartoonists, playfully distort existing styles and mobilize "stereotype as a tool" or "mode of expression" as a function of their critiques of neocolonialism and the corruption of the postcolony (Powell 19). Though political critique comes with risks as evidenced by Pahé's

---

18. For more, see Maurin Abomo, *"Tintin au Congo."*
19. See Repetti, "African 'Ligne Claire,'" "African Wave," and "New Comics."

arrest in 2009 for drawing caricatures of two police officers.[20] Lastly, several artists, like Cameroonian Japhet Miagotar, prioritize innovation, drawing inspiration from local cultures as well as those beyond the francophone world, what Repetti describes as a "creolization of comics" (Repetti, "African Wave" 16).

While most *bandes dessinées* by Black artists work against the visual imperialism of Western popular culture simply by adopting this medium to tell their own stories, many deploy a range of strategies to expose and often critique the necropolitics of neocolonial forms of power, infrastructure, and corruption. Through their countervisuality, they offer new ways of seeing and understanding Black cultures and peoples. I argue that by historicizing their work, we get a better sense of how they respond to and weigh in on their own contexts as well as larger discussions of discrimination, inequity, and representation. When coupled, the political corruption in former French and Belgian colonies and the sustained influence of Global North cultural gatekeepers create a minefield that Black francophone artists must navigate. Their negotiations of such a minefield and their critiques of it can be read in their work. This book argues that reading Black *bandes dessinées* in context helps us unpack the complex relationship between countervisuality and materiality. To put it another way, the choice of the medium and what Black francophone artists do with it are a large part of the message. For instance, serialized publications meant for local audiences prioritize the popular and thus not only focus on and draw from everyday life in the postcolony but also reproduce the local vernacular like the use of Nouchi in the Ivorian weekly *Gbich!* or Kinshasa-based Papa Mfumu'Eto's blend of Lingala and French. Conversely, for album-style *bandes dessinées* accessible to an international readership, artists often favor aesthetic, narrative, and linguistic choices that purposefully temper the blend of mainstream conventions with innovation. *Aya de Yopougon,* by Marguerite Abouet and Clément Oubrerie, is a prime example of this fine-tuning that, through its success, has forever changed comics worldwide.

---

20. "Le dessinateur." Pahé was held in a Gabonese prison for thirty-six hours for his caricatures. Likewise, his work for local newspapers in the late 1990s and early 2000s threatened the viability of the newspapers. However, in contrast to many other political cartoonists in Africa, Pahé's international fame has allowed him to remain in Gabon and has ironically led to him being invited to the presidential palace despite his ongoing caricatures of Omar Bongo and Ali Bongo ("Pahé"). For more on censorship of political cartoons in Africa, see Fagiolo, *Résistants.*

On Black Bandes Dessinées *and Transcolonial Power* recalibrates the existing perception of *bandes dessinées* by Black francophone artists by insisting on the shifting postcolonial dimension of their practices over time. In 2005, French publishing giant and literary institution Gallimard launched a new series dedicated to *bandes dessinées* with the publication of the first volume of Abouet and Oubrerie's *Aya de Yopougon*. The album was quickly translated into English and distributed by Drawn and Quarterly in 2007. In addition to winning many accolades and launching Abouet to international stardom, the series became and remains the indisputable cultural reference point for African comics in French in spite of its collaborative creation and mainstream production *within* France. The continued categorization of *Aya de Yopougon* as an African comic belies its material reality while exposing Global North strategies for shaping and marketing postcolonial exoticism (chapter 2). Moreover, upholding this series, which differs dramatically from the vast majority of *bandes dessinées* produced and distributed in francophone Africa, as the emblem of African comics in French obscures both the breadth of Black *bandes dessinées* published since the 1960s and the often transcolonial complexity of their makeup. It also posits the Global North as the intended audience for all Black *bandes dessinées,* which is far from always the case. *On Black* Bandes Dessinées *and Transcolonial Power,* by attending to the changing impact of racist stereotypes encoded in imperial popular culture as central to reading work by Black francophone artists, reveals that though there has been a stark rise in interest in Black comics from around the world in the wake of Marvel's film adaptation of *Black Panther,* vibrant hubs of Black *bandes dessinées* have generated local, regional, and international audiences across the world since the late 1960s. By filling in the global map of work by Black artists since decolonization, this book demonstrates how Black francophone artists have long theorized and contributed to broader discussions of representation and power.

Chapter Summaries

Organized around key moments, artists and authors, themes, and publications, this book decenters Europe and European gatekeepers as the primary lenses through which to understand Black *bandes dessinées* to highlight the diversity of Black francophone artists and authors, their work, and their audiences. As a result, the objects of analysis under the umbrella term *bandes dessinées* include political and editorial cartoons, serial publications and self-published magazines, anthologies, mainstream and independent albums, blogs, digital comics, and mobile apps. However, though the book proposes a global understanding of Black *bandes dessinées*, it is by no means exhaustive. The bulk of the primary sources come from Africa and Europe, with some discussion of Black *bandes dessinées* from the Caribbean and the Indian Ocean; work by artists in Canada and North Africa (with the exception of Gildas Gamy, based in Morocco), however, is absent and represents a ripe avenue for new research.

Throughout *On Black* Bandes Dessinées *and Transcolonial Power*, I underline the necessity of deep understanding of context and draw from relevant fields to illustrate the need for informed, interdisciplinary approaches, especially given my positionality as a researcher from and trained in the Global North, albeit from a postcolonial context. I am not of African descent, yet my mixed ethnicity stemming from US American imperialism has driven me to interrogate colonialism's mechanisms and ongoing effects. It is in an effort to decolonize what I know about own context that I aim to do the same for the work of Black francophone artists and authors.

Chapter 1, "A Tale of Two Kinshasas, or The Plurality of Everyday Postcolonialism," starts in Kinshasa in the decades following the Democratic Republic of the Congo's independence from Belgium to explore the rich diversity of *Jeunes pour jeunes*, the first African *bande dessinée* magazine, created in 1968, and its impact on Black *bande dessinée* production in the region. Emphasizing the aesthetic, narrative, linguistic, and material diversity of this first magazine and subsequent work by Kinshasa-based artists Barly Baruti and Papa Mfumu'Eto, I argue that the plurality of everyday life in former Belgian and French colonies draws from and participates in local popular culture to cultivate and speak directly to a diverse urban, postcolonial audience. Comparing how Baruti and Papa Mfumu'Eto produce drastically different cultural objects informed by the same sociohistorical and cultural context, I show that artists develop their own sets of practices as a form of innovation and getting by. By doing so, they valorize their own work, their culture, and their audience. Looking at Baruti's formation and reading his textual, aesthetic, and narrative practices in his 1987 album-style biographical chronicle of Congolese singer Papa Wemba's rise to international stardom, which solidified in the 1986 film *La Vie est belle*, I argue that Baruti's harmonious blend of Western and Kinshasa-specific cultural elements and modes of representation can be read as part of the prevalence and importance of self-styling in Mobutu's Zaire of the 1980s. *Papa Wemba: Viva la musica!* not only celebrates Papa Wemba, Congolese rumba, the performance of La Sape, and the film but also showcases Baruti's deft mastery of multiple forms of cultural expression. Conversely, Papa Mfumu'Eto's self-published magazine, *Revue Mfumu'eto*, adapts many of the same strategies of Congolese rumba, especially *libanga* or name-dropping for sponsorship, and blends them with a perpetual proliferation of self-styling that generates a positive feedback network between him and his audience. As the *bande dessinée* version of informal marketing and artistic expression, Papa Mfumu'Eto's magazine continually innovates while celebrating the everyday miracle of such a practice.

The collaborative projects between African francophone artists and European artists and institutions of the late 1990s and early 2000s, alongside increasing diversification of the mainstream Franco-Belgian *bande dessinée* market, created favorable conditions for the French publisher Gallimard to back the release of *Aya de Yopougon* even though author Marguerite Abouet had never been published and artist Clément Oubrerie had not previously worked on a *bande dessinée*. Chapter 2, "The AYA Effect, or Marguerite Abouet's Timely and Timeless Interventions," situates Gallimard's decision within the context of postcolonial francophone literature to expose the unique power dynamics of print culture in French, which have been and remain highly centralized, especially in comparison with the power dynamics of postcolonial print culture in English. The ostensible monopoly of Paris-based publishers since World War II constitutes a powerful hegemonic tool wielded by the French government and institutions to maintain socioeconomic and political influence in francophone regions outside of hexagonal France and also to combat the global prevalence of the English language. Considering this broader context alongside the diversification of the French public over the course of the second half of the twentieth century and into the twenty-first century is essential for explaining the instant success of the first volume of *Aya de Yopougon*. Indeed, the framing of both the series's boutique postcolonialism and its boutique format leveraged the same marketing associated with the fabrication and maintenance of specific nomenclatures such as "La Francophonie" and "African francophone literature" that uphold diversity in the name of bolstering French universalism. At the heart of such marketing is an emphasis on Abouet's identity as an African author and the gendered dimension of her work, both of which have been for two decades repeatedly vaunted as refreshing. In chapter 2, I argue that close attention to Abouet's branding over time—how she is presented and how she develops her own brand—allows us to read her work on its own terms, thereby restoring its critical edge, which has been dulled through translation and repackaging. Through timeless novelty and elusive strategies, to draw from andre m. carrington, that become more explicit over time, Abouet has created and expanded her own Black *bande dessinée* universe driven by what I call the AYA effect, in which all her characters can stand in for her and are marked by a call for a more inclusive and just society regardless of one's geography. Ultimately, as with other successful postcolonial authors in the global marketplace, Abouet has forever changed the mainstream market, as evidenced by imitations of her branding and an increased professionalization and feminization of Black *bandes dessinées*. However, we must keep in mind that Abouet's work represents but one example of restorative processes through this medium.

In chapter 3, "Reframing Migration in the Twenty-First Century," I explore the prevalent topic of northward migration to chart how Black *bandes dessinées* reveal that, contrary to sensationalized media reports in the Global North since the 2010s, migration is not a recent phenomenon. Drawing from Achille Mbembe and Étienne Balibar, I first turn to the one-shot *Une éternité à Tanger*, written by Cameroonian journalist Eyoum Nganguè, illustrated by Ivorian Faustin Titi, and published by the Italian-based Edizioni Lai-Momo in 2004. I demonstrate how many key characteristics that mark the spectral experience of migrants in the face of the increased borderization mechanisms of Fortress Europe were already commonplace in Africa. Moreover, in their visualization of the protagonist's experiences, Nganguè and Titi seek to shed light on migrants' lives while unambiguously exposing the colonial origins of northward migration in the twenty-first century. I then examine other types of publications, moving forward in time, including short vignettes submitted to the annual Africa Comics competition held by the Italian group Africa e Mediterraneo; Beninois Didier Viodé's multiple publications about his fictional avatar Yao, who attempts to emigrate to Europe to pursue a career as an artist; vignettes in the L'Harmattan BD anthology *Nouvelles d'Afrique*, and the long-form Gallimard-published graphic novel *Alpha: Abidjan–Gare du Nord*, written by Franco-Gabonese author Bessora and illustrated by French artist Barroux. Tracking similar tropes and specific aesthetic and narrative strategies across all of the *bandes dessinées*, I argue that while humanization of migrants is an important function of these stories, an equally significant function is the exposure of the necropolitics and imperial debris, to borrow from Ann Stoler, that result from the borderization of Fortress Europe. Taking up Dominic Davies's concept of an "intolerable fiction," I demonstrate how all of these Black *bandes dessinées* critique the presentation of northward migration as an ahistorical crisis while at the same time exploring the physical, psychological, and moral ruination of borderization's anti-Black racism that cordons off who counts as human and transforms nature—the desert and the sea—into agents of death.

Detailing the subgenre of environmental edutainment, chapter 4, "Black *Bandes Dessinées* and Decolonial Ecocriticism," examines how some artists expose the links between today's slow violence and colonialism and how, through innovative artistic practices, they advocate for the restitution of colonial cultural items as a form of decolonial ecology. Thinking with Malcolm Ferdinand and his seminal *Decolonial Ecology* (2022), I compare the work of Congolese artist Barly Baruti and Cameroonian artist Japhet Miagotar to examine how their aesthetic practices are part and parcel of their advocacy for decolonial ways of seeing, representing, and being in the world.[21] In the environmentalist albums *Temps d'agir!* (Time to act!), published in 1982, and *Objectif Terre! Les Aventures de Sako et Yannick* (Goal, Earth! The adventures of Sako and Yannick), published in 1994, Baruti challenges colonial ways of inhabiting and representing the Earth, moving from a Cold War context in which the discourse centered on environmental protection to a global paradigm in which local action plans have the potential to benefit not only people living in former European colonies but the entire human and more-than-human world. On the last page of *Objectif Terre!*, Baruti proposes a planetary call to action to imagine development as detached from the notion of Progress, or a decolonial approach to development. Employing a detail-rich verisimilitude, he presents a countervisuality in which humans are part of their environment rather than its masters. In a similar move, Miagotar develops a new countervisuality predicated on a form of virtual restitution, to expose the interrelated violences of European extraction and dumping. In *Cargaison mortelle à Abidjan* (Deadly cargo in Abidjan), he crafts an allegory about a real environmental crime that took place in August 2006: the dumping and distribution in Abidjan of toxic waste by the crew of the Panamanian-registered cargo ship the *Probo Koala* and local subcontractors. In this retelling, Miagotar purposefully blends two-dimensional renderings of three-dimensional Fang masks and statues with allusions to Hergé's 1958 Tintin album *Coke en stock* to reclaim African cultural production for African artists and, drawing on what Ferdinand refers to as "hold politics," to draw a direct link between the anti-Black death brought about by European ships from different time periods and in different bodies of water (50). In

---

21. The original version of Ferdinand's book, *Une écologie décoloniale: Penser l'écologie depuis le monde caribéen*, was published in 2019.

reclaiming, if only virtually, Fang reliquaries from their decontextualized existence as inspiration for avant-garde European art at the turn of the twentieth century—most famously by Pablo Picasso in his seminal *Les Demoiselles d'Avignon*—and meting out symbolic justice for victims of anti-Black death ferried in ships' holds, Miagotar anticipates the findings of the 2018 *Report on the Restitution of African Cultural Heritage*, more commonly referred to as the Felwine-Sarr Report: that is, that European colonialism's extractivism was violent and constitutes a crime against humanity, one whose ongoing impacts still dictate the world order. Through innovative aesthetic and narrative practices, both Miagotar and Baruti invite readers to rethink how they see the world in order to change how they exist in it.

CHAPTER 1

A Tale of Two Kinshasas, or The Plurality of Everyday Postcolonialism

In 1968, under the leadership of Freddy Mulongo and Achille Flor Ngoye, the first African *bande dessinée* magazine *Jeunes pour jeunes* (Young for youth) was launched in Kinshasa, the capital of the Democratic Republic of the Congo (DRC), and became an important cultural touchstone for its Congolese audience, with print runs up to forty thousand copies by the time of its disappearance a decade later (Cassiau-Haurie, *Dictionnaire* 156). In 1971, under President Mobutu's Zairianization, or "authenticité," campaign to expunge colonial vestiges from the nation, this black-and-white magazine was renamed *Kake* (or *L'Éclair*, "Lightning") (Cassiau-Haurie, *Dictionnaire* 156). Nevertheless, the original slogan, "qui a lu *Jeunes pour jeunes* garde sa jeunesse et qui n'a pas lu *Jeunes pour jeunes* conserve sa vieillesse,"[1] indicated an audience of all ages, not just children, and cheekily proclaimed the transformative fountain-of-youth effect of reading the magazine (Bathy 14). The energy captured by the magazine's two titles and suggested by its slogan mirrored the ambitious team of contributors, who often had other careers and infused their interests into their stories: cofounder Ngoye was also a journalist and later became a novelist, early illustrator César Sinda left for

---

1. "Whoever has read *Jeunes pour jeunes* saves their youth and who hasn't read *Jeunes pour jeunes* conserves their old age."

the United States to pursue his professional boxing career, and Mulongo had previously been a professional footballer, worked as a presidential adviser, and was a journalist as well (Bathy 6–8).

Similarly, the diversity of the eponymous characters whose strips filled each issue reflected the sociolinguistic and cultural diversity of the wide-ranging readership residing in the changing urban, postcolonial context of Kinshasa at the time. Language use and visual style varied from strip to strip as a function of the main characters and their adventures even though strips were written and drawn by various scenarists and artists over the years. For *Apolosa*, the boxer-cum-teacher-local-defender created by Denis Boyau Loyongo, a detail-oriented blend of verisimilitude and comedic conventions instantly emphasized Apolosa's impressively muscular physique in sharp relief with those around him, while the narration in standard French contrasted with the use of Hindoubill in the diegesis. This highly localized Lingala pidgin peppered with some English words included a "propensity for esoteric neologisms and . . . borrowed heavily from Kikongo and French" so as to be "unintelligible to non-initiates such as newly arrived migrants and, particularly, adults" (Gondola 84). Using Hindoubill immediately highlighted the hypermasculine Kinshasa-specific youth subculture of violence that originated in the 1950s and drew from US American Western films from the 1930s and 1940s for inspiration (Gondola 77). The young men, the Bills, took their name from American icon Buffalo Bill, while the portmanteau for their slang, Hindoubill, alluded both to the Westerns' preoccupation with cowboys and "Indians" and to the Hindi of Indian films in competition with American films (Stewart 78). In contrast, the strip *Coco et Didi*, meant for children, was in Lingala and drawn in a simpler style for easy identification with the young sister and brother, while *Vieux pour vieux*, a humorous strip about a bickering couple, also in Lingala, employed a caricatural blackface style for the couple's antics, with the husband's smaller stature pitted against his wife's much larger physique, ostensibly for comedic effect. Likewise, action and suspense strips in Lingala such as *Sinatra*, *Durango*, and *Le Mystère du tombeau de Kalina* took their visual cues from the same genres in *bandes dessinées* and American films, whereas *Le Militant parle*, a strip designed to boost readers' patriotism and sense of civic duty, paired standard French with a crisp, streamlined visual style evocative of how-to-guides or operation manuals (Bathy 25–30). Additionally, strips dedicated to music and the radio like *Top Music* and *La Chanson illustrée* tapped into local popular culture by celebrating musicians and bands familiar to its readers.

As both a magazine and independent publisher, *Jeunes pour jeunes* set an important precedent for Black *bandes dessinées* on the continent, for although Black francophone artists in Africa had produced comic strips for local newspapers and worked with European publishers and authors on ad campaigns in the form of *bandes dessinées* as well as illustrated instructional books, this Kinshasa-based project was locally generated, edited, and distributed. The magazine's creation, development, and popularity indicate positive conditions for a budding *bande dessinée* culture and growing audience in the bustling urban center of postcolonial Kinshasa in the late 1960s. As a hybrid popular-culture medium linked to journalism, literature, film, urban painting, oral storytelling, and music with stories for all ages, its diversity and flexibility attracted a wide readership while its materiality (black ink on newsprint paper) kept costs down, thus making it accessible to its intended local readership. Despite disappearing in the 1970s due to economic hardship and censorship under President Mobutu for, at least in part, its plurality of popular viewpoints not always in sync with the party line, its impact paved the way for contributing artists and new artists to generate new characters, series, and magazines, thus engendering a rich proliferation of Congolese *bandes dessinées* (Cassiau-Haurie, *Histoire* 49).

Though it is easy to classify *Jeunes pour jeunes* as an African *bande dessinée* magazine because of its contributors, the stories told, and the location of its production and distribution, it is important to remember that such classification applies to the medium, in this case, not the format, and that for other Congolese *bandes dessinées,* such a continentally based classification is not as clear-cut. Indeed, a crucial condition for *Jeunes pour jeunes*'s success was the preexisting print infrastructure established and maintained by Belgium- and France-based publishers and Belgian-backed publishers created in the Congo Free State and maintained after independence such as Éditions Saint-Paul (established in the Congo in 1958), which later became part of the global conglomerate Éditions Médiaspaul.[2] Part of this print landscape was also informed by the differences between Belgian colonial rule in central Africa and French colonial rule throughout the world. With an aggressive emphasis on resource extraction and a secondary endeavor to spread Catholicism, first under King Leopold II and then as part of the Congo Free State and the Belgian Congo, Belgian rule in central Africa did not seek to reproduce Belgian society or culture as part of its colonial mission.[3] In sharp contrast, France's civilizing mission as designed by the Third Republic exported the

---

2. For more on this publisher's legacy in the Democratic Republic of the Congo, see Djungu-Simba, "Le fonds."

3. For more on the unique case of the Belgian Congo, see Hochschild, *King Leopold's Ghost.*

French school system as a crucial tool of conquest and assimilation.[4] One outcome of these different approaches is the sustained importance of literature, especially the genre of the novel, in former French colonies, over other forms of print culture. Relatedly, we might also attribute the rise of *bandes dessinées* and other popular-culture art forms in the former Belgian Congo as stemming from the prevalence of religious presses and the prominent role of the Catholic Church in the realms of printing and education in what is now DRC.[5] In spite of these differences, the merging of the French and Belgian *bande dessinée* markets in the 1930s constitutes another important contributing factor, as evidenced by the international popularity of Hergé's *Tintin au Congo*.[6] Meant to encourage support for colonialism at home in Belgium, *Tintin au Congo*'s exotic representations were grounded in real facts such as geographical names and visual cues. Even though, as Philippe Delisle has argued, later editions starting in 1946 ironed out all verbal and visual traces in order to tap into the larger French market, *Tintin au Congo* continued to be an important cultural touchstone in the Belgian Congo (Delisle, *Bande dessinée* 20).[7] In fact, this album's popularity was reignited in a postindependence Congo at almost the exact same time as the birth of *Jeunes pour jeunes*, through the republication of the 1947 version in installments in the semi-glossy Kinshasa-based magazine *Zaïre* in 1969 (Hunt, "Tintin" 93–94). The ubiquity of Hergé's boy-scout adventurer-journalist and of Hergé's *ligne claire* style is undeniable; however, it is but one starting point for Congolese and other Black francophone artists.

Foregrounding the plurality of styles, stories, and languages and the diversity of material formats since the late 1960s, this chapter argues that Black *bandes dessinées*, rather than constituting a classification, describes a range of artists' practices for adopting and adapting this imperially introduced medium to represent themselves, their societies and cultures, and their traditions and histories, as well as their hopes and concerns. This chapter reveals that Black *bandes dessinées* primarily intended for local audiences draw from, participate in, and contribute to regional popular cultures and that this can also happen, albeit using different practices, in *bandes dessinées*

---

4. For more on France's implementation of its civilizing mission, see Conklin, *Mission*.

5. See Cassiau-Haurie, "Littérature"; Naudillon, "Popular Art Forms."

6. It is by no means a coincidence that *Tintin au Congo* was first published in book form in 1931, the same year as both the famous French Colonial Exposition held in Paris and the first publication of Jean de Brunhoff's hit children's book *Histoire de Babar*. For more on the merging of the national markets after World War II, see Vessels, *Drawing*; Grove, *Comics*.

7. See also Hunt, "Tintin."

grounded in a specific cultural context but aimed at a wider audience. This means that, as with other forms of popular culture throughout Africa, many locally produced *bandes dessinées* are concerned with the quotidian experiences and sociocultural realities in formerly colonized regions.[8] It also means that how each artist adapts Franco-Belgian *bandes dessinées* is a function of the artist's relationship with the audience(s). Looking at two key Congolese figures, I argue that artists' individual formations and unique practices are developed in dialogue with those around them and that their strategies are shaped by a range of sociocultural, political, economic, and material factors that can change from project to project. Put another way, Black *bandes dessinées*, though informed by transcolonial power dynamics, are as diverse as their creators. Though banal, this declaration advocates for a deep, contextual understanding of Black *bandes dessinées* on their own terms rather than as only ever seeking legitimacy, especially from European cultural gatekeepers and institutions. Of course, I do not mean to suggest that such gatekeepers have no effect on artists' strategies. Instead, paying attention to form, content, and materiality helps us understand how power impacts artists' decisions, on the one hand, and identify their innovative restorative practices, on the other. Through a comparison between two Congolese icons of Black *bandes dessinées*—Barly Baruti and Papa Mfumu'Eto—I demonstrate how, just like the diversity and plurality of *Jeunes pour jeunes*, the same sociocultural context engaging with the same popular culture references can produce vastly different texts. I read Barly Baruti's *Papa Wemba: Viva la musica!*, a one-shot album that follows the mainstream industry format of a hardback book comprised of forty-eight pages, alongside Papa Mfumu'Eto's self-published and locally distributed magazine to unpack the various factors informing their strategies. For both, other forms of local popular culture—music, self-styling and fashion, film, and photography—inflect their adoption of *bandes dessinées* to represent and showcase the richness of Congolese culture and at the same time their own practices of identity construction. Taken together, the practices of Baruti and Papa Mfumu'Eto find strong affinities with the practices of artists in other urban hubs throughout francophone Africa. Indeed, via important transnational networks often facilitated by festivals, many artists based in different former French and Belgian colonies have influenced each other and even contributed to each other's projects and promotion.

---

8. For more on the centrality of quotidian life in African popular culture across mediums, see Barber, *Readings*.

Barly Baruti's Album about a Film about Music

For many, Barly Baruti's rise to fame, his "emergence as a star of African *bande dessinée*," has played a significant role in the development and international recognition of Black *bandes dessinées* in large part because of his success (and therefore legitimation) in the mainstream Franco-Belgian market (Federici, *L'Entrance* 246). Like many of the contributors to *Jeunes pour jeunes* and later Papa Mfumu'Eto, Baruti works across mediums and forms of expression. In particular, he is also a musician and contributes to the richness of Congolese rumba, which UNESCO added to its list of "intangible cultural heritage of humanity" in 2021 (Pietromarchi; Booty). Baruti's formation as an artist is marked by training at formal institutions in Congo (first in his hometown of Kisangani in northeastern DRC and then Kinshasa) and abroad in France and Belgium (Federici, *L'Entrance* 246–47). Working with Belgian organizations in the DRC on edutainment *bandes dessinées* about the environment in the early 1980s opened important formal apprenticeship opportunities for Baruti, first in Angoulême in France and then at Studios Hergé in Brussels, where he worked with famed *ligne claire* artist Bob de Moor (see chapter 4). The impact of this training on Baruti's work is unmistakable, and at the same time, Baruti's masterful adaptation of European styles to his Congolese context undoubtedly convinced European publishers, artists, and authors of his talent and mainstream appeal. As a result, much of Baruti's early work, in contrast to local *bande dessinée* magazines such as *Jeunes pour jeunes* and later Papa Mfumu'Eto's magazine, was published as albums following the mainstream Franco-Belgian format.[9] While developing his skills as an artist, Baruti also continued working in collaboration in Kinshasa on other projects linked to music, radio, and television, including contributing to the mise-en-scène of the 1986 film *La Vie est belle*, about Congolese rumba superstar Papa Wemba, directed by Benoît Lamy and Mwezé Ngangura (Federici, *L'Entrance* 246). The following year, Baruti released an album-style biographical *bande dessinée* about Papa Wemba and about the film entitled *Papa Wemba: Viva la musica!*, published by Afrique Éditions based in Kinshasa. This film-adjacent forty-eight paged hardback book with a playful lexicon of Kinshasa-specific cultural and linguistic terms at the end presents as a standard Franco-Belgian album yet is rich in intermedial and multicultural practices. For example, Baruti includes a lexicon at

---

9. Baruti has explained that upon his arrival in Kinshasa in the early 1980s, he submitted work to *Jeunes pour jeunes* only to have the team reject it (qtd. in Agnessan 2).

the end entitled "Petit pense-bête à l'intention des 'Non-Kinois'!,"[10] which includes a short description of the Bills as part of the vernacular everyday postcolonial reality of Kinshasa (Baruti, *Papa Wemba* 48). It is worth pointing out that many of Baruti's media-savvy strategies in this one text predate Marguerite Abouet's successful strategies across multiple publications by two full decades (see chapter 2). Indeed, this particular album stands out as a unique display of self-promotion à la Kinois. That is, just like Papa Mfumu'Eto's self-published magazine, Baruti's album about Papa Wemba is informed by, contributes to, and celebrates Kinshasa culture albeit in a more universal way due to its materiality.

Papa Wemba (Jules Shungu Wembadio Pene Kikumba) initially gained local fame as part of the highly popular band Zaïko Langa Langa in the late 1960s at the same time as *Jeunes pour jeunes* was taking off, and, like other Congolese musicians, Papa Wemba splintered off to form other groups, the most important being his band *Viva la musica*, which he founded in 1977 and with which he honed his personal brand and became an international hit (White 6–7). As the front man of the band, Papa Wemba showcased his personal style and solidified his status as the top icon of La Sape, a highly personalized form of self-styling unique to both Congos, whose optimistic ethos is encoded in the acronym, which stands for La Société des Ambianceurs et des Personnes Élégantes.[11] Baruti pays homage to Papa Wemba's status as King of La Sape in the *bande dessinée*, reproducing several iconic looks and newspaper clippings about Papa Wemba's influence (figure 1.1). Thanks to Papa Wemba's local stardom, Congolese filmmaker Mwezé Ngangura selected him as the protagonist in his film *La Vie est belle*, about the Congolese popular music scene. The film, La Sape, and Papa Wemba's music and personal style as well as Baruti's *bande dessinée* about Papa Wemba's rise to fame all celebrate Congolese culture and uplift Kinshasa and its population in ways far removed from the violence, corruption, economic hardship, and political tyranny under President Mobutu. The film is a fictionalized rags-to-riches story imbued with the everyday popular comedy of theatrical sketches on Congolese television at the time (Nasr). In an echo of the film, Baruti's *bande dessinée* purports to be Papa Wemba's own rags-to-riches story that ends with a behind-the-scenes retelling of the musician's silver-screen debut. In the last pages, Baruti shows the film crew preparing to shoot the

---

10. "A little reminder intended for the Non-Kinois."
11. "The Society of Ambiance-Makers and Elegant People." For more on La Sape, see Gandoulou, *Au cœur and Dandies à Bacongo*; Thomas, *Black France*, in particular chapter 6, "Fashion Matters: *La Sape* and Vestimentary Codes in Transnational Contexts and Urban Diasporas."

FIGURE 1.1. Barly Baruti's celebration of Papa Wemba as King of La Sape. *Papa Wemba: Viva La Musica!*, Afrique Éditions, 1987.

opening scene, including Papa Wemba's styling and a zoom in on the clapper board. Then, the final page of the story (figure 1.2) deploys an intermedial layout to imitate the film's opening. Baruti organizes four horizontal panels with rounded corners that correspond to the *La Vie est belle*'s first shots and encloses them in a black frame that is perforated along the outside edges in imitation of actual physical film.

This is but one of Baruti's intermedial mise-en-abyme strategies that simultaneously serves multiple functions by blending local and Western signifiers and modes of representation and subsequently operates as a form of metacommentary. In a similar fashion to Papa Mfumu'Eto's playfully plural approach to layout, *Papa Wemba: Viva la musica!* employs several textual strategies to connote and promote both the talent and fame of both Papa Wemba and Baruti. On the front cover in color, Baruti presents a realistic portrait of Papa Wemba visibly in the process of singing (indicated by the red microphone he holds up and his exuberant expression with eyes closed and a large smile) in front of a drawn wall on which is the poster for the film *La Vie est belle*. Papa Wemba's shoulder and the wall continue to the back cover, where there is also a photorealistic portrait of Baruti in the top left-hand corner (not unlike the proliferation of copied headshots deployed by Papa Mfumu'Eto throughout his magazine discussed below) and a short blurb about the *bande dessinée*, Baruti, the film, and the film's soundtrack. Atop the wall directly below Baruti's portrait is a fedora with a leopard-print band, a coat, and, leaning vertically against the wall, a guitar. Though there is no mention of Baruti as a musician, especially since the

FIGURE 1.2. Last page of *Papa Wemba: Viva la musica!*, which imitates the opening scene of the film *La Vie est belle*. *Papa Wemba: Viva la musica!*, Afrique Éditions, 1987.

FIGURE 1.3. Papa Wemba struggles to compose a song. *Papa Wemba: Viva la musica!*, Afrique Éditions, 1987.

album unabashedly vaunts Papa Wemba as the King of La Sape, Pope of Rumba Rock, and Head Designer of Molokai village (as indicated on the back cover), these items and their proximity to Baruti's portrait nevertheless suggest a personal relationship. In fact, Baruti repeatedly demonstrates his familiarity with music through other textual practices. On the inside covers, a single illustration of various Western and African instruments as well as sheet music and Western musical notations cascading in a diagonal fashion is mirrored on the left- and right-hand sides, creating lots of visual movement (even Baruti's signature on the illustration is mirrored). The multicultural blend of instruments connotes harmony while attesting to Baruti's familiarity with multiple contexts.

This familiarity with Western music also manifests in the story. During the section on Papa Wemba's childhood, when he was part of the choir at a prominent Catholic church in the city, Baruti adds in the actual Western notation for the opening bars of the song "Frère Jacques." Then later, when Papa Wemba struggles with writing the title track for *La Vie est belle*, Baruti uses Western music notation with a treble clef, ellipses, question marks and exclamation points, some notes, and a scribble in thought bubbles to illustrate Papa Wemba's creative process (figure 1.3). There are no scenes in the film that show musicians using sheet music either to perform or create songs, nor is it clear from the *bande dessinée* that Papa Wemba read or used Western musical notation for singing or writing songs. Regardless, Baruti's textual use of Western musical notation acts as a cultural transposition for Western readers and has the effect of universalizing the very localized cultural phenomenon of Congolese rumba (long before UNESCO's recognition of it). Relatedly, the narrative content of this scene and its linguistic plurality connote a harmonious multicultural postcolonial reality. At first, Papa Wemba snaps at his son for interrupting him as he grapples with what to write for the song but quickly changes demeanor upon learning that his son earned a high grade for his recitation of the French poem "The Laborer and His Children," by seventeenth-century classic fabulist Jean de La Fontaine. The short conversation with his son is precisely the pause needed for inspiration, which Baruti indicates through a panel featuring Papa Wemba's delighted expression and a Western treble clef above his head with emphasis lines radiating outward that supplant the function of a drawn lightbulb to convey his new musical idea. La Fontaine's poem, a didactic emblem of French language and culture, becomes the spark for Papa Wemba's song that lifts lines from the poem and mixes them with lyrics in Lingala that refer directly to the practice of *libanga* in which musicians "cite or sing the names of friends or sponsors" in exchange for money or protection (White 170). Taken from the Lingala expression "Kobwaka libanga" meaning "to throw a stone," this practice became necessary for musicians' livelihood following the decline of the record industry in the late 1970s (White 170).

In contrast to Papa Mfumu'Eto, who fabricates endless versions of himself in perpetual play and posturing in his self-made and self-named *Revue Mfumu'eto*, Baruti meticulously stages his identity, at least in his early work, as exemplary of a highly curated blend of Western and local influences. In this way, we might say that his aesthetic and textual approaches align closely with the underlying principles of La Sape. Apart from the portrait on the back cover, there are no images of Baruti in *Papa Wemba: Viva la musica!*, yet his style and, most importantly, the high caliber of his style, marks every aspect of the *bande dessinée*. Indeed, his stylized signature and its mirror image grace the inside covers and run throughout the text punctuating the bottom of each page. Additionally, his mastery of a realistic yet highly legible visual style attests to his talent as an artist intimately familiar with mainstream Franco-Belgian *bande dessinée* conventions and local Congolese culture, just as his textual approach to representing music blends Western modes of representation with conventions of Congolese rumba. Lastly, in his remediation of the film on the title page and then at the end of the text, Baruti demonstrates his insider knowledge of the collaborative filmmaking process. The behind-the-scenes staging that precedes the final page (figure 1.2) foregrounds the many components that go into filming a scene, including all of the equipment needed for the cinematography, lights, storyboarding, blocking, hair and makeup, and, of course, the all-important clapperboard for keeping track of footage. Uplifting Papa Wemba, Congolese rumba, La Sape, filmmaking, and the film *La Vie est belle* in a *bande dessinée* album constitutes Baruti's own performance as an *ambianceur* and *personne élégante*. Though much more restrained than Papa Mfumu'Eto's practices, Baruti's practices nevertheless imitate the sociohistorically and culturally situated politics of self-promotion central to Congolese culture at the time.

Papa Mfumu'Eto's Multidimensional Magazine and Stone-Throwing

Leafing through the impressive archive of *Revue Mfumu'eto,* one cannot help but notice the seemingly endless repetition and variation of Papa Mfumu'Eto's multifaceted self-promotion.[12] While the self-published magazine is named after one of his many self-bestowed sobriquets (and therefore found on the cover of each issue as well as on each page as part of the pagination), the inside cover and the back cover of many issues feature a photocopy of a staged portrait photograph of Papa Mfumu'Eto smiling.[13] This casual and inviting headshot of him in a button-up shirt and tie, as ubiquitous as his name, is a key element of his self-styling and brand. At times, multiple photocopies of the headshot can be found in a single issue of *Revue Mfumu'eto,* and loyal readers expected to see this mechanically reproduced image—Papa Mfumu'Eto's icon—with each new issue. Moreover, since Papa Mfumu'Eto made the magazine himself, part of his practice involved playing with layout and format such that there are sometimes multiple versions of a single issue. Similarly, since he also printed his own magazine, shifts in printing quality could vary over the course of a print run. Consequently, not only was his in-text presence multiplied through endless iterations of his self-presentation (in his self-naming practice and in the proliferation of his own image whether as a photocopy of a photograph or a drawing of the photograph), but the trace of his multimedia practice is encoded in the physical object itself. Indeed, the visual density of his style, often blending multiple visual patterns and layering cartouches horizontally and vertically, is proof of his prolific production. In the stylized lettering for the magazine's title, the uniquely dynamic layout, and chic self-styling as modern (in his dress and his artistic practice), Papa Mfumu'Eto presents as a thoroughly savvy urban superstar of Kinshasa.

Thus, one can imagine how the placement at the end of an issue entitled *Ba latisi ngalula* masque *po abala te / Masque de vieillesse* (Masque of old age) of

---

12. The impetus for this portion of the chapter came from my participation in the 2018 Gwendolyn M. Carter conference hosted by the Center for African Studies at the University of Florida and organized by Nancy R. Hunt and Alioune Sow, during which I was able to sift through the archive of Papa Mfumu'Eto's work amassed by Nancy R. Hunt. Selections from this portion will also feature in the anthology on the archive, which is edited by Nancy R. Hunt and Pedro Monaville (forthcoming from Leuven UP).

13. For examples, visit the "Papa Mfumu'Eto 1er Papers" digital collection held by the George A. Smathers Libraries at the University of Florida located in Gainesville (https://ufdc.ufl.edu/collections/mfumss/). Searching the collection for "back cover" and "self portrait" bring up several examples of the reproduced and imitated photograph.

a full-length photograph of Papa Mfumu'Eto in a traditional African outfit would be simultaneously shocking in its rarity and expected in its playful posturing of identity. The top of the page elaborately and ironically introduces the author in all capitalized letters as SA MAJESTÉ, EMPEREUR PAPA MFUMU'ETO 1ER CE TRÈS CÉLÈBRE INCONNU[14] then gives way to the rare photograph on the right, accompanied on the left by a bulleted list of personal information and elements of Papa Mfumu'Eto's personal taste. The performance of this page and its dense metareferential character sheds light on Papa Mfumu'Eto's posturing with regards to mainstream *bandes dessinées* as well as to his own place within the realm of Congolese *bandes dessinées*. Reading this page in conjunction with other practices across the magazine's run from the 1990s to the mid-2000s helps us better understand how Papa Mfumu'Eto's postures and *libanga*—shoutouts to sponsors, fans, and friends, a practice borrowed from Congolese musicians like Papa Wemba—stages the generative practice of everyday life in Kinshasa as one shared by author and audience alike.

On the bulleted list that accompanies Papa Mfumu'Eto's full-length photograph are preferences including his favorite dishes and his favorite *bédéistes*. This term, which roughly translates as cartoonist or caricaturist, emphasizes the product produced by such artists, namely, a *bande dessinée*. Looking closely at this list provides crucial insight into Papa Mfumu'Eto's own production as a *bédéiste* and, more importantly, his leveraging of the Ninth Art as part and parcel of his "égo-histoire" or his "ego-story/history" (Hunt, "Papa Mfumu'Eto 1er" 268). Taking up from French historian Pierre Nora this concept of writing that blends autobiography and history, Nancy Rose Hunt applies it to Papa Mfumu'Eto and "sa manière de mêler autoglorification, éléments historiques et récits" (Hunt, "Papa Mfumu'Eto 1er" 268).[15] A closer look at the list of *bédéistes préférés* and its performance within the broader context of the page itself and of the specific issue of *Revue Mfumu'eto* reveals an engagement with the history of *bandes dessinées* in the DRC and in Kinshasa in particular, especially when examining the list's mutation across different versions of the same issue; one list appears to be an earlier version due to its handwritten quality, and a later version uses the same page layout but with typed font and additions as well as changes in terms of content. In the early version, the handwritten list of *bédéistes préférés* is as follows: "P'tit Luc (Ptiluc), Hergé, Barly Baruti, Lepas, Aundu Kiala, Waderi Banza, Lepas [sic], Boyau . . . Kiesse, Ekunda, Fifi Mukuna, Al Mata,

---

14. His Majesty, Emperor Papa Mfumu'Eto I, this very famous nobody.
15. "his way of mixing autoglorification, historical elements, and stories."

Pat Masioni . . ." In contrast, the typed list in the later version is as follows: "Barly Baruti, Hergé, P'tit Luc, Tembo Kash, Aundu Kiala, Waderi Banza, Lepas, Boyau, Kiesse, Kabos Ekunde, Fifi Mukuna, Al Mata, Pat Masioni." In both cases, the list is comprised primarily of local Kinshasa-based *bédéistes* (including one woman, Fifi Mukuna) and two Belgian *bédéistes*—Hergé and Ptiluc, a prolific Belgian artist whose career started in the early 1980s. If we consider the ordering of the list as a correlation for Papa Mfumu'Eto's classification, then it is telling that Ptiluc and Hergé—whose respective work is commercially published in Europe—appear at the beginning of the earlier version of the list and are followed directly by Barly Baruti. This foundational triumvirate (inverted in the later version of the list, with Baruti as the first name, but nevertheless intact as a triumvirate) suggests the history of *bandes dessinées* in the DRC as one rooted in Belgian colonialism with continued close-knit ties between the two countries. This triumvirate also reveals Papa Mfumu'Eto's familiarity with the Ninth Art, industry standards, and mainstream commercial *bandes dessinées*, while the shift in ordering in the later version suggests his privileging of Congolese *bédéistes* and their influence on the local *bande dessinée* scene.

It is worth pausing to examine the case of P'tit Luc, or Ptiluc on this list, as his experience and familiarity with African artists and his role as patron and cultural legitimizer resembles that of other European artists and publishers.[16] In the late 1990s and early 2000s, Ptiluc, as a famous artist, was invited to *bande dessinée* festivals in Libreville (Gabon) and Yaoundé (Cameroon); he was also invited to Kinshasa, where he participated in Baruti's l'Espace à suivre, a *bande dessinée* workshop and cultural event hosted by Baruti's Atélier de creation, recherche et initiation à l'art (ACRIA). All of these visits put him in contact with local artists and artists from throughout francophone Africa and the Indian Ocean. In fact, as a result of these cultural and personal exchanges, Ptiluc spearheaded *Ptiluc présente BD Africa: Les Africains dessinent l'Afrique* (Ptiluc presents BD Africa: Africans draw Africa), published by Albin Michel in 2005. Like many other European-published anthologies of *bandes dessinées* by African artists, this collection of vignettes claims to present readers with authentic visions of Africa. However, as with many other such anthologies, there were limitations on the creative freedom

---

16. Ptiluc's promotion of African cartoonists in Europe is not unique and, in fact, closely resembles what has been taking place with regards to African francophone literature. Moreover, how his name and preface dominate the paratextual space of *Ptiluc présente BD Africa: Les Africains dessinent l'Afrique* mimics how French writers' work often inhabited the paratextual space of early francophone novels from Africa, usually in the form of prefaces. For more, see Watts, *Packaging*; Ducournau, *La Fabrique*.

of the participating artists.[17] The narrative impetus for the project—ostensibly faithful representations of quotidian life in Africa—was suggested by Ptiluc, who wanted to share with readers who more closely resembled himself ("les enfants belges et les vieux motards"[18]) his surprise that *bandes dessinées* were just as popular in Africa as in Europe and that there were "dessinateurs cachés quelque part dans cet immense continent"[19] waiting to be discovered (Ptiluc 1–2). Despite the (trans)colonial overtones of Ptiluc's framing of his discovery of African artists, his participation in African *bandes dessinées* festivals and workshops nevertheless developed into active promotion and publication of work by African artists. Perhaps Ptiluc's presence as the only other Belgian besides Hergé on Papa Mfumu'Eto's list of *bédéistes préférés* has more to do with these facts than simply Papa Mfumu'Eto's enjoyment of Ptiluc's style and *bandes dessinées*. While Papa Mfumu'Eto did not contribute to Ptiluc's anthology, three of the four Congolese artists whose work comprises half of Ptiluc's anthology also feature on Papa Mfumu'Eto's lists.

In fact, the majority of the Kinshasa artists on Papa Mfumu'Eto's lists tended to produce *bandes dessinées* in French with highly detailed visual styles leaning toward realism. While many like Baruti and Masioni had albums published in Europe or in Congo via Belgian-initiated publishers such as Éditions Saint-Paul / Médiaspaul, others contributed to collective magazines in imitation of popular Franco-Belgian *bande dessinée* magazines like *Pilote*, *Tintin*, and *Spirou*.[20] The Congolese artists on Papa Mfumu'Eto's lists, with the notable exception of Lepas, also contributed to international anthologies such as the one spearheaded by Ptiluc. Correlating the order of the names with importance, we notice Papa Mfumu'Eto's insistence on Lepas in the early version of the list. Not only does his name appear just after the main trio, but it is the only name to be repeated within the same list. The repetition of Lepas's name on the first list might be a mistake—or not, if we consider Papa Mfumu'Eto's own output, for in contrast to that of the majority of the artists he names, Papa Mfumu'Eto's work never sought to imitate mainstream albums. Instead, *Revue Mfumu'eto* more closely resembles Lepas's "BD de la rue" or "street comics." Lepas, alias of Lepa Mabila

---

17. For more on the creative limitations of such anthologies, see Repetti, "New Comics."

18. "Belgian kids and old motorists."

19. "cartoonists hidden somewhere in this immense continent."

20. In 2009 Pat Masioni became the first *bédéiste* from the Democratic Republic of the Congo to be published by a major anglophone comics publisher—Vertigo comics (a subdivision of DC Comics, Inc.). Masioni's illustrations for Joshua Dysart's reboot of *Unknown Soldier* starting with issue 13 served as the launching pad for a lucrative career as an illustrator and colorist for anglophone comics.

Saye, contributed to *Jeunes pour jeunes* and later began his own magazine, *JunioR* (1985–2007), which he self-published in Lingala and for which he created a direct-to-market distribution model in Kinshasa after many failed attempts. Initially, in 1985 when he decided to produce *JunioR*, he worked with local editors and printing shops who ended up selling his work in Brazzaville without his permission and without sharing the profits; consequently, Lepas took it upon himself to work with printing shops and then personally distributed copies to local vendors, but eventually cut them out as well, deciding to sell his magazine directly to readers (Cassiau-Haurie, "Lépa Mabila Saye"). The Lepas model also alleviated any pressure to produce a luxury cultural object—as with mainstream Franco-Belgian albums—which many African artists have long noted as too expensive to produce or consume in many African countries.[21] Additionally, this model, contrary to published albums and collective endeavors, offers artistic and creative freedom, ensures that profits go directly to the artist, and targets a highly localized audience.

Complete control over *Revue Mfumu'eto* is precisely what makes Papa Mfumu'Eto's work so impressive, intimate, and therefore lucrative in Kinshasa. At the same time, it is what allows for and in fact prompts his endless experimentation and performance. In this regard, Papa Mfumu'Eto's innovative and, most importantly, informal practices closely resemble those of popular Kinshasa-based musicians who developed new practices in the 1970s in response to the decline of record sales. According to Bob W. White, the structure of popular music in Kinshasa changed as a function of the growing necessity of live performances as a crucial source of income.[22] Like musicians' self-styling and self-promotion, in *Revue Mfumu'eto*, each issue, page, formatting element, and margin is a site of potential performance, meaning-making, and self-creation where Papa Mfumu'Eto continually generates new titles, names, and occupations for himself. For example, on the page with his personal preferences in the earlier version, he describes himself as a "dessinateur-journaliste informel."[23] On the back cover of the very same issue, accompanying his reproduced photographic headshot is an expanded self-description. In two text boxes along the vertical and horizontal axes of the photograph, he expounds his many talents and occupations: along the right-hand side of the photograph, he presents himself as an "Artiste-peintre-dessinateur, spécialiste de la face cachée de la peinture

---

21. See, for example, Langevin, "Bande dessinée"; Lent, "African Cartooning"; Repetti, "African 'Ligne Claire.'"
22. White, *Rumba Rules*, see chapter 3, "Made in Zaire."
23. "Informal cartoonist-journalist."

populaire et de la bande dessinée populaire mystico-religio-secrète africaine,"[24] whereas below the photograph, he adds that he is also a "Peintre miniaturiste bantou, historien, philosophe, sociologue, psychologue et chercheur indépendant, évangeliste informel."[25] Accordingly, others attempting to describe him and his work similarly choose a multifaceted approach. For some, he is an "artiste tour à tour bédéiste, peintre et même 'performer'"[26] whose life and work "se confondent, dans une véritable mise en scène, empreinte de légendes et mystère" (Bandibanga et al. 3).[27] This playful tension is clearly on display on the page with the full-length photograph and lists as evidenced by the heading "His Majesty Papa Mfumu'Eto the First, this very famous nobody." This seemingly paradoxical description attests to Papa Mfumu'Eto's decision to eschew producing mainstream album-style *bandes dessinées,* and therefore recognition beyond Kinshasa, in favor of affordable artisanal magazines with a local enthusiastic fan base.[28] Moreover, it features one of the key linguistic strategies deployed throughout all issues of *Revue Mfumu'eto*: it mobilizes the third person to craft and elaborate upon Papa Mfumu'Eto as a character and personality. Again, Papa Mfumu'Eto's practice is derived from his specific context. Like self-aggrandizing musicians who also posture as humble, as White argues, Papa Mfumu'Eto imitates the same "kind of doublespeak for which Mobutu became famous" and that was a key tool of "a genre of political propaganda that became known as *animation politique culturelle*" (White 8).

As part of his performance, Papa Mfumu'Eto blends metanarratives, formal elements, linguistic strategies, and paratextual spaces to comment on what he is doing while he is doing it, so as to include local readers and engender a sense of community and insider status. For example, most cover pages include many different headings, taglines, and even horizontal cartouches that provide metacommentary on the issue at hand. The French term for overlaid text boxes, *cartouches*, seems particularly appropriate for

---

24. "Artist-painter-illustrator, specialist of the hidden side of popular (urban) painting and popular mystico-religio-secrete-African comics."
25. "Bantu miniaturist painter, historian, philosopher, sociologist, psychologist and independent researcher, informal evangelist."
26. "artist in turns cartoonist, painter, and even 'performer.'"
27. "conflate, in a true staging, imprinted with legends and mysteries."
28. This rejection of more mainstream tendencies might be one reason for which Hilaire Mbiye Lumbala all but ignores Papa Mfumu'Eto in his 2009 study *Cases et bulles africaines: Introduction à la bande dessinée africaine francophone* despite allocating a substantial portion of the book to artists from the DRC. This omission is telling, since Mbiye Lumbala nevertheless upholds Chéri Samba as important while only mentioning *JunioR* and *Revue Mfumu'eto* in passing.

describing Papa Mfumu'Eto's use of this formal element, as these overlaid boxes resemble the cartouches of Ancient Egypt, which listed the names and titles of Egyptian monarchs. For *Ba latisi ngalula masque po abala te / Masque de vieillesse*, Papa Mfumu'Eto announces his own comeback in a cartouche along the right-hand side of the cover and declares its impact right away: "Papa Mfumu'Eto 1er revient en force avec 'le feu divin' pour réveiller la bande dessinée Populaire congolaise qui est en train de mourir."[29] This announcement is then meted out toward the end of the story and commented upon on the last page, the one featuring the full-length photograph and Papa Mfumu'Eto's personal information. In both versions, the page offers general information (name, surname, pseudonym, marital status, and religion) before moving to personal preferences, starting with favorite dishes (all of which are local Congolese dishes, with the exception of bread), favorite *bédéistes*, and favorite colors. Starting with food and including colors generates intimacy with readers, since it is easy to relate to such general preferences. While the earlier version of the list stops here (though provides contact information that the later list does not), the later list, in addition to having a different ordering of favorite *bédéistes* (but the same ordering of favorite dishes), expands upon Papa Mfumu'Eto's preferences with more detail and more familiarity. Alongside lists of favorite flowers and drinks, Papa Mfumu'Eto includes what he dislikes ("La Pollution Sonore et tous les bruits nuisibles pendant le sommeil"[30]) and likes ("Le Silence, l'isolement, le Calme"[31]), a description of his "caractère particulier" ("Ne rit pas"[32]), and even what he labels his "signe particulier" ("Artiste Dessinateur qui Possède les doigts les plus fins et les plus souples d'Afrique").[33] Not surprisingly, Papa Mfumu'Eto once again attests to his own talent and dexterity, but he also casts a specific aura of seriousness around himself, all of which is meant to assure his readers of his credentials and at the same time compliment them for choosing to read (and purchase) *Revue Mfumu'eto*.

In fact, his self-promotion on this last page is a metareferential continuation of the narrative content from the end of the issue's story, which ends on the previous page. As a sort of epilogue to the didactic story of the potentially dangerous *Masque de vieillesse*, Papa Mfumu'Eto depicts a scene

---

29. "Papa Mfumu'Eto I returns in force with 'the divine fire' to awaken Popular Congolese comics that are in the process of dying."
30. "Sound pollution and all the harmful noises during sleep."
31. "Silence, isolation, Calm."
32. "Doesn't laugh."
33. "particular sign: Illustrator Artist who Possesses the finest and most supple fingers in Africa."

in a crowded marketplace, where the narration and dialogue, which switch effortlessly between Lingala and French to reflect the linguistic reality of the market and Kinois society, work together to encourage people to pray ceaselessly (to ward off negative spirits) and to demonstrate the importance of local *bandes dessinées* magazines. Through speech balloons, one sees vendors selling food and both Lepas's magazine *JunioR* and Papa Mfumu'Eto's magazine *Revue Mfumu'eto*. At the end of the scene, a visibly happy young woman purchases a copy of *Revue Mfumu'eto* and, in a frontal gaze directed at the reader, explains that she likes it the most since it reflects the reality of her everyday life, thereby endorsing Papa Mfumu'Eto.

This mirrored endorsement between Papa Mfumu'Eto and his readers is but one of the many strategies he uses to engage directly with and flatter his audience, which in turn engenders a loyal fan base eager to discover his newest dynamic creation in which one might find oneself, either through stories to which one can relate or through actual shoutouts within the pages of the magazine itself in an image-text practice that resembles *libanga*. In both versions of *Ba latisi ngalula* masque *po abala te / Masque de vieillesse*, readers' names adorn the left-hand, right-hand, and bottom margins of almost each page; sometimes the names are accompanied by the location of the person mentioned. In the earlier version, the names stop before the page with the full-length photograph of Papa Mfumu'Eto and his personal information. In contrast, the last page of the later, more polished version includes a block of names under the heading "Échangeur LE CHATEAU" (the name of a major market), thus singling people out by their specific geographic location within Kinshasa. While it is unclear whether those named in the margins of *Revue Mfumu'eto* paid to have their names in print, the fact that Papa Mfumu'Eto includes such shoutouts to his readers nevertheless implies an informal form of patronage in that the inclusion of readers' names in the magazine might engender reader loyalty on the premise of potentially seeing one's name in print. This appropriation and adaptation of *libanga* would undoubtedly be familiar to Papa Mfumu'Eto's readers, as would his "tendency towards boastfulness" and his dynamic self-naming practices, which also mimic music culture in Kinshasa (Trapido 64–65). It should come as no surprise, then, that, as with *libanga*, Papa Mfumu'Eto's career as a "very famous nobody" is financially viable because of the local market rather than through international patronage (Trapido 77). As with popular music, "people cited are drawn in by the excitement of hearing [seeing] their own name, and because they are named, they in turn draw in others by buying extra copies" and sharing "(or giving it to) friends and relatives" (White 177). This textual practice generates "a degree of liveness and warmth by placing [creators] (and by extension their fans) in a live network of social reciprocity" (White 178). Furthermore, as with Congolese musicians, who have inspired other African musicians to name drop their names, other African artists pay homage to Papa Mfumu'Eto in their work. Of particular note, Gabonese Pahé includes a *clin d'oeil* to Papa Mfumu'Eto on the first page of the second volume of his autobiographical *bande dessinée* (*La Vie de Pahé: Paname*) when describing a trip to Kinshasa. In both volumes of *La Vie de Pahé*, Pahé plays up his own cosmopolitanism and prowess as a famous artist by starting with his participation in *bande dessinée* festivals in countries other than Gabon (Cameroon and DRC). Pahé starts off the second volume with a splash page of Kinshasa, where he traveled to participate in Barly Baruti's l'Espace à suivre cultural event. Attesting to Papa Mfumu'Eto's local influence, Pahé includes his name as part of the local graffiti. At the same time, Papa Mfumu'Eto's local impact manifested in his return to *bande dessinée* in the form of contributing to the fifth installment of *Kin label*, a local *bande dessinée* magazine started by Asimba Bathy (an original contributor to *Jeunes pour jeunes*) and featuring the regular participation of many of the *bédéistes* from Papa Mfumu'Eto's list (Cassiau-Haurie, *Dictionnaire* 234).

Ultimately, Papa Mfumu'Eto's polyvalent, multimedia, and hands-on approach to *bandes dessinées* leverages ostensibly simple strategies laden with metareferential, narrative, and local sociocultural content, all of which he uses to create his own story and identity. This "chaotically pluralistic" process and its resulting product—the *Revue Mfumu'eto*—tell of the postcolonial reality of daily life in Kinshasa (Mbembe, *On the Postcolony* 108). Just like local musicians, especially the *atalaku*, or bands' hype man, who fabricates his own instrument from recycled insecticide cans, adapting and recycling existing materials including the Ninth Art and Congolese *libanga*, Papa Mfumu'Eto presents himself and his readers as savvy cultural consumers and producers who make names for themselves and who name-drop the famous and influential around them (White 11–12).

Conclusion

Barly Baruti and Papa Mfumu'Eto represent two sides of the same coin, and a close, contextualized analysis of their practices demonstrates how similar influences can result in a rich diversity of Black *bandes dessinées*. Both, like Congolese musicians, are *débrouillards*; that is, they are skilled, self-reliant artisans who take what is around them and, through a range of multimedia and intermedial artistic practices, create dynamic stories that highlight and celebrate everyday people who are also adept at *se débrouiller,* or getting by. Rather than focus on the negative socioeconomic and political constraints of the postcolony that produce the necessity to hone informal tactics, Baruti, Papa Mfumu'Eto, their audiences, and other Black francophone artists working throughout Africa valorize the talent and agility needed to make do.[34] We see this in the popular Black *bande dessinée* heroes of West Africa such as the eponymous character in T. T. Fons's *Goorgoorlou* in Dakar, and in *Gbich!*'s Ivorian businessman mascot, Cauphy Gombo, whose slogan "No pitié in bizness" instantly captures his suave and global aptitude for getting by. We also see this in the political cartoons of artists working in Cameroon and Gabon in spite of potential censorship and serious retaliation by government representatives and law enforcement.[35] More recently, this same prized tactic, of getting by through using what is around you, has tapped into global fan culture, in particular through the imitation of manga and anime heroes instead of Franco-Belgian icons or Anglo-American superheroes. A prime example of this is the downloadable digital comic *Narinto,* written by Ivorian Nandy Diabaté and illustrated by Cameroonian Saïd Fochivé (2017–present), in which an Ivorian boy styles himself after his favorite manga character, Naruto, as he makes his way through his daily life. Baruti and Papa Mfumu'Eto as well as several contributors to *Jeunes pour jeunes* are still producing work, though Papa Mfumu'Eto has turned his attention exclusively to painting. Thanks to their innovation in the last quarter of the twentieth century, there are new audiences and more opportunities for more experimentation, self-styling, and storytelling.

---

34. My reading of Kinshasa in the 1980s and 1990s is indebted to Mbembe's *On the Postcolony.*

35. See, for example, Mbembe, *On the Postcolony,* especially chapter 4, "The Thing and Its Double"; Pahé, *Gabonaises* and *Les Choses.*

CHAPTER 2

The AYA Effect, or Marguerite Abouet's Timely and Timeless Interventions

In 1993, unrest mounted in the Ivory Coast following the death of President Félix Houphouët-Boigny, who had ruled since independence in 1960. Previously, following World War II, Houphouët-Boigny was elected to the French National Assembly and held several government positions alongside other prominent figures from France's empire, including Aimé Césaire (Martinique), Léopold Senghor (Senegal), Sékou Touré (Guinea), Léon M'ba (Gabon), Modibo Keïta (Mali), and Philibert Tsiranana (Madagascar), all of whom participated in France's Commission on Overseas Territories to decide the future of the country's colonial possessions.[1] Some regions remained part of France as overseas departments and territories, while others negotiated for independence. Concerning the latter group, France lobbied to retain power through economic and military agreements. The response among soon-to-be-independent nations varied. Houphouët-Boigny advocated for maintaining ties with France, publicly declaring support in 1955 for la France-Afrique, a positive view of France's continued involvement

---

1. For more on the debates facilitated by this commission and how they shaped contemporary race relations in France and the francophone world, see Marker, "Obscuring."

with African nations.[2] Working closely with the French (Jacques Foccart, central architect of la Françafrique, and French presidents), Houphouët-Boigny boosted economic development in the newly independent Ivory Coast, resulting in the "Ivorian Miracle." Researchers have exposed the aspirational performativity of this concept and its restrictive limitations, but the alluring possibility of social change led the country to become one of the most stable nations in West Africa in the two decades following the "era of independences."[3]

Eventually, the economic trouble that had already started toward the end of Houphouët-Boigny's three-decade reign, as well as his death, increased instability. Mistrust in the democratic process grew under the new president, Henri Konan Bédié, and ethnic tensions rose, spurred by his concept of "Ivoirité," a supposed common Ivorian identity that he used to exclude key rival Alassane Ouattara from politics. In December 1999, Robert Guéï, former head of the military under Houphouët-Boigny, led a coup d'état that ousted Bédié. Guéï's supporters terrorized the Ivorian public, and he ruled until losing the presidential election in October 2000 to Laurent Gbagbo, leader of the primary opposition party under Houphouët-Boigny. The election took place amidst protests, since both Bédié and Ouattara were unauthorized to run for office and postelection violence resulted in hundreds of deaths. In December 2000, Ouattara and his party boycotted subsequent legislative elections, and protests led to more deaths and arrests. Despite attempts at reconciliation in 2001 and 2002, a failed coup on Gbagbo in September 2002 transformed into a rebellion that occupied the north. Gbagbo and his forces fought back, targeting both the rebels and political opponents. Continued fighting between the north (under the rebels) and the south (under Gbagbo, his supporters, and the Ivorian army), known as the First Ivorian Civil War (2002–7), also included attacks on United Nations peacekeepers and French nationals living in the Ivory Coast.

---

2. Contrary to Houphouët-Boigny's positive notion of *France-Afrique*, the multivalent portmanteau *"Françafrique"* became a pejorative term to describe France's aggressive neocolonial designs in francophone Africa. As François-Xavier Verschave has noted, the alternative spelling *"France à fric"* (France with money) immediately points to France's sustained imperial interests, whose embeddedness is easily read in the currency of several francophone African nations; though "CFA" currently stands for the franc of the Financial Community of Africa, its designation has changed several times since World War II as a function of decolonization and neocolonialism. For more, see Verschave, *La Françafrique*; Diop, "Françafrique"; Diallo, "Félix Houphouë-Boigny"; Taylor, "France à fric."

3. See in particular Boone, "Commerce"; Bamba, *African Miracle*.

In 2007, following an international workshop held in Abidjan the previous year on the role of political cartooning to bear witness to the violence in the Ivory Coast, Olvis Dabley, founder of the Coco Bulles festival, and Lassane Zohoré, cofounder of *Gbich!* (one of the most successful *bande dessinée* magazines in francophone Africa), curated an anthology of political cartoons entitled *Côte d'Ivoire, on va où là?* (Ivory Coast, where are we going?), with the tagline "1993–2006: 13 ans de crise politique en dessins de presse."[4] This sixty-five-page softback compilation featuring glossy paper and lively colors was published in Abidjan with the assistance of the French embassy. Its thematized chapters with short introductory explanations foregrounded key figures and factors that shaped the nation's turmoil: Houphouët-Boigny (deemed "le père de la nation"), Ivoirité, la Françafrique, power, the nation's division in two, the role of the press, and, to promote peace, what unites Ivorians. These sections both attest to cartoonists' robust and sustained work to expose the corruption plaguing the Ivory Coast and to inform the Ivorian public (literate and illiterate) of politicians' machinations that polarize and exploit people for their own benefit.[5] The anthology also boasts a robust annex of supporting texts that contextualize the situation leading up to 2007.[6] Together, the many components combat reductive narratives about the nation's instability, which are summarized in the preface by a quote from celebrated Ivorian reggae singer Alpha Blondy: "Si vous comprenez quelque chose à la crise ivoirienne c'est qu'on vous l'a mal expliquée."[7]

Peace was brokered and Gbagbo was reelected in 2008, but violence erupted once again in response to the November 2010 election when Gbagbo refused to accept defeat despite Ouattara's internationally recognized

---

4. "1993–2006: 13 years of political crisis in political cartoons."
5. In Nicoletta Fagiolo's 2009 documentary *Résistants du 9e Art* (Rebels of the 9th art), Zohoré explains that one of *Gbich!*'s unwavering objectives is to fight for peace by celebrating difference while also exposing how politicians attempt to aggravate ethnic tensions. For Zohoré and his team, their work is essential because, unlike newspapers, *Gbich!* is (at least partially) accessible to all Ivorians, allowing the illiterate public to keep up with current affairs.
6. The annex includes a journalistic *bande dessinée* about the First Civil War, by Lebanese-Swiss cartoonist Patrick Chappatte, who traveled to the Ivory Coast in 2006; a parable about the lamentable state of Ivorian society, by journalist Venance Konan; descriptions of seven politicians presented as principle actors of the Ivorian crisis, accompanied by grayscale caricature portraits of each; a lexicon of important groups and acronyms; and a timeline of key political events in the Ivory Coast, from independence in 1960 to December 19, 2006, when, in a national address, President Gbagbo proposed an end to the crisis through negotiations with his opponents.
7. "If you understand anything about the Ivorian crisis it's that someone has poorly explained it to you."

victory. The fighting between Gbagbo's forces and Ouattara's, who were supported by French troops, known as the Second Ivorian Civil War (2010–11), escalated in Abidjan, where Gbagbo was holed up, and ended with his arrest in April 2011. Ouattara has remained in power since, in spite of boycotts to his successive reelections. Meanwhile, Gbagbo went into exile in France. In 2016, he was charged by the International Criminal Court (ICC) with crimes against humanity for the deaths during the Second Ivorian Civil War. In 2019, the ICC acquitted Gbagbo, and in 2021 he returned to the Ivory Coast, where his supporters, many in the Abidjan suburb of Yopougon, welcomed him with joy, while some victims of the postelection violence in 2010 saw his return as a failure of justice.[8]

At almost the same time as the two Ivorian civil wars, the first six volumes of the most well-known Black *bande dessinée* series—*Aya de Yopougon*, written by Marguerite Abouet and illustrated by Clément Oubrerie—were published in France, to instant and sustained acclaim. Since the release of the first volume in 2005, the series continues to be framed as offering a refreshingly vibrant vision of everyday life in contemporary Africa even though it is set in a specific Ivorian neighborhood in the late 1970s and 1980s. In the first volume's preface, award-winning French novelist Anna Gavalda joyfully praises Abouet's script, which is based on childhood memories, and Oubrerie's graceful visual rendition of the characters and Yopougon. Though she alludes to a cultural signifier from the past that is central to the story—the American soap opera *Dallas*—Gavalda uses the present tense throughout, thus minimizing the story's time displacement. Of course, the representation of life during the Ivorian Miracle in *Aya de Yopougon* stands in sharp contrast with that which emerges from the political cartoons collected in *Côte d'Ivoire, on va où là?* And while the Ivory Coast was still in the midst of the First Civil War, the first volume of *Aya de Yopougon* was awarded the prize for Best First Album at the 2006 Angoulême International Comics Festival. The series has since become and remains the paragon of African comics in French even though, in significant ways, it was unlike anything else published in francophone regions of Africa or Europe at the time and despite its contested status as African or French.

Repeatedly upheld for presenting a universally relatable vision of Africa removed from negative clichés, *Aya de Yopougon* is unequivocally the most widely distributed, written-about, and commented-upon Black *bande dessinée*. Christophe Cassiau-Haurie and others drawing from his work refer

---

8. For more on Gbagbo's trial and return to the Ivory Coast, see Maclean, "Ex-Ivory Coast President"; Aboa and Coulibaly, "Former Ivory Coast President"; Kouassi, "Gbagbo Acquittal."

to the series' phenomenal success as "the Aya effect," which, though considered a legitimizing boon for what Cassiau-Haurie and Sandra Federici classify as African *bandes dessinées*, is seen by some as problematic and potentially inhibitory (Cassiau-Haurie, *Quand la BD* 13; Federici, *L'Entrance* 283). In her analysis of whether Abouet is a "bédéiste francophone *africaine*" or francophone African comics creator, Rosemonde Assanvo-Kadjo considers the impetus to categorize as itself a deception (7). Underlining the universalist themes across Abouet's first three series (*Aya de Yopougon, Bienvenue*, and *Akissi*), and their collaborative production, Assanvo-Kadjo concludes that all of her work is but "le simple reflet d'un projet interculturel" (7).[9] At the same time, in contrast to Cassiau-Haurie's affirmation that "the Aya effect" proved that a *bande dessinée* written by an author from the Global South with African protagonists could succeed, Cameroonian artist and publisher Simon Pierre Mbumbo laments that thriving in the conservative Franco-Belgian *bande dessinée* market is not easy for African creators and, moreover, that "*Aya de Yopougon* est l'arbre qui cache la forêt"[10] (qtd. in Michel). In fact, for internationally renowned Paris-based Congolese artist Pat Masioni, *Aya de Yopougon* "fait désormais partie des classiques de la B.D. franco-belge,"[11] an estimation that aligns the series with Europe more than Africa (qtd. in Federici, *L'Entrance* 284). In contrast, Ivorian author and literary activist Edwige-Renée Dro, who translated the seventh volume of *Aya de Yopougon* from French to English and who is based in Yopougon, considers the series an Ivorian classic despite its meager distribution in the Ivory Coast (qtd. in Peltier).

Odile Cazenave and Patricia Célérier explain that the enormous success of *Aya de Yopougon* "is quite symptomatic of the fact that, in general, international recognition still comes through Europe and the West" and highlight that the series "is often critically isolated from the wider context of African production in Europe and on the continent" (139–40). Concerning production on the African continent, they describe the "imbalance in distribution, readership, and reception" by comparing *Aya de Yopougon* to Dakar-based *Goorgoolou*, by T. T. Fons (pen name of Alphonse Mendy), given the similar narrative focus on an everyday hero in West Africa (140). For the European context, they explain that *Aya de Yopougon* regularly receives media praise "for breaking away from the usual clichés" in contrast to works that address more serious topics, like *Malamine, un africain à Paris*, by Christophe Edimo and Mbumbo (see chapter 3), and overtly "politically committed cartoons,

---

9. "the simple reflection of an intercultural project."
10. "*Aya de Yopougon* is the tree that hides the forest."
11. "is from now on part of classic Franco-Belgian *bandes dessinées*."

such as the Senegalese Samba Ndar Cissé's *Oulaï*, addressing female genital mutilation" (140). These broad observations capture the general assessment in the Global North of supposedly "African" comics in French, but there is little attention paid to the differences between the various objects lumped together. *Goorgoolou* is a serialized newspaper strip, *Malamine, un africain à Paris* is an independently published softback one-shot, and *Oulaï* is a short vignette published in an anthology. Cazenave and Célérier's discourse performs the ambiguities inherent to "the Aya effect" and Black *bandes dessinées* more broadly. In their discussion, what constitutes "African" is unclear, and graphic novels, comics, and cartooning are interchangeable. The placement of their discussion of *Aya de Yopougon* (preceded by African art and followed by short mentions of Nigeria's video industry and the role of music in Africa) cordons the series off from literature in favor of linking it to African cultural production, yet they describe it as a comic book "in France" (139). They acknowledge the collaborative effort of Abouet and Oubrerie, but there is no discussion of the series's publisher or materiality. It is ironic that they pay close attention to the transcolonial geography of legitimation but not its mechanisms concerning *bandes dessinées*, despite doing so for texts unambiguously belonging to the category of literature.

This chapter prioritizes such mechanisms to investigate what "the Aya effect" reveals about the transcolonial factors informing Black *bande dessinée* production, distribution, and reception and also the range of interrelated strategies and practices of authors, artists, and publishers. As is evident from the discussion above, the stakes of categorizing Abouet and her work are, for some, very high. In this regard, Abouet resembles other postcolonial cultural producers in general and, in particular, other francophone authors. A key element for understanding "the Aya effect," in fact, is the uniquely unavoidable centrality of literature in the French-speaking world. The French language, a primary tool of nation-building within France, became instrumental for empire-building (especially during the Third Republic) as the lynchpin of the nation's civilizing mission.[12] As a result, in the French-speaking world, much social and cultural capital derives from literary success; this is evident in the prestige of literary prizes and the dominance of French publishers. Thus, the growing number of publications by authors from former French colonies in the late 1990s and early 2000s; their accolades, which transformed the metropolitan literary scene; and their regular appearances in the media and on the literary festivals circuit greatly diversified French public awareness of postcolonial realities. All of this serves as a

---

12. For more, see Conklin, *Mission*.

crucial backdrop informing the calculated decision by Paris-based publisher Gallimard to work with famed artist Joann Sfar to launch Bayou, a collection of *bandes dessinées,* with the first volume of *Aya de Yopougon,* even though Abouet had never been published and Oubrerie had worked as an illustrator but had never produced a *bande dessinée.*

Drawing from the large body of research about postcolonial authors in the global marketplace and about African francophone authors in the field of French-language literature, this chapter is less interested in categorizing Abouet and her work than it is in understanding "the specific knowledge practices and contexts that produce the object and occasion and color its analysis" (Brouillette and Thomas 512). Situating Abouet's timely interventions not only sheds light on the cumulative impact of what andre m. carrington describes as the "novelty" of her work but also exposes the primary mechanisms of recognition that work in concert to perpetuate Abouet's dominance of Black *bandes dessinées* worldwide. Thinking with Sandra Ponzanesi, Sarah Brouillette, and Graham Huggan, I insist that the materiality of Abouet's multiple series is paramount to her success and that "each moment in [her] marketing . . . becomes a part of the paratext of [her] subsequent works' reception," which themselves "become opportunities . . . to engage in acts of self-construction and critique" (Brouillette 2).[13] I argue that, on the one hand, Gallimard's initial decision to back *Aya de Yopougon* simultaneously served two goals—to claim a substantial portion of the *bande dessinée* market by tying the medium to literature and to further solidify its position as a prominent global institution through its diverse roster of award-winning authors and artists—and, on the other, Abouet's timely interventions and timeless novelty constitute a set of practices that lean on the postcolonial exotic to "claim space in the dominant field," which has allowed her to "be more effective in [her] strategies of subversion, contestation and resistance" (Ponzanesi 107). Through branding, genre mixing, translation, and expansion to transmedia storytelling, Abouet has generated her own graphic universe for Black *bandes dessinées,* in which postcolonial self-fashioning—at the narrative, material, and personal levels—is valorized as the epitome of twenty-first-century universalism. Yet, as Mbumbo's lament about the hyperpopularity of *Aya de Yopougon* illustrates, this reality "give[s] the lie to globalization paradigms that mistake the visibility of individual Francophone African authors for broader and substantial material shifts in the book economy" (Thierry 77–78). Thus, while Abouet's success has radically

---

13. For more, see Brouillette, *Postcolonial Writers*; Huggan, *Postcolonial Exotic*; Ponzanesi, *Postcolonial Cultural Industry.*

changed the market and boosted "the emerging of a new community of readers and consumers," we must keep in mind that her oeuvre, stemming from a specific set of practices, does not represent all Black *bandes dessinées* (Ponzanesi 78–79). Furthermore, continuing to frame her work in the same way after two decades not only hinders our ability to read her work on its own terms but, more significantly, runs the risk of drastically skewing how we understand other artists' practices and how we value their work.

Black *Bandes Dessinées* and/as Literature

Two key developments linked to diversification in France in the 1990s primed Gallimard's decision to launch Bayou with *Aya de Yopougon*: an increasingly visible diversification of the French population since World War II and the rise of small presses dedicated to experimentation and an expansion of material, artistic, and narrative possibilities for *bandes dessinées*. The independent Paris-based publisher Amok, founded in 1994 by French artists Olivier Marboeuf and Yvan Alagbé, marks an early example of the overlap of these two developments and of Black *bandes dessinées* created in Europe (see introduction). Amok's successful merger with the Belgian alternative publisher Fréon in 2002, resulting in the establishment of Frémok, demonstrates that important changes to the Franco-Belgian *bande dessinée* market were already underway in the years leading up to *Aya de Yopougon*'s debut. At almost the same time, there was another example of doubled diversification that became a watershed moment: Marjane Satrapi's autobiographical series *Persepolis*, published in four volumes from 2000 to 2003 by L'Association, the most influential new *bande dessinée* publisher in France of the 1990s and early 2000s.[14] Satrapi's immediate success with a new material format (closer to a graphic novel) and a sophisticated artistic and narrative approach forever changed the industry. Significantly, *Persepolis*'s multicultural subject matter, female author, and unique style not only created space in the market for new voices, it also broadened and diversified the audience. Likewise, the relatively quick translation of the series into English drastically changed comics worldwide and strengthened inroads to international (non-French-speaking) audiences for *bandes dessinées* beyond a select canonical few.

Part of *Persepolis*'s initial appeal in France came from Satrapi's palatable representation of growing up in Iran, particularly her account of

---

14. For more on the rise and significance of independent publishers, see Beaty, *Unpopular Culture*.

having to wear a hijab in the wake of the Islamic Revolution in the late 1970s. At the time of *Perspolis*'s publication, public debates in France about the place of hijabs in schools served as a proxy for broader tensions stemming from French colonialism's many legacies.[15] The "headscarf affairs" in France (1989–2004) tested Republican universalism by way of *laïcité* (the French version of secularism), and, with the passing of the 2004 law under President Jacques Chirac that banned "ostentatious" religious symbols in public institutions, resulted in reinscribing the importance of assimilation despite the reality of an increasingly multicultural French population.[16] The three decades following World War II, known as Les Trente Glorieuses, saw the rapid economic development and modernization of France thanks to migrant workers from France's colonies at the same time that many such places were fighting for independence.[17] In addition to diversifying the hexagonal population, the bifurcated project of modernization and decolonization led to ostensibly conflicting domestic and international policies. At home, the government physically and socially marginalized visible minorities by relegating them to subsidized housing projects on the periphery of major cities. Abroad, the mobilization of developmental aid linked particularly to the French language supposedly celebrated cultural diversity. The crucial role played by French culture, especially literature, as a form of soft power during decolonization and since is most evident in President Charles de Gaulle's appointment of celebrated author André Malraux as the first Minister of Culture (a key position he held from 1958 to 1969) and in the establishment in 1970 of the Agency for Cultural and Technical Co-operation among French-speaking countries, which eventually became the International Organization of La Francophonie (OIF; Organisation Internationale de la Francophonie) in 1998.

Recent scholarship has convincingly established not only how the field of French-language literature is highly concentrated in Paris but also how

---

15. In the 1990s, the French media and President Jacques Chirac referred to growing unrest, especially among the youth, as a *fracture sociale* but declined to examine the relationship between the unrest and colonialism. For critics and scholars working on postcolonial France, the *fracture sociale* is akin to a *fracture coloniale*. For more, see Blanchard, Bancel, and Lemaire, *La Francture coloniale*; Bancel, Blanchard, and Thomas, *Colonial Legacy*.

16. President Chirac established the Stasi Commission in 1998 to investigate possible interpretations of *laïcité*, and while the final report advocated for religious tolerance and national measures to accommodate multiculturalism (e.g., the recognition of religious holidays other than Catholic ones), such recommendations were ignored. For more, see Scott, *Politics*; Winter, *Hijab*.

17. For more, see Ross, *Fast Cars*; Shepard, *Invention*.

it and literary prizes have been instrumental in making, or, more precisely, manufacturing specific taxonomies such as the African francophone novel and La Francophonie to "safeguard the universality of the French language during the period of decolonisation" and since (Bush and Ducournau 206).[18] As Ruth Bush and Claire Ducournau explain, French-language literary prizes, through their specific criteria, allow the French state, organizations, and cultural institutions to bolster the hegemony of French monolingualism and maintain the "Empire de la langue française" by awarding books that "appeal to universal values [which] reinforces the nature of those values' symbolic bind to the French language" (202–3). Unlike world literature in English, which is no longer restricted to the United Kingdom and the British Commonwealth, world literature in French has yet to be decoupled from France in spite of the public debate sparked by the *Manifesto of the 44*, an open call for a world literature in French, published in *Le Monde* on March 16, 2007, and signed by forty-four well-known authors from around the world.[19] In her astute analysis of the OIF's literary prize (Prix des Cinq Continents), Madeline Bedecarré foregrounds how the "façade [of] heterogeneity" and the "staging of internationalness or decenteredness" are mobilized to "maintain Paris's hegemonic position within the French-language literary space" and to promote and protect *"French* publishing" and "the book industry *in France"* (301–12). As she and others point out, the portmanteau "Galligrasseuil," a combination of the Paris-based publishers Gallimard, Grasset, and Le Seuil, underscores the dominance of these three institutions and the monopoly they have on the literary scene and prizes.[20] Furthermore, the OIF, which receives the bulk of its funding from the French government, "co-opts the prize winners to conduct a literary campaign on their behalf . . . to promote the French language . . . as a universal language with a global presence" (Bedecarré 315). Promoting the diversity of La Francophonie has been and remains an important outward-facing campaign supported by French publishers and the French government in an effort to dismiss the global dominance of English.[21]

In the late 1990s and early 2000s, while the *bande dessinée* industry expanded thanks to the small-press movement, the sharp rise in literary

---

18. For more, see Bush and Ducournau, "Francophone African Literary Prizes"; Ducournau, *La Fabrique*; Bush, *Publishing*; Bedecarré, "Prizing"; Watts, *Packaging*.

19. For more on the manifesto and the debate it sparked, see Le Bris and Rouaud, *Pour une littérature-monde*; Kleppinger, "What's Wrong"; Hargreaves et al., *Transnational French Studies*; and Mabanckou and Thomas, "Francophone Sub-Saharan African Literature."

20. See Bedecarré, "Prizing"; Spear, "(R)Evolutions."

21. For a detailed discussion, see Salomone, *Rise of English*, chapter 6, "'New Scramble' for Africa."

awards going to postcolonial francophone authors (some born to parents from former French colonies and some from former French colonies) attested to the diversification of the audience as well as the maneuvering of French institutions to shape the changing literary scene. In the promotion and recognition of primarily cosmopolitan authors and their work, French publishers market the margins by playing up elements of the postcolonial exotic. For example, in 2000, editors at Gallimard created the series Continents Noirs (Black Continents), meant to celebrate the innovative literary style of Black authors. However, in an effort to highlight difference, the publisher effectively segregates non-White authors, ostensibly based on geography. As Dominic Thomas notes, "Gallimard publishes 'black' authors in its series 'Continents Noirs' (Black Continents) and 'major' authors in 'La Blanche' (the White series)—a hierarchy now complicated by the inclusion of 'successful' Black writers such as Alan Mabanckou, Patrick Chamoiseau, Ananda Devi and Marie Ndiaye in 'La Blanche'" (Thomas, "Introduction" 4). Thomas's point highlights that the hierarchy is constructed along racial lines under the guise of geography. At the same time, while this hierarchy strengthens the bifurcation between the center and the periphery, carried over from the colonial era, the reality is that these diverse authors are all nevertheless published in France by French publishers. Thus, as Claire Ducournau's exceptional study of the fabrication of African literary classics in French illustrates, the concept and criteria for such a category are ambiguous and obfuscate the dominant role played by cultural brokers and institutions in the Global North to bestow and reinforce classification.[22]

Considering this broader context, it is easy to read Gallimard's launch of the Bayou collection with *Aya de Yopougon* as achieving many goals at once through the mobilization of a boutique format to package boutique postcolonialism, to borrow from Ponzanesi. To direct the new Bayou series, Gallimard selected Joann Sfar, who had become a prominent figure for his prolific and innovative work with L'Association.[23] For Bart Beaty, this was the inverse of "selling out"; instead, "the co-optation of the independent cultural producer . . . reduces the status of the 'independent' to a brand within the field of consumption" (181). According to editors at Gallimard, Sfar could deliver what they wanted: *bandes dessinées* that resembled the rest of Gallimard's brand, that is, public-oriented works that were simultaneously original, literary, and innovative (Severin). Sfar prioritized bringing new voices to the mainstream market, and while there is much diversity among the creators and the stories told, the collection's common denominator is a specific format, which

---

22. See Ducournau, *La Fabrique*.
23. For more on Sfar's impressive body of work and its impact on the industry, see Leroy, *Sfar*.

became a brand in and of itself. Though Bayou was phased out by 2018, having successfully served its purpose by engendering the establishment of Gallimard Bande Dessinée, the collection's short description on Gallimard's website tersely conveys what is most important: a long-form graphic novel in color with a hardback cover and rounded spine, measuring 175 by 247 millimeters, overseen by Joann Sfar. While Sfar's star power ignited the collection, it was *Aya de Yopougon* that catapulted it to widespread success, and Gallimard's prospects in the *bande dessinée* market to global proportions.

Though *bandes dessinées* by artists from African countries were gaining traction in Europe in the early 2000s, *Aya de Yopougon* was decidedly different. Instead of promoting an African artist's talents, as in the cases of Barly Baruti's work on Frank Giroud's *Eva K.* and *Mandrill* and collaborative projects like Ptiluc's *BD Africa*, *Aya de Yopougon* flipped the script to center the writing of an author originally from an African country, supported visually by a French artist. Indeed, one of the key mechanisms of legitimation represented by Abouet is the elevation of Black *bandes dessinées* to the status of literature by one of the leading French publishers.[24] The Gallimard boost not only comes with the best chance at large-scale distribution, but it can also dictate market trends and influence how other texts are perceived. It is no surprise, then, that Abouet's only coauthored *bande dessinée* not published with Gallimard, *Terre gâtée: Ange, le migrant*, is prefaced by none other than award-winning author Alain Mabanckou. The copresence of these two Gallimard superstars attracts a wide readership by lending the combined forces of their own brands and that of Gallimard to bestow prestige on the independent publisher Éditions Rue de Sèvres.

The sustained promotion of Abouet as a writer, instantly signaled through Galvada's preface and later reinforced by Mabanckou's, cannot be overstated. In many ways, Galvada's preface corresponds to Richard Watts's analysis of the paratexts of novels by francophone African women: "if the works themselves often blur the boundary between fiction and testimonial autobiography, their paratexts do not. They simply vouch for the reliability of the woman writer and of her appropriateness as witness to a particular event or, more often, sociological condition" (146). For Watts, the result of such paratexts "is that the women of the francophone world and their narratives are presented, at the moment of their emergence in the 1960s and far beyond, as transparent and immediately accessible vessels for transmitting, rather than reflecting on, experience" (146). Reading the publicity of

---

24. Pushing *bandes dessinées* more toward literature through specific packaging and materiality with the creation of the album—a hardback book with high-quality paper and color—had already proved an effective legitimizing mechanism for the Ninth Art in the late 1960s and 1970s. For more, see Lesage, *L'Effet livre* and *Ninth Art*.

Abouet's work and her public appearances as always part of the paratext, we see how she is continually lauded as a new, authentic voice from Africa despite having lived in Paris since the age of twelve. This is especially the case when it comes to *Aya*, the 2007 English translation of the first volume. A significant part of the Gallimard boost is access to a global market through translation, as books published with Gallimard and Le Seuil are statistically the most translated into English.[25] In the anglophone context, the series similarly benefits from the prestige of the Montreal-based comics publisher Drawn & Quarterly. Additionally, since no other Black *bandes dessinées* had been translated into English in full at the time and few have been translated since, it is no wonder that Abouet and her work dominate the global perception of Black *bandes dessinées*, given the ongoing quick translation of the *Aya de Yopougon* and *Akissi* series.[26] It is also worth emphasizing the French state sponsorship of *Aya de Yopougon*. After the international popularity garnered by the English translation of the first two volumes, subsequent translations were funded in part by the French Ministry of Foreign and European Affairs as well as the Institut français; it is easy to imagine why the French government would invest in the global promotion of *Aya de Yopougon* and its vision of a prosperous Ivory Coast at almost the same time as French troops assisted in Gbagbo's capture in Abidjan. Ultimately, thanks to this institutional support and its resulting global distribution and recognition, Abouet, like other successful postcolonial authors, enjoyed more freedom to experiment and explore new topics as time went on. According to Ponzanesi, the economy of prestige resulting from awards and branding allows authors, artists, and their work to "participate in the promotion of new aesthetic and political parameters of appreciation and evaluation that open up new venues for emancipating the postcolonial from its niche market" (47). In order to understand Abouet's contributions, it is necessary to analyze her strategic practices over time, thereby restoring the critical edge to her work that has been dulled through translation and (re)packaging.[27]

---

25. The high volume of English translations from these two publishers dominates the outsider perception of French literature. See Sapiro, "Translation."

26. By 2010, when the first six-volume run of *Aya de Yopougon* ended, only a handful of other Black *bandes dessinées* had been translated into English, and only in part. Examples include the excerpts in *Africa Comics*, the catalog accompanying the Africa Comics exposition held at the Studio Museum in Harlem from 2006 to 2007 and the short excerpts presented annually online by Words Without Borders as part of their Graphic Literature roundup. For comparison, it was not until 2021 that any of Barly Baruti's work appeared fully translated in English.

27. Romain Becker's insightful analysis of how German translations of specific series such as *Aya de Yopougon* flatten out authors' intentions and strategies also applies to the English-language translations of Abouet's work. See Becker, "How a German Publisher."

Timely Interventions and Branding: The AYA Effect

Paying close attention to Abouet's branding—both how her work is branded and how she creates her own brand—we see that in conjunction with the boutique materiality of the Bayou format, the female-centered boutique postcolonialism that abounds in the first volume of *Aya de Yopougon* was a crucial initial strategy to spark interest and remains important, yet, even by the second volume of *Aya de Yopougon*, Abouet quickly expanded beyond such a narrow focus.[28] In the first volume, the female-centered boutique postcolonialism coalesces through the plot, which focuses on Aya and her close girlfriends, and through the bonus section, "Le Bonus ivoirien," which presents local cultural tidbits to enhance readers' experience of Yopougon. A lexicon of local slang and recipes serve as the enticing backbone of the bonus sections. However, it is worth pointing out that even since the start, Abouet's treatment of cultural diversity is elusive, to use carrington's description. For instance, just as the characters' names reflect the ethnic and religious diversity of the Ivory Coast without explicit commentary about it, Abouet weaves Nouchi throughout but downplays its status as a local creole language in favor of casting it as a quirky and adoptable set of slang expressions (which Galvada playfully models in her preface) (Grossi 282). To emphasize the gendered lens of the series, the initial bonus sections focus on women's quotidian experiences, and the inside covers of each volume, with the exception of volume 4, are decorated with varying repeating colorful patterns created by Oubrerie that mimic fabric used as *pagnes*, or wrappers, and are therefore associated more with women's experiences.[29]

The most explicit marketing strategy, however, is also the most immediate. The enticing, feminine Otherness of the first volume is encoded on the cover in Aya's name in large, red, all-capital letters and reinforced by her intriguing expression with raised eyebrows looking to something on her left. The reduction of the character into her name is most obvious in the English translation, for while the French title remains *Aya de Yopougon*

---

28. Portions of this section first appeared in my chapter in *Drawing (in) the Feminine: Bandes Dessinées and Women*, where I also explain how Abouet focuses more on the community around Aya than Aya herself, and I argue that Abouet's genre-blending narrative and textual strategies (e.g., borrowing conventions from soap operas, a brief photo-roman in the style of popular West African women's magazines, and speaking directly to readers in the bonus section) mimic the dynamic range of characters' self-fashioning in the story (Bumatay, "Feminine Plural").

29. For volume 4, which features the character of Innocent on the front cover instead of Aya, Oubrerie supplies profile portraits resembling urban paintings for hairstylists and barber shops. This textual practice reinforces the shift in narrative focus toward Innocent's experience of migration.

(with *de Yopougon* always in a smaller font spanning the width of the character's name), the title of the first English translation is simply *AYA*.[30] This initial collapse has subsequently become an icon that simultaneously represents the series and Abouet. Consequently, in place of Cassiau-Haurie's "Aya effect" that only mentions the series' impressive print run as indicative of its popularity, it makes more sense to speak of Abouet's AYA effect, since the all-capitalized name supplanting the eponymous character is the central force of Abouet's brand, so much so that Abouet and AYA have become intertwined almost to the point of collapsing into one. The resulting ambiguity, when instrumentalized, employs the same novelty from *Aya de Yopougon* that carrington argues is "an elusive rather than resistant strategy" (2). This elusive strategy allows Aya (and the entire cast of characters) to stand in for Abouet. In fact, in both name and practice, AYA echoes the Dakar-based women's magazine *AWA: La revue de la femme noire* (1964–73), which, as Ruth Bush argues, "presents a singular, personified point of identification and aspiration" through metonymy but also "acts as a repository for multiple ideas regarding feminine identity in post-independence francophone Africa" (Bush, "Mesdames" 226). Mapping the development of AYA as a brand reveals how Abouet's timely interventions expand beyond the realm of Aya and her friends to become a repository for a universalist, inclusive, and multicultural community informed by but not limited to geography. As with its other award-winners, Gallimard developed packaging materials to market Abouet's subsequent work, which initially took the form of a circular sticker affixed to the front cover of the second volume of *Aya de Yopougon* informing readers of the Angoulême prize for "AYA 1." Then, in 2010, when Abouet branched out from *Aya de Yopougon* to two equally autobiographically inspired series—*Bienvenue*, published in the Bayou collection, and *Akissi*, published as part of Gallimard Jeunesse and eventually as part of Gallimard Bande Dessinée—a new circular sticker was introduced that enacts the collapse between Abouet and Aya: "Par l'auteur de AYA de Yopougon."[31] All the letters are capitalized, but the name AYA is dramatically larger than the rest of the text and centered in the circle. As a guarantee of quality through star power, the circular icon has also been incorporated

---

30. Abouet, *Aya* (translated by Helge Dascher).
31. "By the author of AYA of Yopougon." The eponymous character at the center of the three volumes of *Bienvenue*—a White, French art student—shares many personality traits with Aya (she is committed to helping the members of her chosen community) while living a personal growth trajectory inspired by Abouet's life prior to *Aya de Yopougon* (Federici, *L'Entrance* 290). Conversely, *Akissi* represents the stories Abouet had originally wanted to tell. Both series illustrate Abouet's freedom to explore stories and themes of her choosing while working with new artists, Singeon and Mathieu Sapin, whose unique artistic styles lend themselves to the respective tones of the different series.

into the layout of some covers of Abouet's work instead of added later as a sticker.³²

Following her contributions to the Bayou collection, Abouet expanded her brand to other mediums and venues while continuing to work on her *Akissi* series. From 2012 to 2013, she wrote a *bande dessinée* cookbook, codirected the animated adaptation of *Aya de Yopougon*, which was accompanied by a Gallimard-published coffee-table behind-the-scenes book about the film, and collaborated with curators at the Musée de l'Histoire de l'Immigration in Paris on the important exposition Albums: Des histoires dessinées entre ici et ailleurs; Bande dessinée et immigration 1913–2013. It is easy to see the film adaptation as following in the footsteps of the successful adaptations of Satrapi's *Persepolis* and Sfar's *The Rabbi's Cat*, and the cookbook as following market trends.³³ At the same time, Abouet's seemingly different projects are all interlinked and further blur the difference between her and Aya in the name of promoting a positive view of migrants in France, claiming space for them, and celebrating multiculturalism. In *Délices d'Afrique: 50 recettes pour petits moments de confidences à partager* (African delights: Fifty recipes for little secretive moments to share), Abouet convivially and confidingly speaks to her readers, whom she calls her girlfriends, while presenting anecdotes alongside recipes, all of which is abundantly illustrated by Agnès Maupré in a watercolor style evocative of *Aya de Yopougon*. The implied setting is the Ivory Coast, as an avatar of Abouet interacts with Ivorian women, while the implied audience is cast as residing in France through Abouet's discussion of how easy it is to find African ingredients in Paris. In this prime example of marketing the postcolonial exotic, Abouet shares her Ivorian experiences around food and provides the means to spice up everyday metropolitan life. Her double insider status is signaled through her chic cosmopolitan

---

32. In a promotional article for the long-awaited release of *Aya de Yopougon*, volume 7, a photo of Abouet shows her wearing an outfit made from bespoke fabric featuring the repeating figure of Aya (sporting her own vibrant light-blue-and-white patterned dress with arms casually crossed in a confident yet relaxed pose, looking directly at the viewer) next to the title "AYA de Yopougon" in the same font as all the stickers. Abouet's easy smile and relaxed posture in the photo, paired with Aya's repeating figure, creates a kind of mise en abyme of the two confident women (Morand).

33. While the original version of Abouet's cookbook, published by Éditions Alternatives, followed trends in 2012, the increased interest in the subgenre of *bande dessinée* cookbooks and in Abouet's return to the *Aya de Yopougon* series in 2022 resulted in a second edition in 2023 with an imitation of the Gallimard circular icon incorporated into the cover design. Unsurprisingly, reviews of the second edition repeat the same "newness" discourse as reviews of the original edition, with little deviation other than to acknowledge the second printing despite there being more than a decade between the two editions.

avatar with a straight bob, form-fitting sleeveless pink dress, and matching hoop earrings. And, in an elusive manner, she claims both the Ivory Coast and France as her own and at the same time normalizes and celebrates different identities through the plurality of who could be included in her use of the term "girlfriend." The following year, Abouet made this claim at the national level in France through her contributions to the exposition about immigration and *bandes dessinées* held as part of a rebranding campaign for the Musée de l'Histoire de l'Immigration. The exposition's poster prominently features a confident Aya dressed in a pink dress reminiscent of Abouet's from the cookbook even though in the original drawing, taken from the film poster and the film's book, Aya wears an orange dress.[34] One could argue that the shift from orange to pink is nothing more than a design choice to offset the blue and yellow of the rest of the poster. However, the choice of pink for Abouet's avatar in the cookbook and Aya's dress on the poster immediately connotes Paris, and a feminized version at that. Furthermore, Aya never leaves the Ivory Coast, nor does she want to, but, like her name, she stands in for Abouet, and, in a pink dress, she stands in for Abouet's successful immigration story.[35] In fact, color is a crucial element of the branding practices Abouet developed with the *Akissi* series.

The longest-running of Abouet's series (also translated into several languages), *Akissi* attests to the market-savvy of her innovative practices. In interviews, Abouet repeatedly explains that the impetus for *Aya de Yopougon* had been to write about her childhood, but advice from the editorial team at Gallimard encouraged her to refocus the series on young adults. Thanks to the global success of *Aya de Yopougon*, Abouet returned to her original plan with free reign in terms of materiality, narrative structure, and aesthetic style. Understanding the importance of brand recognition, Abouet created new boutique formats, via packaging and attention to aesthetics through artist selection, to distinguish each of her other Gallimard series while also signaling their link with *Aya de Yopougon*. *Akissi*, intended for children, looks and feels more like a children's picture book, though it is a *bande dessinée* consisting of short vignettes. It employs a wider hardback format, gloss lamination, and thematized bright color combinations for the outside cover,

---

34. An oversize version of the film poster with Aya in the orange version of the dress served as an anchor for the physical exposition. Nevertheless, since the exposition poster remains on the museum's website, Abouet, by way of the Parisian version of Aya, continues to be a key role model for successful immigration in France: https://www.histoire-immigration.fr/albums-bande-dessinee-et-immigration-1913-2013.

35. For more on Abouet's participation in the rebranding of the Musée de l'Histoire de l'Immigration, see Bumatay, "African *Bande Dessinée* Festivals."

title, inside covers, and title page of each vignette, all of which highlights Mathieu Sapin's playful interpretation of Oubrerie's "graphic universe" (as indicated on the title page of each volume). Like the banjo-wielding icon created by Sfar for the Bayou collection, the character of Akissi is deployed as this series's indefatigable logo, in imitation of the layout of the classic French and Belgian *bande dessinée* magazines *Pilote* and *Spirou*. In fact, in place of Tintin's Milou, Akissi adopts a small monkey whom she names Boubou and treats like a sibling more than a pet. A small silhouette of Akissi running at the top of each volume's spine instantly conveys her boundless energy, while adorning each cover and vignette title page is a small icon of her with arms crossed and a confident smile, superimposed over a jagged-edged cartouche of her name. Like other successful children's series, "repetition is an aesthetic mode which cannot be reduced to a simplified narrative structure [and constitutes] a poetics of the serial [that] raises questions about the nature of beginnings and endings, which is often connected with the issue of fulfilling and foiling expectations" (Kümmerling-Meibauer 171). A unique example of this is in volume 10, which is about the global coronavirus pandemic (figure 2.1). The page layout resembles that of every previous vignette, but now, the header icon of Akissi is wearing a face mask to protect herself as the large introductory panel presents her whole family watching their flatscreen television as President Outtara addresses the nation to inform them of the lockdown. *Akissi* also includes a bonus section like in *Aya de Yopougon*, which Abouet uses to generate community among children worldwide and to encourage learning and play through recipes and a lexicon of slang used by Ivorian children, as well as games, jokes, and activities. The evolution of Abouet's brand through *Akissi* informs the newer volumes of *Aya de Yopougon* and demonstrates Abouet's successful transformation of niche practices into mainstream innovation. No longer tied to the Bayou collection, volumes 7 and 8 retain the size of the original series but without a rounded spine and with the juxtaposition of bright colors for the outside covers instead of the black used for the Bayou format.

In a similar fashion, Abouet's approach to her detective series *Commissaire Kouamé* is informed by its genre. Though originally published in 2017, subsequent editions of *Commissaire Kouamé: Un si joli jardin*, the first volume of this series illustrated by Donatien Mary, include both the AYA sticker and a black circular sticker with white lettering announcing that the *bande dessinée* received the Prix SNCF du Polar in 2019. That the French National Railway awarded Abouet this prize for detective fiction for her first stab at a completely new genre attests to her mainstream recognition and appeal. Each volume is approximately the same length as a volume of *Aya de*

FIGURE 2.1. Vignette title page about the pandemic lockdown. *Akissi: Enfermés dedans*, vol. 10, Gallimard Jeunesse, 2020.

Yopougon but is physically larger than the Bayou format, allowing for more experimentation of page layout and pacing. Like the branding of *Akissi*, each volume features an icon of the protagonist at the top of the spine and a stylized icon-title combination on the front cover. Here, instead of youthful energy, the commissioner's frontal discerning stare paired with his hallmark glasses, wide brim fedora, and matching suit immediately connote the investigative preoccupation of the series. While Sapin's artwork leans toward the cartoonish through simplification and exaggerated proportions for *Akissi*, Mary's style, like Oubrerie's, toggles between stylized realism and exaggeration, depending on the narrative situation and tone. Likewise, the bright multicolored pages of *Akissi*, evoking animated cartoons, attract young eyes, whereas Mary's use of muted colors—thematized black for interrogation scenes—and crosshatching in *Commissaire Kouamé* borrow from film noir conventions to connote the adult subject matter of the series, including the seedy undertones of violence and corruption.

Timeless Novelty: Past(s) and/as Present(s)

Given the cameos in and crossovers between *Akissi* starting in volume 8 (2018), both volumes of *Commissaire Kouamé* (2017, 2021), and volumes 7 and 8 of *Aya de Yopougon* (2022, 2023), Abouet's return to *bande dessinée* after writing for the telenovela series *C'est la vie* (2015) undoubtedly marks a significant shift in her work, at the heart of which is an approach that builds upon the timeless novelty of *Aya de Yopougon* while also becoming more purposefully situated in the twenty-first century.[36] We see this in the aforementioned volume 10 of *Akissi*, whose subtitle "Enfermés dedans," or "Stuck inside," and the comedic depiction of home life during the coronavirus lockdown unambiguously indicate its contemporaneity (2020). Previously, the series's historical setting was less obvious due to the presence of a CRT television in Akissi's home starting in the first volume, like the one on the first page of *Aya de Yopougon*; it was not until the sixth volume that a flatscreen television and cellphones were depicted. A similar shift from timelessness to an explicit reference to the present occurs between volumes one and two of *Commissaire Kouamé*. In his attentive review of the first volume, historian Romain Tiquet rightly observes that while it is difficult to discern the plot's historical setting, what is more important is that Abouet leads her reader through different historical moments that marked both her and the country, by blending the era of the Ivorian Miracle (the setting of *Aya de Yopougon* and Abouet's childhood) with that of the growing economic crisis of the late 1980s (due in part to the devaluation of the price of cacao) and with the more recent past, including a direct reference to a real terrorist attack that

---

36. From 2015 to 2016, Abouet worked as a scenarist for the pan-African telenovela *C'est la vie* (That's Life!) set in Dakar about women and children's health, distributed by TV5 Monde Afrique on Canal France International (Federici, *L'Entrance* 282).

occurred in Grand-Bassam (a beach resort just south of Abidjan) on March 13, 2016, that left nineteen dead (Tiquet 419).

In spite of such inclusions of events from the Ivory Coast's recent history, the overall aesthetic of the first volume aligns this newer series most closely with that of Abouet's childhood, buttressed by cameos of the commissioner and his right-hand man Arsène zooming past Akissi and her friends in volume 8 of her series, and the commissioner's crossover role in the newer volumes of *Aya de Yopougon*, on the lookout for Moussa at his mother's behest. A key component of the nostalgic feel and callback to the 1970s is the character of Arsène, the commissioner's right-hand man, who is a tall, imposing White man comedically obsessed with small classic cars and dedicated to assisting Marius Kouamé in his quest for justice even if that means aggressively roughing people up for information. Arsène's obsession with classic cars drives much of the physical comedy and boosts the ambiguity of the historical context. The running gag of various distorted car roofs with two bumps indicating the heads of the commissioner in the back and Arsène in the front makes the two figures comical as the work they undertake is anything but. Similarly, Arsène's big frame hunched over small steering wheels, his speedy driving, and halting stops generate high energy to dramatize the procedural tropes of solving crimes, such as identifying and following leads, tracking people down and conducting interviews, and, after piecing together the bigger picture, revisiting old leads. Additionally, the deliberate styling of Arsène and Kouamé not only provides insights about their personalities but also harkens back to the 1970s, cueing readers in to Abouet's homage to the genre-defining American television series *Columbo*, starring Peter Falk, that ran from 1971 to 1978, which, unsurprisingly, overlaps with the historical setting of the start of *Aya de Yopougon*. Abouet's initial adherence to timelessness, and shift away from it in *Commissaire Kouamé*, can be read in his cameos in the newer versions of *Aya de Yopougon*. Kouamé is visibly the same age in volume 7 of *Aya de Yopougon* even though the plot predates the first volume of *Commissaire Kouamé* by three decades, whereas in volume 8 of *Aya de Yopougon*, he is drawn as decades younger, with black hair instead of his iconic silver coif. This continuity correction between the two new volumes of *Aya de Yopougon* parallels the shift between the two volumes of *Commissaire Kouamé*.

Abouet's narrative choices, amplified by Mary's artwork, play up elements of timelessness in the first volume of *Commissaire Kouamé* to welcome readers back to Yop City, a familiar place changed by violence; however, by the second volume, subtitled *Un Homme tombe avec son ombre* (A man falls with his shadow), Abouet includes concrete references to the present in an explicit critique of corruption at all levels of Ivorian society. In both volumes, Abouet thwarts expectations and undermines stereotypes in an appeal for social change, advocating for a more just and inclusive Ivory Coast. For instance, the leitmotif of Arsène's presence and subordinate role to Kouamé, as contrary to the stereotypical socioeconomic hierarchy based on race in the postcolonial setting, is remarked upon by several characters but deemed so entirely outdated by the two protagonists that they refuse altogether to respond to such comments. Likewise, Abouet crafts the central mystery of each volume to highlight socially marginalized and exploited groups in the Ivory Coast and uplift them and their rights through Kouamé's morality and drive for justice. In the first volume, Kouamé's support and protection of people who are transgender, people who are victims of domestic violence, and children enacts what José Esteban Muñoz describes as "queer futurity" in a vision of a new, inclusive Ivorian society akin to that constructed anew by Cameroonian-born, Abidjan-based author Werewere Liking in her 1983 song novel, *Elle sera de jaspe et corail: Journal d'une Misovire.*[37] Indeed, just as Liking's critique of gender politics in postcolonial Ivory Coast demands the creation of new Ivorians, all of Abouet's work—especially *Aya de Yopougon*—normalizes individuals working together toward a possible utopic Ivorian society. For Abouet, as for Liking, such change can only happen when women are included and when men redefine their roles in society.

The urgent necessity of an inclusive Ivorian society manifests in the uncharacteristic inclusion of an in-text reference to the year of the diegesis—2021—in the second volume of *Commissaire Kouamé* (figure 2.2). As with the first volume, the central mystery of the second volume—locating the nefarious individual behind a string of kidnappings of people with albinism for rituals meant to ensure power—purposefully foregrounds a marginalized group. During his investigation, Kouamé visits Gor, a local gang leader invested in protecting his community since the government will not. As with other scenes focused on dialogue, Abouet and Mary opt for a simple layout consisting of four strips of two panels that repeat a similar framing of stylized silhouettes (Mary denotes the Commissioner's glasses and button-up shirt with white) of the two characters in profile, with an orange background behind the characters in lieu of a detailed setting. Even though Kouamé is a beacon of morality throughout the two volumes and never fails to call

---

37. See Muñoz, *Cruising Utopia*. In *It Shall Be of Jasper and Coral (journal of a misovire)*, Werewere Liking coins the term "misovire," meaning "man-hater," yet, while the journal details a woman's reflections on her daily life, it also optimistically announces the future creation of a new type of Africa of mixed composition, of jasper and coral and of mixed gender roles.

FIGURE 2.2. Conversation between Kouamé and Gor. *Commissaire Kouamé: Un homme tombe avec son ombre*, vol. 2, Gallimard Bande Dessinée, 2021.

out corruption when he notices it, this page stands as one of Abouet's most explicit discussions about the interlinked socioeconomic and political reality of the Ivory Coast and corruption's pervasiveness. In response to Kouamé's inquiry as to whether he recognizes the suspect from a police sketch, Gor explicitly states that in the year 2021, when even the humblest person has at least one cellphone if not several, there are still those who continue to believe that human sacrifice is necessary to gain wealth and power. Kouamé attempts to brush this off, explaining that such a practice is of the past, when people lived in obscurity and obscurantism. Mary underlines the word "obscurantism" in Kouamé's speech bubble to suggest that lack of education is no longer the case. But in fact, this is Gor's point—and Abouet's as well—that young people need something to hope for and that charlatans out for power will exploit that, since the government has failed to instill hope, especially since access to education is not guaranteed. Gor's closer proximity to the average Ivorian public, that is, his remoteness from Kouamé's privileged social echelon, in which his teenage children attend a wealthy racially mixed school, means that he can better understand the people. Gor's critique of the government is not empty; he represents a strong, direct response to the government official on the first page of the first volume who blames the youth for the nation's instability. In opposition to those in power, Gor advocates for the youth since they are the future, but he explains that they need to be empowered and educated and that consequently, the government should build schools (instead of going after children for what they do while under the sway of other adults). Though Gor sees Kouamé as a government representative, he agrees to work with him to make sure that the children are not harmed and to step in on their behalf by taking them under his wing once the suspect is apprehended. Ultimately, both men as well as Arsène serve as models of new types of people in twenty-first-century Africa.

As evidenced by the two volumes of *Commissaire Kouamé*, Abouet has become more politically engaged, and this applies to the newer volumes of *Aya de Yopougon* as well as to her cowritten non-Gallimard *bande dessinée*, *Terre gâtée*. All of these more recent publications target key issues that impact Africans' lives whether living on the continent or abroad, including corruption, persecution, and northward migration. *Terre gâtée*, cowritten with Charli Beleteau, blurs the distinction between the past and the present while adapting an existing genre—the American Western—to reflect on current events. The context of the American Wild West is transposed to the Sahara via Christian de Metter's realistic digital artwork to explore the spectral existence of migrants and the complex global system of borderization that marks northward migration in the twenty-first century (see chapter 3). At the same time, Abouet's treatment of migration in *Aya de Yopougon* is triangulated through a twenty-first-century lens via Innocent's ongoing experiences as the only immigrant of the series in Paris. In the catalog for the 2013–14 exposition at the Musée de l'Histoire de l'Immigration, Abouet confessed that Innocent is her; like him, she arrived in Paris innocent, unaware of what awaited her and afraid of what might happen to her when she started looking for a job, because she lacked the appropriate working permit until 1998 (Olivier 148–51). Indeed, the introduction of Innocent in volume 3 of *Aya de Yopougon* is complemented in the bonus section by a staged conversation between Aya and Abouet herself about the difference between community in the Ivory Coast and psychiatrists in France. At first glance, this cultural comparison seems in line with other strategies to play up the postcolonial exotic of the series, yet upon closer inspection, it can be read as Abouet's elusively couched introduction of her own experience of immigration. She continues this paralleled story in volume 4 when Innocent arrives in Paris, and she includes an explicit account of her trajectory from the Ivory Coast to France in the bonus section. Reading her work intertextually, we notice the reworking of these reflections about northward migration in the *Akissi* series, of which volumes 7, 8, and 9 all take up Akissi's fear at being forced by her parents to leave for Paris. In fact, the playful oversimplification of Abouet's adolescent anxieties about migrating, recounted in the bonus section of *Aya de Yopougon* volume 4, becomes a full-page gag in *Akissi*, volume 7, subtitled "False departure." In the bonus section of *Aya de Yopougon*, Abouet linguistically sketches out her complex mix of emotions upon learning that she was to leave the Ivory Coast, a moment marked by extreme sadness and also a juvenile and naïve excitement at the prospect of meeting her favorite French *bande dessinée* character, Rahan. As a conclusion to this autobiographical insert, Abouet provides two observations—that France was not as cold as she thought it would be and that not all French men looked like Rahan. In the *Akissi* vignette, Akissi has a nightmare about a snow-covered and dangerous France, which swiftly becomes a glorious encounter with Rahan and just as quickly reverts to being dangerous.

In the newer volumes of *Aya de Yopougon*, Abouet foregoes a sense of timelessness and includes explicit references to important events in France and the Ivory Coast. In France, Abouet addresses immigrants' rights, including material about church sit-ins and increasing activism throughout the 1980s, and thus points to the deeper history of migration beyond the elevated media attention of the 1990s.[38] In a bold move, Oubrerie draws an adult Abouet shoulder-to-shoulder with Innocent sporting a *Purple Rain*

---

38. For more, see Thomas, *Africa and France*; Freeman, "French 'Sans-Papiers' Movement."

FIGURE 2.3. A cameo of Abouet next to Innocent. *Aya de Yopougon*, vol. 7, Gallimard Bande Dessinée, 2022.

Prince-inspired outfit as they get swept up in a pro-immigrant demonstration with fliers for a concert by Rock Against the Police (RAP), a real group headed by the members of the band Carte de Séjour (figure 2.3).[39] The crowd's chants against extrajudicial killings of ethnic minorities in the *banlieues* (metropolitan project-housing suburbs) and the presence of an adult Abouet reinforce a direct through line from the 1980s to contemporary France. At the same time, through Aya's more active narrative arc driven by social justice, Abouet weaves in elements of Ivorian her-story, which comes to a head in volume 8 with a footnote. In the middle of volume 8, Aya confesses to her mother, Fanta, that she doubts having the courage to return to

---

39. The band's name translates as "residence permit," colloquially known in the American context as a "green card."

her studies at the university because of intimidation from other students angry with her for advocating for change. In response, Fanta, looking pointedly at Aya, reminds her that she is the daughter and the granddaughter of women who marched on Grand-Basam to liberate Ivorian men who had been wrongfully imprisoned by the French colonists. Just below this panel, a footnote tells the reader to go to the bonus for more details. In the bonus section, the reader finds a single page for the lexicon of slang and a three-page entry entitled "La Marche des femmes sur Grand-Bassam." Abouet stages the recounting of this important moment in Ivorian history as a *bande dessinée* scene in Aya's family courtyard where she and her mother collaboratively tell the story of when, in 1949, Ivorian women marched to Grand-Bassam from Abidjan since no drivers would take them. Many brought their children with them, and when they got to the courthouse, they were beaten and some were arrested. Though their efforts were repressed and it took months for some women to be liberated, the regional and international media took notice and harshly criticized the French colonists' repression. Abouet ends the entry with a short paragraph in a standardized font (in opposition to the handwritten font for the retelling) that informs readers that Ivorian women played an important role in Ivorian politics (and can do so again) and that if they happen to be in Grand-Basam and see the statue commemorating the women who marched, they might also be able to meet Ivorian women who can show them an old 1,000 CFA bill with the portrait of Marie Koré, one of the key figures of the march. These unambiguous sociopolitical and historiographic commentaries are a far cry from Abouet's previously elusive strategy predicated on playing up the postcolonial exotic. Thanks to her international platform, she has expanded the universe of her own work and simultaneously created space for others in the *bande dessinée* market, all while modeling the benefits of inclusive and multiethnic communities regardless of geography.

The AYA Effect and (Black) *Bandes Dessinées*

Abouet's many projects, linked more with literature than cartooning, have been instrumental in creating space in the mainstream market for Black *bandes dessinées*, albeit primarily for texts more aligned with her oeuvre. Like shifts in African francophone literature, this has been marked by increased professionalization and feminization. One key example is that of Elyon's, pen name of Congo-based Cameroonian Joëlle Epée Mandengue, whose BD blog-turned-crowdfunded-series *La vie d'Ébène Duta* incorporates media-savvy branding throughout.[40] Trained in Belgium, Elyon's has become an international spokesperson for Black *bandes dessinées* as the founder of the Bilili BD Festival in the Republic of the Congo and as the primary curator of the exposition Kubuni, les Bandes Dessinées d'Afrique.s, which premiered at the Angoulême Cité International de la Bande Dessinée et de l'Image and has subsequently been hosted worldwide via the Institut Français (see the coda).[41] Professionalization and femininization of Black *bandes dessinées* can also be read in the surge of collaborative projects in which stories are penned by Black authors and illustrated by artists based in France. Prime examples include *Pari(s) d'amies,* by author Rokhaya Diallo and artist Kim Cosigny (2015); *Alpha: Abidjan–Gare du Nord* (2018), by author Bessora and artist Barroux (see chapter 3); Jessica Oublié's works *Peyi an nou,* illustrated by Marie-Ange Rousseau (2017), and *Tropiques toxiques: Le scandale du chlordecone,* illustrated by Nicola Gobbi and with photography by Vinciane Lebrun (2020) (see chapter 4); and *Ouagadougou pressé,* by Roukiata Ouedraogo illustrated by Aude Massot (2021).

Related impacts of the AYA effect include more emphasis on materiality and the adoption of conventions specific to Abouet's oeuvre. Cassiau-Haurie's *bande dessinée* series at L'Harmattan initially prioritized softback matte paper albums for affordability, but since 2017, in the wake of Abouet's success, titles are now released simultaneously as downloadable PDFs and hardback, large-format albums with high-quality paper. This applies to new titles and reissued ones. Thus, while Cassiau-Haurie does not explain the role of materiality in his discussion of "the Aya effect" in his work as a researcher, as an editor, he has implemented lessons learned from it. Similarly, artists, some of whom were active prior to the publication of *Aya de Yopougon,* have adopted key conventions from it, particularly the use of splash pages that present nuanced visions of specific locales in Africa while serving as narrative pauses and transitions. Beninois artist Didier Viodé's multiple publications about his fictional character Yao serve as a useful example, as his later work, still organized around short vignettes, incorporates more watercolor splash pages (see chapter 3).

---

40. On the correlation between Abouet, Elyon's, and their respective series, see Bumatay, "Feminine Plural." For more on the professionalization and feminization of African francophone literature, see Ducournau, *La Fabrique.*

41. Relatedly, Elyon's was also one of the four co-organizers of "Afropolitan Comics: From South Africa to the Continent," an important virtual exposition and series of events in 2019 that showcased comics production across the continent and facilitated discussions across language barriers, media formats, genres, and practices.

Another key impact is the recognition of branding's importance, especially in terms of packaging. While the Bayou collection had a fixed format, the branding tactics for Abouet's non-Bayou series at Gallimard—*Akissi, Commissaire Kouamé,* and the newer volumes of *Aya de Yopougon*—have generated their own symbolic capital and have therefore been imitated. The use of vibrant, nonprimary, and high-contrasting colors for covers has become an instant signifier of Black *bandes dessinées* through the marketing of the postcolonial exotic. Several Black *bandes dessinées,* such as the aforementioned works written by Black women authors and the new hardback albums published by L'Harmattan BD, have adopted this branding tactic. Similarly, *bandes dessinées* about Africa and the African diaspora by authors and artists not of African descent also take up these branding tactics for immediate identification of their subject matter. Examples include the series *L'association des femmes africaines* (2020, 2021), by Swann Meralli and Clément Rizzo, and *L'Argent fou de la Françafrique* (2018), by Xavier Harel. Ironically, these packaging practices that allude to tropical elsewheres echo "the exotic staging of colonial literature" from the 1950s at the *salon de vente de livres* in Paris, where the enticing "multicolored covers" sufficed to "evoke the tropical sun" (Bush and Ducournau 212).[42] However, in place of the 1950s colonial nostalgia, these *bandes dessinées* that market the postcolonial exotic through their packaging, like Abouet's work, present self-aware narratives that claim space for Black francophone identities and Black Frenchness, critique the effects of French colonialism and its ongoing imperial formations, and often offer a blend of the two, as in the case of Jessica Oublié's work. Obviously, the AYA effect has done much more than legitimize Black *bandes dessinées* in the Global North, yet we must keep in mind that legitimation from the Global North is not always artists' guiding principle or primary objective.

Conclusion

Held in Grand-Bassam just outside Abidjan in 2017, the Coco Bulles festival finally returned for a fourth edition after a hiatus of ten years, and Marguerite Abouet was one of the many headliners, alongside famed French political cartoonist Plantu (founder and president of the French organization

---

42. For more on the importance of literary salons for francophone literature, see Bush, *Publishing,* especially chapter 3, "Literary Prize Culture."

Cartooning for Peace).[43] Given Abouet's fame and return visits to the Ivory Coast, one might assume that her participation in the Coco Bulles festival would be a natural outcome, yet the cumulative portrait of her in the festival's promotional materials reinscribes tensions that run through Black *bandes dessinées*. Although she gets first billing among the many international invitees on the main flyer, her presence in the rest of the materials is barely noticeable. Moreover, given the centrality of branding throughout Abouet's career, Aya is almost entirely absent, appearing only in writing in Abouet's bio. There are two main reasons for Abouet's marginalization. First, the Tâche d'encre group have conceived of Coco Bulles as a "Festival international du dessin de presse et de la bande dessinée,"[44] with an obvious emphasis on political and editorial cartoons, which in this instance is separate from rather than a subset of *bandes dessinées*. The strong preference for cartooning is easily legible in the prominent presence of other cartoonists, especially Plantu, whose Cartooning for Peace was a major festival sponsor and who gets a full page in the promotional materials to celebrate the reinstatement of the festival and the importance of the Tâche d'encre team. Second, Abouet's relegation to the end of the invitees' section in the program stems from her role as scenarist rather than artist. This is emphasized by the fact that the drawn portrait of her has been provided by one of the Tâche d'encre members, in contrast to all of the other artists, whose self-portrait immediately clues us in to their personal and visual style. Ironically, the grayscale portrait for Abouet is done by the same artist who provided portraits of key Ivorian politicians in the annex of the 2007 anthology *Côte d'Ivoire, On va où là?*; this literally and figuratively generates an image of Abouet far removed from her carefully curated brand linked to Aya. Instead, the grayscale portrait, by aligning her with Ivorian politicians, casts her as an important influence on the Ivory Coast albeit removed from daily life. One can detect this distance in the short blurb accredited to her in the festival's catalog, in which she repeatedly states how surprised she was by the number of international and Ivorian artists at the festival as well as by the Tâche d'encre team and their work (Abouet, "Ce festival" 7).

---

43. Plantu is the penname of Jean Plantureux. The page for the Coco Bulles festival on the official Cartooning for Peace website has no mention of Abouet's participation, though links to the festivals' own promotional materials are included, where Abouet is mentioned.

44. One possible translation is "International Festival of Cartooning and Comics," though "dessins de presse" has also been translated as newspaper drawings and, as this book illustrates, the translations of *bande dessinée* are many.

Together, Abouet's participation in the 2017 Coco Bulles festival and the organizers' framing of her participation capture the heterogeneity and changing reality of Black *bandes dessinées*. For Abouet, telling palatable personal stories that have wide appeal is well facilitated by a format along the lines of a graphic novel, whereas cartoonists providing social and political commentary on current events are better served by periodical publications and social media. In spite of differences in materiality, accessibility, and intended audiences, Black *bandes dessinées* are nevertheless framed by French-language institutions in the Global North as part of (if not always stemming from) the Ninth Art's global reach, with the broadest understanding of the term "Ninth Art." This is explicitly evident in the case of Abouet's oeuvre, its quick translation, and its self-propelling success regardless of its categorization as Ivorian, African, or Franco-Belgian. Though it might not seem like it, this is also the case for many Black francophone political cartoonists such as the Tâche d'encre members. For while Cartooning for Peace rallies under an anglophone title, the French government and cultural institutions supporting it—and by extension events like the Coco Bulles festival—are deeply invested in perpetuating France's soft power through upholding Republican universalism via the discourse of human rights as defended through political cartooning and caricature.

CHAPTER 3

Reframing Migration in the Twenty-First Century

In his 1959 novel, *Un Nègre à Paris* (translated in English as *An African in Paris*), Ivorian author Bernard Dadié presents satirical observations about the French via protagonist Bertin Tanhoé, who receives a round-trip ticket from Dakar to Paris. In this pseudo-ethnography of the colonial metropole and its residents, published in France on the eve of Ivorian independence, Dadié catalogs many observations shared by others from the French empire in the first half of the twentieth century who, once in France, were shocked into disillusionment by the hypocrisy of the myth of cultural superiority driving France's justification for colonialism. *Malamine, un africain à Paris*, a softback *bande dessinée* album published in France in 2009, written by Franco-Cameroonian Christophe Edimo and illustrated by Cameroonian Simon Pierre Mbumbo, follows another titular African who also journeys to Paris. Though the title echoes Dadié's, and though Malamine follows a colonially established trajectory, his reasons for being in Paris, as well as the city itself and its inhabitants, are far removed from the situation five decades prior. Whereas Tanhoé's touristic observations are often comedic in their astute critique of postwar French society and culture, Malamine's failed attempts at social mobility while connecting with a diverse Black population are cast in a somber tone. Indeed, as Binita Mehta argues in her astute reading of this *bande dessinée*, even the protagonist's name, translated as "someone who 'looks bad/gloomy,'" attests to the story's "dark quality," which is further boosted by Mbumbo's "*noir*-ish" artwork (Mehta, "Reluctant Migrant" 131–62). The *bande dessinée* opens with Malamine's arrival in Paris in 1997, which we assume is his first time in France though this is not the case. Turning the page, the reader is presented with two very different versions of the same studio apartment. On the left, we see Malamine's friends helping him move in, and on the right, we see the same studio ten years later. Throughout the *bande dessinée*, Mbumbo depicts the past with borderless panels, and for the present, he encases panels with thick, uneven, hand-drawn frames. This visual convention lends the past an open optimism that stands in stark contrast with the present's enclosed fixity. This psychological effect is enhanced by Mbumbo's choice of gray scale rather than color or even black and white. The light-filled apartment of the past has become gloomy; the close-ups of a computer and of a bucket under a leaky faucet on the noticeably darker right-hand page, with the rest of Malamine's meager possessions, connote a utilitarian life in which he has been trapped for the last decade. The only window in the apartment, which bookends the two pages diagonally, transforms the studio into a virtual prison cell. Through flashbacks, we learn that 1997 marks Malamine's return after having earned an economics doctorate at the Sorbonne only to fail to obtain a job in his unnamed West African home country due to discrimination and corruption. Through Malamine's struggle to become more than a hospital porter, Edimo and Mbumbo demonstrate how systemic racism, anti-immigrant sentiment, and the absence of a close-knit community within the diaspora, resulting from a lack of a singular shared past, generate a frustratingly lonely situation of unbelonging.[1] Moreover, they illustrate how Malamine's anger toward France stems from the powerlessness he experienced in his home country, which they posit as linked to colonialism.

Despite the stark difference in tone between the novel and the *bande dessinée*, the five decades separating them, and the differing conditions of the protagonists' journeys, the similarities highlight imperial practices that shape the movement, experiences, and self-awareness of individuals from the (former) French empire. Considering how both texts critique

---

1. Though the Black diaspora in Paris has become more inclusive of diversity since the publication of *Malamine,* its earlier fragmented nature is cataloged in the 2009 novel *Black Bazar,* by famed author Alain Mabanckou. Additionally, writing about Black France in 2011, Mabanckou foregrounds how the unevenness of both colonization and decolonization prevents a strong, close-knit community ("Preface" 7). For more on the affinities between *Malamine, un africain à Paris* and Mabanckou's *Black Bazar,* see Mehta, "Reluctant Migrant."

the hypocrisy of French universalism in their respective historical contexts helps us think through what Ann Stoler refers to as "imperial formations," that is, the heterogeneous and dynamic mutations of imperial structures following the formal end of colonization (2). In contrast to a distinct *before* and *after* implied by the term "postcolonial," and the lack of clarity of the term "neocolonial," Stoler urges us "to track the uneven sedimentations in which imperial formations leave their marks" so that we can interrogate "how empire's ruins contour and carve through the psychic material space in which people live and what compounded layers of imperial debris do to them" (Stoler 2). Comparing travel in Dadié's novel with that in the *bande dessinée* exposes ongoing imperial sediment as well as new layers that exacerbate existing debris. In *Un Nègre à Paris*, Tanhoé notes the indifferent attitude he encounters at the airport when trying to reserve a seat, explaining that "all those titles I spent twenty years acquiring, that I thought I could use one day as a way in, as an 'Open, Sesame!'—none of them counted," and adding that such discriminatory treatment could "drive you to despair" (10). Though this represents an outdated practice, as Bertin is trying to get a seat on a flight for which he already has a ticket, the underlying implication remains the same: that the regulation of travel, or movement, is an exercise of power and that gatekeepers' discriminatory practices can have lasting psychological effects on travelers. In *Malamine*, vestiges of French colonialism continue to function as strong push factors for migration, but restrictive immigration policies and intensified border control not only generate despair but also produce undocumented individuals (known in French as *sans-papiers*) and a host of new psychological and physical dangers.[2]

While postcolonial (im)migration and the lived experiences of (im)migrants in France have become key topics since the 1970s, when the French government increasingly limited immigration and Jean-Marie Le Pen established the extreme-right party Le Front National, this chapter moves away from Europe to explore northward migration itself and thus investigate these new dangers.[3] Focusing on work in which characters rarely set foot in Europe (and if so, not for long), this chapter examines how Black *bandes dessinées* about migration reframe broader discussions about movement in the twenty-first century, which, for Achille Mbembe, is marked by "borderization," or "the process by which world powers permanently transform certain spaces into

---

2. Already in 1999, French philosopher Étienne Balibar wrote about the increasingly strict immigration laws in France, particularly those eroding avenues for regularization, as contributing to apartheid (Balibar, "Le Droit").

3. See, for example, Hargreaves and McKinney, *Post-Colonial Cultures*; Hitchcott and Thomas, *Francophone Afropean Literatures*; McKinney, *Postcolonialism*.

impassable places for certain classes of people" (Mbembe, *Necropolitics* 99).⁴ The selection of *bandes dessinées* includes albums and vignettes published in Europe by African artists and collaborations by African and French authors and artists. With the exception of the mainstream award-winning album published by Gallimard in 2014, *Alpha: Abidjan–Gare du Nord*, written by Swiss-Gabonese author Bessora and illustrated by French artist Barroux, the texts come from the two most prolific publishers of African *bandes dessinées* in Europe: the Italian Africa e Mediterraneo and Lai-momo collective (responsible for the annual Africa Comics competition since 2002) and Paris-based L'Harmattan BD.⁵ The corpus includes the softback album *Une Éternité à Tanger*, written by Cameroonian journalist Eyoum Nganguè and illustrated by Ivorian Faustin Titi (2004); three vignettes from the anthology *Africa Comics 2005–2006* by artists from francophone Africa, including Didier Viodé; two of Viodé's subsequent albums published by L'Harmattan BD; two vignettes from the 2014 anthology *Nouvelles d'Afrique*, published by L'Harmattan BD; and the aforementioned *Alpha: Abidjan–Gare du Nord*.⁶

As many have argued, migration has long been central to comics worldwide as a common theme and a formative experience for many artists, but it has become even more ubiquitous since the turn of the twenty-first century.⁷ Though the reasons are manifold, in the European context (what Jan Vederveen Pieterse referred to as Fortress Europe as early as 1991), one particular event plays a central role: the Schengen Agreement of 1985, which

---

4. I use the broad term "migration" to include graphic narratives about immigrants, migrants, and refugees, since the shifting legal definitions of these terms are themselves often a mechanism of "borderization."

5. Coauthors Sandrine Bessora Nan Nguema and Stéphane Barroux publish under their respective pen names. Their *bande dessinée* won the Prix Médecins Sans Frontières in 2015 and the Pen Promotes Award in 2016.

6. Though there are other Black *bandes dessinées* that deal with migration, such as Malamine, Abouet's *Terre gâtée* (see chapter 2), both volumes of *La Vie de Pahé* (see chapter 1), and Christophe Edimo and Al'Mata's *Les Tribulations d'Alphonse Madiba dit Daudet*, the corpus of this chapter brings together texts that explicitly address characters in the process of trying to migrate from Africa to Europe. It is also worth noting that there are several examples of Black *bandes dessinées* that look at the complexities of migration *within* Africa, including entries in *Africa Comics 2005–2006* and *Nouvelles d'Afrique* as well as Florent Kassaï's album *Destination le Tchad*. Likewise, there are Black *bandes dessinées* that address migration internal to France, from the overseas departments to the metropolitan areas, including Lilian Thuram's *Notre Histoire* and Tehem's *Piment Zoizos: Les Enfants oubliés de la Réunion*.

7. See, for example, Marie and Olivier, *Albums*; Serrano, *Immigrants*; Bigelow and Singer, "Introduction"; Kauranen et al., *Comics*.

began reducing borders internal to Europe (Pieterse, "Fictions" 5).[8] The subsequent ever-intensifying processes of securing and surveilling Europe's external borders have forever reconfigured migration and how it is framed by European media and political discourses. In reaction to such framing that employs the rhetoric of a so-called "migrant crisis" and traffics in what Albert Memmi identified in the 1950s as "depersonalization" through "the mark of the plural," authors, artists, and activists mobilize cultural production to raise awareness about migrants and create space for them to speak for themselves (85). Graphic narratives constitute a particularly rich and prolific segment of such cultural production.

Generally, the work of comics scholars on such graphic narratives (including my own previous work) has focused on the ways in which artists leverage formal conventions to humanize migrants, thereby engendering empathy in readers, but this approach has its limitations.[9] Summarizing scholarship on refugee comics, Dominic Davies explains that the thrust of such an approach pits the slowness and subjective nature of comics against "a visual culture of proliferating decontextualized images of violence and suffering" (257). Central to this approach is an acute preoccupation with the practices artists use to authenticate a story's veracity and legitimize witnesses' testimony, which Davies pushes against. Similarly, in *Ethics in the Gutter: Empathy and Historical Fiction in Comics* (2017), Kate Polak valorizes fictional comics about real-world events, what she calls "historiometagraphics," as more effective at generating a critical response, for they leverage readers' "awareness of the graphic narrative as something *produced* . . . which gives comics the possibility of engaging in commentary on the production of history and its violences" (11). Building on this assumption, she argues that this awareness "cues the reader into an engagement more ethically nuanced than he might have had otherwise" (14). Though reading ethically is important, Davies warns against assuming that the "solicitation of empathy or action is the singular purpose of any such image [or text]" because it "foreclose[s] more expansive ways of reading [and] thinking"

---

8. Another key event that contributed to the shifting discourse around migration was American President George W. Bush's declaration of a "Global War on Terrorism" directly following the September 11, 2001, attacks on the World Trade Center and the Pentagon by members of Al-Qaeda. Since the scope of this chapter is limited to migration from the continent of Africa to primarily Fortress Europe, the specificities of the North American context are not discussed, though the analytical approaches here provide rich comparative opportunities.

9. See Bumatay, "Picturing" and "Plural Pathways." For key examples of comics' innate ability to humanize characters, see Versaci, *Book*; Mickwitz, *Documentary Comics*; Chute, *Disaster Drawn*.

(258). Drawing from Susan Sontag's *Regarding the Pain of Others* (2003), he insists we consider "what [images] *are* actually telling us" and explains that their "intervention is not always to disrupt the status quo but sometimes more simply to reveal its machinations" (263). Put another way, we gain new insights about the multivalent critiques at work in migration comics by realigning our analytic priorities. To push our understanding further, Davies proposes a new concept that expands upon Jacques Rancière's notion from *The Emancipated Spectator* (2008) of an "intolerable image": an intolerable fiction. Identifying the intolerable fictions artists expose and working through how they do so, Davies argues, helps us destabilize them, thus paving the way for change beyond empathy.

This chapter examines Black *bandes dessinées* from 2004 to 2019 that reframe migration from the vantage point of the African continent. Though some are close to autofiction and others are informed by interviews, the primary concern is investigating what artists do in and with their *bandes dessinées*, rather than evaluating their authenticity claims. In reading with Davies and Stoler, I focus on the intolerable fictions these *bandes dessinées* present and examine artists' strategies for conveying the compounded consequences of imperial formations' ongoing corrosive processes. Consequently, this chapter argues that while an important function of such *bandes dessinées* is to give a human face to individual migrants, at the same time, an equally yet contradictory function is precisely to represent dehumanization, but not just that of European discourses about migrants. Instead, this chapter foregrounds the multifaceted dehumanization of borderization. What emerges from an attention to artists' treatment of dehumanization is a concerted effort to historicize and contextualize migration in the twenty-first century, a condemnation of the necropolitics and anti-Black racism foundational to borderization, a nuanced critique of borderization's wide-ranging physical, psychological, and moral ruination (to use Stoler's terminology), and a critical reframing of concepts such as "human," "universal," and "rights" that exposes the intolerable fictions of Global North ideologies and institutions.

An Eternity in Tangiers, or The Long History of Twenty-First-Century Migration

One crucial intolerable fiction about migration to Europe is its characterization as a supposedly recent and ahistorical crisis. Writing in 2017, prominent Black Mediterranean studies scholar Ida Danewid explains that left-wing activism, academic debate, and the far right in Europe all contribute to a "veil of ignorance" (1676) that "disconnects connected histories and turns questions of responsibility, guilt, restitution, repentance, and structural reform into matters of empathy, generosity, and hospitality" (1675). The result is a framing that "confirm[s] rather than disturb[s] colonial relations of power" and "divorces the contemporary Mediterranean crisis from Europe's long history of empire and racial violence" (1679). Moreover, through the fetishization of the stranger and a "focus on bodies in pain," left-liberal activists and interventions produce a "politics of pity rather than justice" that "not only decontextualises and dehistoricises the ongoing tragedy, but also contributes to the construction of a particular cultural narrative—of European goodness, humanity, and antiracism" (1681). For Danewid, the central problem is "an ethics based on mourning and welcoming migrants as universal humans—rather than as victims of a shared, global present built on colonialism, racism, and white supremacy" (1683). Danewid's critique exposes how European discourses across the political spectrum have developed intolerable fictions about migration and migrants to justify ongoing yet mutated forms of imperial ruination. Indeed, the "veil of ignorance" she describes purposefully obscures the *longue durée* of European colonialism as well as the last three decades of Europe's recent past.

At the turn of the twenty-first century, even before the establishment in 2004 of the European Border and Coast Guard Agency (known familiarly as Frontex), scholars astutely pinpointed the colonial underpinnings of emerging forms of borderization. In 2001, French philosopher Étienne Balibar argued that Western Europe's treatment of asylum seekers and so-called clandestine immigrants draws from "the persistence of administrative methods and habits acquired during contact with 'indigenous' populations" and reactivates colonial-era hierarchal categories, which results in the "'racialization' of processes of globalization" (Balibar, We 38–39). For Balibar, borders have become "essential institutions in the constitution of social conditions on a global scale"; however, "the most decisive borders . . . are no longer 'lines': instead they are *detention zones* and *filtering systems*" (Balibar, We 111–13). These new zones and systems thus become "instrument[s] of security control, social segregation, and unequal access to the means of existence, and sometimes as an institutional distribution of survival and death" (Balibar, We 117). At almost the same time, in 2003, Mbembe introduced the concept of necropolitics, which describes "the ultimate expression of sovereignty [as] the power and the capacity to dictate who may live and who must die" (Mbembe, "Necropolitics" 11). Like Balibar, Mbembe argues that "the problem is neither the migrants nor the refugees nor the asylum seekers. Borders. Everything begins with them, and all paths lead back to them" (Mbembe, *Necropolitics* 99). For both, filtering systems and borderization derive directly from European colonialism and its schemas of knowledge, but with adjusted mechanisms of dispossession and abstraction that have led to "a systemic use of various forms of extreme violence and mass insecurity" (Balibar, *We* 116) as well as mainstream "indifference to objective signs of cruelty" (Mbembe, *Necropolitics* 38). In the name of national security post-9/11, the surveillance state is allowed to apply such violence and cruelty on people deemed noncitizens, a status manufactured in large part through anti-Black racism. According to Mbembe, "race is one of the raw materials from which difference and *surplus*—a kind of life that can be wasted and spent without limit—are produced . . . [it] is an instrumentality that makes it possible both to name the surplus and to commit it to waste and unlimited spending" (Mbembe, *Critique* 34). Racism's attendant dehumanization results in both "a generalized cheapening of the price of life" and "a habituation to loss" (Mbembe, *Necropolitics* 38). Consequently, the dominant matrix of migrants' existence in these detention zones and filtering systems is one that distorts life in favor of death, which is at the core of what the *bandes dessinées* under consideration here theorize through the multimodal conventions of the medium. Via fictional characters, they invite readers into the midst of such filtering systems and attempt to convey borderization's multiple processes of dehumanization and ruination.

That the earliest *bande dessinée*—*Une Éternité à Tanger*, published in 2004—was translated into English and rereleased in 2017 speaks both to the long history of northward migration in the current century and the urgency of reframing our understanding of it. Already in 2004, author Eyoum Nganguè and artist Faustin Titi highlighted key aspects of migrants' experiences and their use of certain formal techniques to convey the protagonist's situation have become common tropes. Published by Lai-momo and Africa e Mediterraneo five years before *Malamine*, this album centers on Gawa, a migrant from the fictional port city of Gnasville, and toggles between his present life trapped in Tangiers and flashbacks of his multiple attempts to migrate to Europe.[10] Whereas Mbumbo alternates between frameless and noticeably framed panels in *Malamine*, Titi, working in ink and watercolors,

---

10. Prior to the publication of *Une Éternité à Tanger*, Nganguè and Titi introduced Gnasville in their submission to the 2003 Africa Comics competition organized by Africa e Mediterraneo and Lai-momo, entitled "Le Flic de Gnasville" ("The Cop of Gnasville"), which exposes police corruption. In the densely packed, grayscale three-page entry, a cop on the verge of retirement reflects on his twenty-year career of meager pay during which he was obliged to extort money, grossly overcrowd jails where prisoners were routinely beaten and malnourished, and imprison, torture, and rape journalists, intellectuals, and students critical of the ruling party. Additionally, that Nganguè hails from Cameroon and Titi from the Ivory Coast reinforces Gnasville's function as a placeholder for any city in francophone West Africa.

plays with color palette to differentiate Gawa's past from his present and blur the lines between the two. He employs a mauve-tinged gray scale for the past, which, like a sepia wash, connotes Gawa's memories. During these flashbacks, the repetitive use of shadows and black silhouettes attests to the logistics of migrating clandestinely from shady deals with traffickers and traveling at night to hiding and waiting for indeterminate lengths of time in cramped spaces. In sharp contrast, Titi uses color for Gawa's present in Tangiers, but the city and his existence in it appear drained of life. The yellow- and brown-based grays of Tangiers's cobblestones and the rare blue of the sea and the sky do little to combat the dominating whiteness of the buildings, whose long corridors seem to emphasize Gawa's effective imprisonment. What does stand out in Tangiers are peoples' clothes and especially Gawa's frayed yellow pullover. This makes him easy to identify and highlights his loneliness. The legibility of Gawa's predicament also derives from Titi's style, which reads as a nuanced, more realistic take on the *ligne claire* style. In fact, while the settings, characters, and precise use of watercolors telegraph Titi's insistence on realism, some exaggerated representations of Moroccans who exploit migrants verge on caricatures reminiscent of the stereotypical Arab figures in Hergé's Tintin series. Ultimately, Titi's meticulous style derives from the serious nature of Gawa's experience; the highly legible realism he achieves is essential for communicating the life-threatening dangers of Gawa's every step and his half-life in Tangiers.

Through Gawa's situation, author Nganguè introduces key components of migrants' experiences, including the complex reasons for leaving one's home. Hallmarks include an unending series of negotiations with unreliable traffickers and not being in control of one's movement or time. The repetition and variation of these scenes illustrates the vast distances migrants travel, the various modes and unpredictability of how they travel, the juxtaposition of long stretches of time and hurried urgency for each leg of the journey, and the precarity and uncertainty of each moment. The flashbacks in the first half of the album trace Gawa's northward journey through the western part of the Sahara, featuring scenes of cramped trucks, full boats, and dangerous treks on foot after being stranded by traffickers. At the album's midpoint, Gawa explains that he and a small group of other migrants decided to stay in Tangiers to plan their next move, since "turning back and going home was completely out of the question!" (24). Instead of explaining outright why Gawa cannot return, the flashbacks go further back in time, effectively reframing Gawa's migration thus far. While in Tangiers, Gawa receives a letter informing him of the deaths of his cousins who were in a plane about to land in France. This letter and the deadly risk his cousins took prompt

Gawa to think back to his time in Gnasville, when he was a university student and demonstrated against the government's corruption. Law enforcement's response was a violent suppression that included harm, humiliation, and rape, which, as suggested by the subsequent ransacking of the local League for Human Rights' office, was nothing out of the ordinary. Gawa was arrested following the incidents and told by the police captain that he had only two options: either become an informant or be crushed with no job prospects whatsoever. In actuality, the two options are equally shaped by necropolitics. Staying would mean living under the constant threat of violence while becoming part of a corrupt system, and though leaving might lead to a better life, it also spells danger and corruption for migrants.

Gawa chooses, unsurprisingly, to leave, and it is in the last section of the album that Nganguè reframes migration to expose its colonially influenced necropolitical infrastructure. By this point, readers have witnessed Gawa's clandestine trek to Tangiers, but his journey had begun much earlier with exhausting all legal options first. Panels depicting him waiting in long lines for days and nights in the sun and torrential rains outside various European embassies echo across the rest of the *bandes dessinées* and convey how filtering systems are themselves a form of detention zone. Far from Europe, these institutions constitute the outsourced labor of borderization. The recurring trope of a White woman employee tasked with systematically denying every applicant's visa begs the questions of the legality of her presence in Africa and the authority of her ruling, which subsequently calls into question the legal basis for all migration policies, regardless of their uneven enforcement. The string of denials suggests that the only viable option for Gawa is to deal with traffickers. Yet again, Nganguè challenges stereotypes, as Gawa's first clandestine attempt is aboard a cargo ship in his hometown. As with his journey through the Sahara, Gawa is betrayed, and the African crew manhandle him as they throw him overboard. That they leave him to die in the Atlantic forces us to recognize that what happens in the Mediterranean is also happening in other bodies of water. It also exposes how part of borderization's ruination is its ability to transform people and environments into agents of death. Gawa survives long enough for local fishermen to rescue him, but the resulting trauma prompts him to vow never to attempt leaving again. Sustained corruption nevertheless pushes him to gather money from his family to undertake the journey recounted in the first half of the album. In the present, Gawa must contend with other agents of borderization; he must evade the Moroccan police with whom European countries have brokered deals to secure Fortress Europe, while dealing with corrupt locals who exploit his clandestine status. Caught in the detention zone that Tangiers has become for him, he oscillates between dreaming of a new life in Paris and of drowning in an overcrowded boat in the Mediterranean. Titi's use of wavy borders and the same color palette from the flashbacks for these dreams and nightmares gives them equal psychological weight as Gawa's memories, all of which overshadow his effective imprisonment in Tangiers.

As final commentary, the story jumps even further back in time to the colonial era but productively blurs the distinction between the past and the present. Starting at the bottom of the penultimate page and continuing to the top of the last page (figure 3.1), Titi's tinted panels depict an early scene of European colonial contact in Africa, featuring an unending procession of African men and women transporting natural resources under the watchful eye of a colonial administrator. In the accompanying text boxes, Nganguè first employs the present tense, juxtaposed over a colonial village as he conveys Gawa's lament: "They [Westerners] steal from us, but they also want to make us look like beggars!" (44). He then switches to the past tense in the first panel of the last page to summarize the violence of resource extraction, slavery, and cultural imperialism enacted by European colonizers, who, in contradistinction to the current paradigm, arrived without visas or advance notice (figure 3.1). The last two horizontal panels slowly seep back to the present: the middle panel, slightly smaller than the other two, is a wide shot of an offshore oil rig, and the final panel presents Gawa at the Moroccan shore with a flock of seagulls in flight behind him. In the second panel, Titi employs the same tint as for the past, presenting the oil rig as a direct continuation of colonial-era practices. Once again, the text box creates tension by criticizing how Europe rejects Africans while reaping African resources. In the final panel, Gawa's yellow pullover unquestioningly returns us to the twenty-first century and, more importantly, his eternal state in limbo. The setting of the Moroccan shore fixes him at an intersection of multiple edges. His daily life is spent on the edge of Moroccan society, just as the port city itself sits on the threshold of land and sea as well as that of Africa and Europe. Psychologically, as indicated by the final text box, he lingers between not knowing if he "will one day return home, or die with Fortress Europe still in sight" (45). The flock of seagulls in motion at his back visually emphasize the constructed nature of his imprisonment; they can traverse human-made borders, but Gawa is bound in a half-life by borderization.

The complexity of Gawa's situation crafted by Nganguè and Titi can be read as using the multimodal form of comics to theorize the same conclusions about necropolitics that Mbembe makes, especially those pertaining to the racialized surplus essential to how borderization operates. According to Mbembe,

FIGURE 3.1. Gawa's static life at the edge. *An Eternity in Tangiers*, Phoneme Media, 2017.

> sovereignty consists in the power to manufacture an entire crowd of people who specifically live at the edge of life, or even on its outer edge—people for whom living means continually standing up to death, and doing so under conditions in which death itself increasingly tends to become spectral. ...
> As a rule, such death is something to which nobody feels any obligation to respond. Nobody even bears the slightest feelings of responsibility or justice toward this sort of life or, rather, death. (Mbembe, Necropolitics 37–38)[11]

Though Titi's depiction of Gawa anchors him in the present, his death-life at the outer edge of Moroccan society transforms him into a kind of haunting presence in Tangiers. Similarly, the other *bandes dessinées* employ a range of strategies to theorize the ignored spectral reality of migrants' lives that, like in *Une Éternité à Tanger*, is instantly signaled through titles and aesthetic choices, which roughly fall into two camps. First, texts focused on rendering the compounded experiences of migration easily accessible similarly adapt the *ligne claire* style for their own purposes. Second, texts highly attuned to the psychological ruination resulting from death's spectrality lean heavily on gray scale and watercolors to emphasize the persistent and precarious instability of such a state. Working chronologically through artists' and authors' choices for theorizing necropolitics' processes of dehumanization allows us to track change over time. However, the echoing similarities across the different *bandes dessinées* illustrate how the emergent intolerable fiction of migration's ahistoricity is a function of borderization's globalization. In other words, the spectral existence Mbembe describes, and the imperial debris that both produces and ignores such an existence, has not changed; what has changed is the dramatic increase in scale, efficacy, and normalization of necropolitics.

Borderization: Between Life and Death

Following the publication of *Une Éternité à Tanger*, Africa e Mediterraneo chose migration as the theme for the 2005–6 edition of its biennial Africa Comics competition; as with Nganguè and Titi's 2004 album, several short-form entries in the resulting *Africa Comics 2005–2006* anthology raised key concerns and critiques about borderization long before abstract statistics and sensationalized reporting became part of the European media landscape in the early 2010s. One of the winners, Beninois artist Didier Viodé, eventually

---

11. Mbembe even refers to the people at the edge as the living dead (*Necropolitics* 40).

continued the story from his entry "Visa Rejeté" in two subsequent albums published by L'Harmattan BD—*Vive la corruption* (2011) and *Yao visa refusé* (2019)—to examine the ongoing practice in the twenty-first century of European nations' systematic rejection of African visas. In the span of only a few pages, the entries in *Africa Comics 2005–2006*, including Viodé's short piece, enhance the insights about borderization presented in *Une Éternité à Tanger*, especially pertaining to death's ever-present spectrality for migrants.[12]

The title of Cameroonian artist Daniel Severin Ngassu's entry, "Entre la vie et la mort" (Between life and death), immediately signals migrants' in-between status, which is reinforced by his use of grayscale watercolor and ink. The migrants resemble ghostly living dead as they struggle to keep walking. Ngassu threads this in-betweenness throughout the four-page entry highlighting the ambiguity of migrants' spectral existence. The dried-out landscape and incomplete human remains of the first panel blur the line between beings and the environment and suggest that the setting starts in the Sahara. However, the accompanying text boxes of the first and second panels put into question the geographic location by informing readers that inhabitants from a region in Cameroon hit by misery and drought have no option but to migrate to lands less poor. The specific wording of "des terres moins pauvres" could mean an area richer in its capacity to produce crops and, relatedly, a land with a stronger economy (Ngassu 62). In both cases, the subtext is the substrata: the push factors for migration—desertification resulting from climate change and the attendant eroding means of socioeconomic survival—derive from imperial formations. Right away, then, Ngassu demonstrates necropolitics' spectral ubiquity for certain people, even within their own homes. For some, leaving can result in the same fate as that of staying, that is, turning to dust in the dust, or as Stoler would put it, degraded personhoods bound to degraded environments (6). This tragic end is confirmed, at least for some, on the adjacent right-hand page, where two travelers fall victim to fatigue and are subsequently left by those who must continue for their own survival. Though the others pity those who perish, because they are also at the outermost edge between life and death, such spectral deaths quickly become part of the landscape. When the migrants arrive at their ostensible land of refuge, it is unclear if what awaits them will be any better, as Ngassu's only indication of the new home is a chain-link fence. Though the migrants' dialogue implies that they are saved and entering into an ordered system, Ngassu undermines their relief in the

---

12. While there are several other francophone entries about migration in the anthology, I focus on the three that deal explicitly with various facets of borderization. The entries vary from one to five pages in length.

FIGURE 3.2. Spectral migrants entering a detention zone. "Entre la vie et la mort," *Africa Comics 2005–2006*, Africa e Mediterraneo, Lai-momo, 2006.

final panel, which happens to be silent (figure 3.2). In this horizontal panel, one migrant looks directly at the reader with a blank expression as he is about to cross the threshold into the darker fenced area with other equally spectral figures behind him. This final panel resembles that of *Une Éternité à Tanger* with the difference that these migrants are on the cusp of learning that detention zones generate their own kind of in-between existence. Not indicating where the chain-link fence is allows Ngassu to allude to all detention zones and their dehumanizing effects, regardless of their location.

The two-page entry "Si la Mer Méditerranée pouvait parler . . ." (If the Mediterranean Sea could speak . . . ; figure 3.3), by Congolese artist Valéry Bakida Nzila (penname Badik'art) features similar hallmarks, including groups of migrants crossing the Sahara, chain-link fences, and blurring the distinction between human and environment (in this case, both the Sahara and the Mediterranean); however, instead of fluid watercolors, he maximizes legibility to eliminate any ambiguity regarding anti-Black racism's centrality to borderization. In this densely packed double-page spread, image and text as well as layout and style work efficiently in tandem. Employing a nuanced *ligne claire* style, Badik'art repeats horizontal panels to convey the scale of migration, the vast distances migrants travel, and the dangers they encounter. Interspersed with these panels, he includes a map detailing the possible routes from Gao in eastern Mali to Melilla and Ceuta (the Spanish enclaves in Morocco) and compact panels depicting the risks migrants face at the hands of borderization's various human and nonhuman agents.

Traffickers and Moroccan police extort, beat, rob, and chase migrants, leaving them to die of hunger, dehydration, and drowning. They are assisted in their death work by harmful human-made obstacles (towering metal fences topped with razor wire) and nature (the desert and the sea).

Through the layout and content of the second page, Badik'art theorizes the anti-Black death work central to borderization, or what Lucinda Newns has termed "necropolitical ecology" (figure 3.3) (1). Badik'art insists on the active role of nature through the personification of the Mediterranean Sea in the title and repeatedly on the second page, where a vertical panel spanning the left side establishes the Mediterranean as a central figure of twenty-first-century migration, simultaneously a witness and an actor. Moreover, the unique perspective and increased verisimilitude of the vertical panel emphasize the Mediterranean Sea's significance. In the text box at the top, Badik'art introduces the Mediterranean Sea as the one who engulfs or guzzles migrants in its hostile depths, and he guesses at the number of victims. He ends the text box by pondering, "If only the Mediterranean Sea could speak," and uses a squiggled bottom edge that blends with the wavy lines for the sea, thus drawing the reader's attention downward (107). At first, the reader encounters natural ocean flora and fauna, which gives way to human skeletal remains and eventually ends with human skulls, the large scale of which foregrounds their presence on the seabed. The accompanying panels to the right, depicting other forms of violence and death, seem to create parallels with the sea's hostile depths. For instance, the Moroccan police, like the sea flora and fauna, do with migrants what they will and extract what they can.[13] Additionally, the wavy text box halfway down the page that straddles the vertical panel of the sea on the left and, on the right, the horizontal panel of migrants left for dead in the Sahara links these environments as twinned accomplices. Likewise, Badik'art's thematic use of oranges, yellows, and tans for the Sahara, North Africa, and the sea paint all three zones as equally deadly. As early as 2006, Badik'art "call[ed] attention to the shared complicities in the death and disposal of human victims of necropolitical border policies" between humans and more-than-human nature (Newns 8). Interestingly, he places panels depicting human-made borders and their effects at the bottom of the page, adjacent to the skeletal remains and skulls of the vertical panel. In contrast to Ngassu's decontextualized chain-link fence, Badik'art's extreme low-angle point-of-view panel places

---

13. It is worth reiterating that this two-page *bande dessinée* was published in 2006. Over a decade before award-winning Armin Greder's wordless graphic novel *Mediterraneo* (2017) was published to much acclaim, Badik'art pointed to the complicity and interconnectedness of the African continent, the Mediterranean Sea, and Europe.

FIGURE 3.3. Borderization's human and more-than-human agents. "Si la Mer Méditerranée pouvait parler . . . ," *Africa Comics 2005–2006*, Africa e Mediterraneo, Lai-momo, 2006.

readers at the foot of such borders. Though already anxiety-inducing, the danger and trauma of trying to scale the razor-wire-topped fence is amplified because it is confined on all sides by death. To mirror the large skulls on the left, Badik'art ends the page with a text box on the right in which he calls out the anti-Black racism undergirding all of borderization's death work.

Speaking directly to readers in the final panel, he explains that migrants from "Black Africa" (the term he uses in the first panel) will continue to take their chances in spite of borderization's potentially fatal dangers. He then concludes by declaring that international decision-makers, African leaders, and enthusiasts of "Négrologie" should, moving forward, use the lessons learned by migrants' plight. In a footnote directly below, he explains that "Négrologie" comes from journalist Stephen Smith's 2004 book *Négrologie: Pourquoi l'Afrique meurt* (Negrology: Why Africa is dying), thereby already pointing to the anti-Black racism of both the push factors to migrate and the mechanisms to prevent it.

In contrast to the other *bandes dessinées* in this chapter, the works by Beninois Didier Viodé featuring his fictional alter ego, Yao, take a comedic approach to the necropolitical dimensions of borderization. Considering Viodé's distinctive style and cheeky satire, it is no surprise that his *Africa Comics 2005–2006* entry "Visa rejeté" won first prize, which enabled later opportunities with European publishers. In this entry and the subsequent L'Harmattan BD albums *Vive la corruption* (2011) and *Yao visa refusé* (2019), Viodé's unique blend of comedic conventions (exaggerated features, action lines, and ideograms) with watercolors generates a playful yet precise style. His fusion of expressive line work reminiscent of other famous caricaturists (André Franquin, Georges Wolinski, Pahé) and a pastel-forward palette of watercolors creates a self-contained form of legibility removed from realism. As a productive middle ground between the two main aesthetic camps of the other migration *bandes dessinées*, Viodé's style allows him to present biting sociopolitical critiques to which readers are particularly receptive because of the levity achieved through his unique style (see, for example, figure 3.4). Starting in the four-page entry and continuing through the subsequent albums, he concentrates his critique of borderization's intolerable fictions through repetition and variation in the daily life of Yao, an artist specializing in painting, like Viodé himself.[14] "Visa rejeté" starts with Yao in line at the French consulate at four o'clock a.m. where he waits for hours during a heat wave. In the bottom strip, Yao finally makes it to the counter, only for the White woman clerk to angrily tell him that he should have gotten up earlier since the office is closed for the day. On the adjoining right-hand page, Viodé sandwiches Yao's second attempt (which is rejected due to a supposed lack of adequate documentation, in spite of the exaggerated stack

---

14. In addition to making *bandes dessinées*, Viodé is a multimedia artist working in paint, photography, and video. *Étrangers sans rendez-vous*, his 2011 *bande dessinée* about his experiences as a migrant in Besançon, France, showcases his talent as an expressive painter and is far more contemplative than his work on the character Yao.

FIGURE 3.4. Didier Viodé exposes the racism of borderization. "Visa rejeté," *Africa Comics 2005–2006*, Africa e Mediterraneo, Lai-momo, 2006.

of papers he carries) with the direct opposite of his situation (figure 3.4).[15] In the top strip, a blond-haired White man easily gets a visa from a Black woman clerk, who approves his on-the-spot fabricated reason for traveling (ostensible humanitarian aid). Then, in the bottom strip, accompanying a panel of the White man on a beach being pampered by two Black women in bikinis, Viodé sardonically explains that far from Yao's frustrating situation (the detention zone of filtering systems), some people pursue humanitarian work under Africa's palm trees.

The juxtaposition of these experiences exposes the gross inequality and racial biases of borderization in the twenty-first century. Like Gawa, Yao vows to stay in his home country rather than leave, but the lure of potential opportunities in Europe for artists eventually spurs him to reapply. Unsurprisingly, his demand is rejected, this time because one of his ears is not visible in his passport photo. In *Vive la corruption* and *Yao visa refusé*, Viodé further critiques the complicit systems of local corruption and borderization that perpetuate the trapped half-life witnessed in the *bandes dessinées* discussed above, yet the recentness of the 2019 publication date of *Yao visa refusé* and the change from a rejected visa to a refused one telegraph the spread of necropolitics' ubiquity. Instead of seemingly arbitrary grounds for rejecting a visa, borderization's agents can simply refuse visas altogether.

This shift toward increased normalization of borderization and the anti-Black necropolitics central to it has amplified the attendant processes of physical, psychological, and moral ruination. Though artists since the early 2000s have generated articulate representations and critiques of borderization, Europe's mobilization of intolerable fictions—Danewid's "veil of ignorance"—obscures to thus neutralize such insights. Consequently, migrants face a bleaker reality, in which dehumanization is no longer an ongoing process but rather the bedrock of their existence. As part of a racialized surplus, they are altogether excluded from notions of humanity, universalism, and rights. Turning now to the *bandes dessinées* published in 2014, a decade after *Une Éternité à Tanger*, we witness a move toward increased despair, destruction, and death. Instead of migrants in stasis, characters are now the ruined debris of imperial formations with more impunity. An important indicator of the worsening conditions is the change in titles, from ones that refer to detention zones and the state of being in them to individuals' identities (as seen in Viodé's work, from "Visa rejeté" to *Yao Visa refusé*). It is in these more

---

15. Viodé's award-winning entry, "Visa rejeté," was featured in the 2006–7 exposition Africa Comics at the Studio Museum in Harlem, and an English translation of the vignette is included in the accompanying catalog, including the translation of figure 3.4 (page 213 of the catalog).

recent *bandes dessinées* that the tension between the urgency to humanize migrants while exposing the intolerable fictions that fuel their dehumanization is the most poignant.

Les damnés de la terre, la mer, et l'air

Though migration in the twenty-first century has a long history, as indicated above, significant political events starting in 2010 and 2011 (the Arab Spring, the Syrian Civil War, and the reemergence of the Islamic State) and their destabilizing effects throughout Africa and the Middle East have mobilized more people to seek refuge and asylum in Fortress Europe. By 2014, attention-grabbing headlines claiming each year as the deadliest on record for migrants were already sounding repetitive. The vignettes about northward migration ("Un Congolais au Maroc" and "Le voyage de Bouna") in L'Harmattan BD's anthology *Nouvelles d'Afrique* and the mainstream album *Alpha: Abidjan–Gare du Nord* have subsequently aimed to reframe migration for readers in Europe and beyond by delving into individualized situations. Indeed, that all three are the result of creative collaborations between French publishers and French and African authors and artists attests to the entangled transnational reality of imperial formations and at the same time draws attention to the unevenness of the circulation of ideas, people, and goods. The two vignettes in *Nouvelles d'Afrique* are written by Morocco-based French author and illustrator Jean-François Chanson and center on male protagonists who meet tragic ends; "Le voyage de Bouna" is illustrated by Ivorian artist Koffi Roger N'Guessan, and "Un Congolais au Maroc" is illustrated by Burkinabe artist Gildas Gamy, and both employ their own adapted form of the *ligne claire* style to maximize legibility and reader identification. Conversely, the album *Alpha: Abidjan–Gare du Nord*, published by Gallimard in the wake of Marguerite Abouet's success, marries dynamic first-person narration by award-winning Swiss-Gabonese author Bessora with French artist Barroux's deceptively simple watercolor-based multimedia artwork. This luxury item—a hardback long-form album larger in size than the Bayou Series launched by *Aya de Yopougon*—constitutes a major intervention in the European debate about migration.[16] Gallimard's calculated risk in bringing this story to a broad audience relies on the feminization of Black *bandes*

---

16. Additionally, the 2018 English translation, *Alpha: Abidjan to Paris,* alongside the digitization of both language versions, has expanded the reach of the authors' intervention about migration to a global scale.

dessinées by supporting Bessora, who, by 2014, had already won several prestigious literary awards for her novels, some of which Gallimard published. Like *Une Éternité à Tanger*, this album and the two vignettes operate on multiple levels and present many of the same critiques, yet the spread of borderization's mechanisms means that characters, including borderization's agents, suffer increased levels of ruination. Moreover, these later texts go further in their depiction of how such processes of ruination affect people differently based on their age and gender. While the adult men are ruined beyond what Gawa and Yao experience, the women and children are even more at risk of being devastated.

Ruination's spread can be read in the fact that "Le voyage de Bouna" closes the collection in *Nouvelles d'Afrique*. With the exception of "L'esprit de famille," all the vignettes paint devastating stories of life in francophone Africa, and while many end on a sad note, the final vignette, which leaves readers alone in the dark with a dead body, also leaves little room for hope. Bouna, a Senegalese adolescent dazzled by the possibility of life in France, stows away in an airplane's landing gear in Dakar. He quickly loses consciousness and when he awakens, he is handcuffed to a hospital bed in Lyon. Though the doctors intend to help Bouna stay since he is a minor, he is deported because his father recognized him on the news and contacted local authorities. Back in Dakar, Bouna, wearing the knit cap he was given in Lyon in spite of the excessive heat, reads in a newspaper that Belgian authorities in Brussels found two Guinean youths dead in a plane's landing gear. Bouna is saddened by their deaths, but neither their fate nor his father's pleading prevent him from returning to the Dakar airport to try again. The final page of the vignette (and the entire anthology) is silent except for the very last panel. The top two strips depict Bouna sneaking into the airport under the cover of night and climbing into a plane's landing gear. Then the four panels of the bottom strip fade to all black (figure 3.5). In the first three, Bouna huddles closer into himself to keep warm as the plane takes off. The increasing black in the panels signals both the fading light as the landing gear retracts and Bouna's fading consciousness. Since Bouna is positioned in the top half of each panel, by the fourth all-black panel, his absence is unmistakable. Accompanying this visual obliteration, the text box in the bottom half of the panel explains that Bouna's body—not Bouna—was found the next day in Abidjan and that his family, who had reported him missing, recognized him from his photo in the media. Bouna's tragic end in Abidjan contrasts starkly with the vignette's title; his journey, devoid of leisure, can only lead to harm and death. The only positive aspect

FIGURE 3.5. Bouna's final moments in a plane's landing gear. "Le voyage de Bouna," *Nouvelles d'Afrique*, L'Harmattan BD, 2014.

is the up-to-date reporting on migrants in Europe and Africa that staves off complete erasure by bringing such tragic news to international publics and providing closure for Bouna's family.

Like "Le voyage de Bouna," "Un Congolais au Maroc," generates tension between the sense of adventure suggested by the title and the main character's outcome.[17] In addition to the title, Chanson and Gamy mobilize a visual style and tropes akin to Hergé's Tintin series (such as a point-of-view panel of the protagonist reading a letter) to expose the ubiquitous dangers of anti-Black racism in the detention zone of North Africa. In some ways, this vignette continues Gawa's situation in *Une Éternité à Tanger*. At the end of the 2004 album, Nganguè and Titi allude to those in Tangiers who exploit undocumented migrants, but rather than explore what Gawa must do to ensure his survival, they end by emphasizing his liminality. Conversely, Chanson and Gamy's vignette starts with Bernard and his girlfriend, Gislaine, in Rabat on the verge of their long-awaited attempt to cross into Fortress Europe, having each earned enough to pay exploitative traffickers. Bernard must still go into work at a marble depot and decides to take his precious savings with him. Unlike the empty corridors of Gawa's Tangiers, Rabat is unwelcoming and dangerous for Bernard. On his way to work, a

---

17. Though the title foregrounds Bernard's Congolese identity instead of his name, it nevertheless evokes the formulaic titles of Hergé's Tintin albums to highlight how experiences of elsewheres differ as a function of necropolitics.

Moroccan boy walking with his mother angrily throws a racial slur at him. In this replay of Frantz Fanon's disembodying experience of Blackness, Bernard thinks to himself that it is bad enough that adults treat him thusly, but such unchecked racist behavior from a child is difficult to take.[18] Yet this is just the start of his problems. In the busy streets, he is the target of fearful and suspicious looks from locals, and he must falsely claim to be Muslim for a taxi driver to give him a ride. At work, when a large piece of marble severely injures his leg, his boss is more concerned about the well-being of the material than Bernard and warns him to heal quickly or lose his job. After being treated for his injuries, and now with a crutch, Bernard is easily stopped by a cop, who frisks him, pockets all of his savings, and knocks him out. When Bernard comes to, he is on a bus with other migrants, whom the Moroccan police strand between Algeria and Morocco. Another migrant explains that while there are several routes back, given Bernard's injury, his best option is to head for Oujda, where a group of Nigerians can house him and provide false documents. The migrant adds that if Bernard has no money, other arrangements are possible. At the supposed refuge, Bernard is denied entry until he confirms via telephone that his brother has wired money on his behalf. As he is led to an overcrowded bedroom, he passes by a room in which a woman's rape constitutes her ostensible arrangement. On the last page, when he finally makes it back to his own room in Rabat, he finds a letter from Gislaine, who went in search of him. That their paths did not cross likely means that she has met her own string of detrimental events and is potentially lost to him. The final panel is a frontal close-up of Bernard covering his eyes as he weeps. Unlike Tintin, Bernard, who can only ever travel in circles at the margins, is no adventurer. Furthermore, ruination accumulates with each cycle; Bernard has returned to where he started, but now is physically injured, penniless, and alone.

In *Alpha: Abidjan–Gare du Nord*—by far the longest of all the *bandes dessinées* analyzed here—Bessora and Barroux also exploit discrepancies between different genres of travel and travelers to combat stereotypes about migrants and expose the necropolitics at the heart of borderization. The primary focus is on the eponymous protagonist, who calls himself an adventurer in an attempt to remain positive as he tries to join his wife and son (Patience and Badian), who already left for Paris but from whom he has had no word. Along the way, Alpha becomes close with three others—Antoine, Abebi, and Augustin—whose importance is indicated by their names starting with the letter *A* and who facilitate exploration of how migration impacts

---

18. See Fanon, *Black Skin*, chapter 5, "The Lived Experience of the Black Man."

individuals differently. Antoine serves as Alpha's foil, while Abebi and Augustin supplant Alpha's actual wife and son. Through this central quartet and everyone they encounter including migrants living in camps, migrants-turned-traffickers, borderization agents, benevolent individuals, and tourists, Bessora and Barroux foreground differing forms of ruination, which fall into three interrelated categories: being ruined physically, morally, and psychologically. As I argue elsewhere, the substantial length of this *bande dessinée* derives from the authors' goal of conveying how migrants' experiences of detention zones warps their sense of time, place, and self.[19] Instead of repetition and variation or frequent flashbacks, readers spend a long time with Alpha in a linear fashion, which allows them access to his experiences as if in real time. Readers follow his progression, or rather degradation, with particular attention to his changing psychological state as he struggles to go on while bearing witness and sometimes contributing to others' ruination.

Alpha stands as a culmination and expansion of the previous *bandes dessinées* about migration in that it presents many of the same hallmarks while going further in its depiction of the interconnectedness of imperial debris and borderization. Bessora's captivating first-person monologue laced with oral storytelling conventions, which caption Barroux's hand-drawn panels as handwritten text, make identification with Alpha easy. The vast majority of the pages are comprised of two horizontal panels featuring Barroux's grayscale watercolors with selective pops of color and rare instances of photo collage. This layout and absence of word balloons generates a contemplative mood as Alpha strives to remain optimistic despite being racked both with anxiety about the potential loss of his wife and son and with guilt about what he must do to try to reach them. Bessora's blend of frank observations, innuendo, questions, pep talks, and white lies produce a complex psychological portrait of Alpha, who facilitates an intimate experience of filtering systems, detention zones, and their rippling effects. As with Gawa and Yao, his attempt at traveling legally to France is denied, and Bessora's narration captures his frustration in the face of consulate employees' linguistic gymnastics and bureaucratic machinations that traffic in the intolerable fiction of French universalism's colorblindness. Similarly, Alpha must deal with traffickers and find ways to secure transport along each leg of his journey, but his interactions and decisions paint a vastly more complex picture than previous *bandes dessinées*, in which migrants are exclusively cast as victims of human and more-than-human borderization agents and opportunists. From Alpha's point of view, everyone has their own problems, some more

---

19. Bumatay, "Picturing."

dire than others. Before leaving and during his trek toward Gao, he closely notes individuals' methods for coping while living at the margins and for extracting what they can from migrants for their own survival, important lessons he later uses to shape his own decisions. For instance, while he is quick to judge scammers in Gao upon his arrival, after eight months of trying to cobble together enough money through manual labor to cross into southern Algeria, Alpha comes to the conclusion that trafficking is the only viable option. This moral gray zone weighs on him as he points out that his exploitative rates are lower than other scammers and that, unlike them, he is reliable. Relatedly, Alpha's reflections on Augustin and Abebi, the surrogates for his son and wife, are riddled with guilt for lying to Augustin and effectively becoming his trafficker and with anxiety for Abebi's quickly deteriorating state.[20] He describes her sex work in a matter-of-fact way that nevertheless belies his concern for her. While he is glad that her means of getting by is much more lucrative than his, he has no illusions of the physical and psychological toll it exacts from her. Moreover, he is devastated by her compounded ruination. Not only does she lose faith when Algerian border guards who deny her passage are her most frequent customers, but she contracts AIDS and, in spite of trying to have another abortion, gives birth to a stillborn girl, after which she never regains consciousness and dies. Their twinned plight prompts Alpha to think about his mother, and the unstated subtext points to his reflection on the fate of all women and children he has encountered. Indeed, this *bande dessinée* goes furthest in theorizing "what it might mean to live through, with, and as bricoleurs around" imperial debris (Stoler 22). Alpha's recognition of others' humanity is a powerful strategy for highlighting both necropolitics' dehumanizing effects and people's agency in spite of them.

Like Bessora's narration, Barroux's artwork employs several of the same stylistic features of previous *bandes dessinées* but innovates on them in ways that push our comprehension of necropolitics' spectrality. In her attentive analysis of *Alpha*, Agnès Schaffauser argues that it "draws attention to the gravity of the migrant subjects' loss of personhood," which is most evident in the ruination of Abebi and Alpha, for whom Barroux supplies the most portraits (102). At first glance, Barroux's style appears simplistic, but his meticulous attention to framing, shading, and watercolors' properties masterfully captures characters' complex moods and their varying spectrality.

---

20. Barroux's frontal portraits of Alpha, with varying expressions from guarded to distraught, work with Bessora's text to generate critical gaps so that readers grasp that what he tells (about) himself is sometimes at odds with what he actually thinks and how he feels.

Schaffauser also argues that Barroux's visual treatment of Alpha works with his name to present him as a hero who stands in for any and all men, while his red shirt (akin to Gawa's yellow pullover), like that of the little girl in Steven Spielberg's *Schindler's List*, singles him out as a victim (107). Though Schaffauser highlights this potential intertextual reference, she falls short of exposing the intolerable fiction of racial hierarchies foundational to both fascism and colonialism (articulated by Aimé Césaire in his seminal 1950 *Discourse on Colonialism*), which are reactivated through borderization, thus creating this visual echo across time and space. Similarly, her reading of Barroux's choices provides keen insights about migrants while missing some of the authors' important critiques. For Schaffauser, Barroux's use of watercolors, a fluid element, is a metaphor for migrants "who must remain agile and fluid, in perpetual displacement" and whose "precarious uncertainty" is reflected in watercolors' "blurry sections and imprecise contours" (109). Additionally, she reads the "drops of water often found scattered on the illustrations" as a mechanism to "recall the tears shed by migrants" (111). This exclusive focus on migrants demonstrates the important symbolism of Barroux's choice, but it fails to account for the implications of this style when applied to other people. One of the most striking features of Barroux's style is his intricate play between shades of black and white. With the exceptions of a White tourist whose skin is noticeably bright pink (figure 3.7) and a beaten migrant who succumbs to his wounds and is painted with a red face emphasizing his physical degradation, Barroux portrays all people as having the same skin color (though differing physical features and clothing) and uses grays and blacks to connote varying emotional, physical, and psychological states. Barroux's choice has a twofold impact: first, it downplays racial difference, and second, all the characters in this necropolitical matrix are on a spectral continuum, not just migrants. This highlights Alpha's habituation to loss as the lens through which to view the world, but it also speaks of Césaire's boomerang effect, for it exposes the dehumanization—for Césaire, the "decivilization"—of borderization agents, "to whom the lucrative business of administering brutality can be subcontracted" (Mbembe, *Necropolitics* 98–99).[21] Just as Bessora's complex narration foregrounds the human dimension of migration, Barroux's repetitive yet varied use of frontal portraits implicates the reader in recognizing their humanity like Alpha does.

At the same time, specific moments in the text work to theorize how the intolerable fiction fueling necropolitics (anti-Black racism) cordons off who is recognized as human and who is not. This is most evident when

---

21. Césaire famously described this boomerang effect in *Discourse on Colonialism*.

Barroux includes collaged photographs of children. Schaffauser rightly reads this practice as linked to Augustin's fate and as a way to "reveal invisible children, or rather 'invisibilized children,' who, on the road, lose their innocence, frequently subjected to sexual exploitation, forced labor, or . . . to trafficking organized by unscrupulous smugglers" (113). Additionally, when we consider the placement of these photographs, particularly their striking juxtaposition with the watercolors and the tension they provoke through ironic gaps with Bessora's narration, a critique of universal humanism emerges. The most effective instance of this occurs across a two-page spread with two similar horizontal panels on the left and a rare splash page on the right (figures 3.6 and 3.7). Turning to these pages, the reader's eyes automatically go to the White tourist centered on the right-hand page, due to Barroux's use of bright pink for his skin and equally bright colors for his vacation souvenir T-shirt (figure 3.7). The saturated grayscale palette of the rest of these two pages, including the collaged photograph of a boy in the bottom left corner of the splash page, effectively blur the distinction between the landscape and all the people who are not the tourist. Their existence is visibly muted by the White tourist's presence. In fact, according to the logic of the diegesis (informed by necropolitics), his pink-marked whiteness trumps the photograph's indexicality. This is not to say that the authors suggest that he is more human than those around him; rather, the composition of this splash page and its caption about Western tourists' access to leisurely travel exposes universalism as a construct predicated on systemic racism. The harmful effects of this are explored on the left-hand page that readers must move backward to read (figure 3.6). Here, the two figures representing Patience and Badian in the top panel are barely recognizable as human and, in the bottom panel, dissolve indistinguishably into the landscape through Barroux's increased use of water. In the captions for these two panels, as usual, Alpha mobilizes his observations and rationality to quell the increasing sense of dread at what might have happened to his wife and son because no one has news of them. Ironically, in his explanation that it is normal for no one to remember Patience or Badian in Gao because the population and size of such places constantly change, he also highlights the ease of their erasure. In these phantom villages made to return to the dust without a trace—as reinforced visually by Barroux's bottom panel—people also disappear. Alpha concludes that these places only persist in the minds of those who lived in them. Thus, while the tourist's humanity might shine brightly on the right-hand page, for Alpha, other peoples' existence (Patience and Badian), even in their absence and in spite of the many forces enacting their erasure, are more real.

J'ESPÈRE QU'ILS SONT PASSÉS PAR LE MAROC. MAIS JE NE TROUVE PERSONNE À GAO QUI SE SOUVIENNE D'EUX. C'EST NORMAL: ICI, LA POPULATION CHANGE TOUT LE TEMPS, LES CAMPS SE MONTENT ET SE DÉMONTENT ET SE REMONTENT. CERTAINS FONT DES PETITES VILLES QUI DURENT UN PEU PLUS LONGTEMPS.

CES VILLES SONT FAITES POUR ÊTRE DÉSERTÉES ET RETOURNER À LA POUSSIÈRE, SANS LAISSER DE TRACES NI DE SOUVENIRS. VILLES FANTÔMES. SAUF DANS LA TÊTE DE CEUX QUI LES ONT HABITÉES.

FIGURE 3.6. Left-hand page depicting two figures' dissolving personhood. *Alpha: Abidjan–Gare du Nord*, Gallimard, 2014.

FIGURE 3.7. Right-hand page highlighting a White tourist. *Alpha: Abidjan–Gare du Nord*, Gallimard, 2014.

Because readers spend so much time with Alpha and his companions, the one-page text-only epilogue detailing Alpha's eventual deportation from France to Abidjan after learning that Patience and Badian never made it to Paris, is nothing but devastating. Like the vignettes from *Nouvelles d'Afrique*, this tragic end leaves little room for hope. The switch to an omniscient third-person narrator echoes the final all-black panel of "Le voyage de Bouna," while Alpha's degrading circular trajectory mirrors that of Bernard. All three, like Abebi's aborted and stillborn children, and other migrants are the wretched of the Earth, sea, and air; the allusion in *Alpha* to Fanon's pivotal 1961 anticolonial *The Wretched of the Earth* exposes how migrants' fates remain entangled with imperial formations and shaped by necropolitics.

Conclusion

All of the Black *bandes dessinées* about migration discussed above undoubtedly rely on reader identification with fictional characters to generate empathy for migrants in the twenty-first century, yet this is but one key component of what they do. As this chapter argues, prioritizing analyses of the humanizing efforts of these *bandes dessinées* can prevent us from recognizing artists' and authors' intricate critiques of borderization and their innovative multimodal approaches to investigating the physical, psychological, and moral ruination of imperial debris. By historicizing borderization, these *bandes dessinées* counteract the intolerable fiction of a so-called migrant crisis. Through repeated scenes of rejected visas and brutality at the hands of borderization's human and more-than-human agents, they condemn the spreading necropolitics of Fortress Europe. Even prior to leaving, the difference between life and death is blurred for migrants since many former colonies have become themselves detention zones because the European Union's multifaceted securitization and borderization mechanisms effectively criminalize leaving by refusing visas and forestalling access to processes for requesting asylum. Rendered illegal and clandestine through state and suprastate entities, migrants persist consequently in a state of exception, a dynamic condition that points to the continuation of colonial-era dehumanization processes. Through repeated scenes with borderization agents and traffickers, these *bandes dessinées* call attention to their blatant and therefore banal impunity with regards to the 1948 Universal Declaration of Human Rights, thereby unmasking the anti-Black racism that informs filtering systems and detention zones. When read chronologically, these *bandes dessinées* demonstrate the increased amplitude and scale of borderization. The correlating increased insistence on individuals, their spectrality, and their demise in the *bandes dessinées* (and the increase in volume of such *bandes dessinées*) suggests a growing awareness of intolerable fictions about migration. However, though the response of empathy in the face of such fictions is a first step, the hope is to reframe our understanding in order to make change possible.

CHAPTER 4

Black *Bandes Dessinées* and Decolonial Ecocriticism

On August 19, 2006, during the First Ivorian Civil War (see chapter 2), the Panamanian-registered cargo ship *Probo Koala* docked in the port of Abidjan. In the next twenty-four hours, its crew unloaded over five hundred cubic meters of toxic waste produced on board from treating coker naphtha with caustic soda, a crude refining process banned by many countries. This toxic waste was then dispersed throughout the city by a local company created just months earlier. Within weeks, tens of thousands of people were treated for exposure to chemical waste, and the dumping eventually led to more than a dozen deaths. Though many steps and intermediaries contributed to the generation and dumping of toxic waste, ultimate responsibility lies with the multinational trading company Trafigura, for whom, in this case, profit superseded the well-being of those in the Global South. Trafigura's disregard for the inhabitants of Abidjan is but one egregious example of the Global North's continuing exploitation of the Global South. In Paris a century earlier, Pablo Picasso, having discovered cultural objects imported from the French colonies including Fang masks and sculptures, began work on *Les Demoiselles d'Avignon*, which he would unveil the following year in 1907. Many art historians identify this large-scale oil painting—featuring five women of different ages, each posed differently and each with a face resembling a mask from different world cultures—as a crucial turning point in the development of Western art, the beginning of what would become Cubism.

Though separated by time and space, these two events are closely related. The toxic dumping in the Ivory Coast, for those paying attention to climate justice, exemplified the Global North's ongoing violence toward the continent of Africa and its peoples: activists and scholars have articulated twenty-first-century extraction and dumping as twinned exploitations carried over from European colonialism.[1] However, while climate justice activists are perhaps less likely to observe the connection with European high art, Felwine Sarr and Bénédicte Savoy, authors of the 2018 *Report on the Restitution of African Cultural Heritage: Toward a New Relational Ethics*, which was commissioned by French President Emmanuel Macron, posit Europe's pillaging of cultural objects from its colonies (especially in the late nineteenth century and into the twentieth century) as an integral mechanism of colonial violence and a crime against humanity.[2] Moreover, the evacuation of meaning from these objects through abstraction, enacted by European artists such as Picasso, can also be read as a form of "dumping" of toxic ideology predicated on racial superiority. Cameroonian artist Japhet Miagotar brings these two events into contact in his 2012 album, *Cargaison mortelle à Abidjan* (Deadly cargo in Abidjan), thus anticipating the Sarr-Savoy Report's findings. Adapting three-dimensional Fang art into a two-dimensional form—a foundational process for Picasso's move toward Cubism—he mobilizes an allegorical retelling of the 2006 international scandal to expose the necropolitical link between colonial extraction and the "slow violence" of neocolonial dumping.[3]

With a particular focus on Miagotar, this chapter examines artists' use of *bandes dessinées* since the 1980s as a means of decolonial ecology. It focuses primarily on Miagotar's strategies for exposing and challenging the sustained legacy of Western ideology that repeatedly (and purposefully) casts Africa as a blank canvas conveniently situated for European needs. Since the beginning of the seventeenth century, Europeans have crafted and mobilized the notion of a blank Africa devoid of culture, civilization, and history to justify their unfettered extraction of resources, goods, labor, and people from

---

1. For more on the transcolonial links between modernity's extractive processes and environmental degradation, see Bauman, *Wasted Lives*; Nixon, *Slow Violence*; and Ferdinand, *Decolonial Ecology*.

2. The original title is *Rapport sur la restitution du patrimoine cultural africain—Vers une nouvelle éthique relationnelle*. It is colloquially referred to as the Sarr-Savoy Report.

3. See Nixon, *Slow Violence*.

the continent.[4] More recently, this notion has been reformulated to project an image of the continent as ostensibly "under-polluted," which has fueled the Global North logic that Africa deserves the "slow violence" of being a dumping ground for modernity's waste.[5] At first glance, it is evident that Miagotar activates visual citations of Hergé's 1958 album *Coke en stock* to attract mainstream readers to thus inform them about the 2006 scandal. Yet Miagotar's deliberate allusion goes well beyond a simple bait-and-switch tactic to raise awareness of the toxic dumping. It signals continuity in practices of exploitation more than just aesthetic continuity. In Hergé's album, the "coke in stock" refers to African Muslims who have been captured during their pilgrimage to Mecca by Arab slave traders and euphemistically refers to a source of energy. A half-century after *Coke en stock*'s publication, the *Probo Koala* treated another energy source—coker naphtha—on board and dumped the toxic waste of this process in Abidjan. Miagotar's allusion to Hergé reminds readers that both albums' Panamanian-registered cargo ships are ships laden with cheap fuel that spell demise for African people. He thus draws attention to the ship's hold, the site Malcom Ferdinand identifies with "hold politics": in this ongoing politics of exploitation, Black colonial enslavement and environmental changes are inseparably linked, and past violence toward other humans comes from the same place as present destruction of the earth and its beings (50). With *Cargaison mortelle à Abidjan*, Miagotar simultaneously illustrates the transcolonial dimension of hold politics and enacts multiple forms of symbolic justice. Just as Daniel Severin Ngassu and Barroux deliberately used watercolors to denote the instability and change inherent to migrants' experiences, as explored in the previous chapter, Miagotar develops a countervisuality derived from Fang art to combat the ongoing forms of dehumanization and Black death resulting from hold politics.

Black *Bandes Dessinées* and Environmentalism

Miagotar's *Cargaison mortelle à Abidjan* emerges from a long tradition of environmentalist Black *bandes dessinées*. Like migration, the environment has long been a key topic linked with postcolonialism. Since the early 1980s, free

---

4. For more on the role of discourse in this endeavor, see C. Miller, *Blank Darkness*.

5. As an epigraph to his seminal *Slow Violence and the Environmentalism of the Poor*, Rob Nixon quotes a confidential 1991 World Bank memo in which Lawrence Summers cites the underpolluted state of countries in Africa as justification for outsourcing "the dirty industries to the Least Developed Countries" (qtd. in Nixon, 18).

pamphlets, NGO-driven projects, collaborative anthologies, and one-shot albums have tackled problems stemming from urbanization and modernization, developing themes of transportation, pollution, deforestation and desertification, and conservationism, sometimes alongside issues of personal and community health in francophone regions of Africa. Key 1980s examples focusing on environmental threats and protection include albums by Congolese artists Mongo Sisé (his Tintin-esque *Bingo* series from 1982–84, especially volume 4, *Bingo au Pays Mandio, ou La Lutte contre la desertification* (Bingo in the Land of the Mandio, or The fight against desertification) and Barly Baruti (*Temps d'agir!* [Time to act!], 1982). Key 1990s examples include *Sokrou, ou Les Méfaits des sacs plastiques* (Sokrou, or The dangers of plastic bags; 1998) by Beninois artist Joseph Akligo and several didactic albums by Gabonese artist Ly-Bek (*La merveilleuse aventure de João* [João's marvelous adventure], 1998; *L'empreinte de la tortue* [The turtle's footprint], 1999; and *Défense d'ivoire* [Ivory tusk], 2000).[6] Since most of these edutainment texts are aimed at children and young people, they tend to be overtly didactic. Yet in presenting parts of Africa as they are alongside how they could be—for better or for worse, and in some cases both—some veer toward postcolonial critique. They point to links between local corruption, the hardships of everyday life, and extractive and exploitative practices that have continued since the days of European colonialism. Some go further and propose a form of environmentalism predicated on struggle that "[challenges] the colonial ways of inhabiting the Earth and living together," what Ferdinand calls "decolonial ecology" (175). Those who advocate for decolonial ecology in their Black *bandes dessinées* reject forms of development exported by the Global North that prioritize profit over the well-being of people and also the well-being of the environment. Through their work, such artists insist that challenging neocolonial and neoliberal forms of development necessarily involves challenging the ways we represent and see the Earth.

Barly Baruti's 1994 album *Objectif terre! Les Aventures de Sako et Yannick*, for example, directly challenges colonial ways of inhabiting the Earth and also colonial ways of representing it. Though the album is geared toward school-age readers (it was even distributed to instructors in Belgium by the Belgium-based Administration Générale de la Coopération au Développement [AGCD]), it also serves as a manifesto, demanding a shift in local and global human activity that prioritizes maintaining a balance with the environment instead of exploiting it. Over a decade earlier, in 1982 (also with the assistance of AGCD), Baruti had published *Temps d'agir!* The front

---

6. For more, see Langevin and Tramson, "Cinquante titres."

cover of that earlier work features a realistic drawing of a rhinoceros and the tagline "For the protection and improvement of the natural environment in the third world."[7] Baruti's use of exclamatory directives for both titles—*Temps d'agir!* and *Objectif terre!*—points to the ongoing and arguably increasing urgency of environmental awareness. When considered together, these two environmental Black *bandes dessinées* suggest a move from a postcolonial Cold War paradigm, which emphasized protecting the natural environment in the so-called Third World (embodied in the cover's rhinoceros, a species visually associated with formerly colonized regions), to a global one, in which a global action plan would benefit not only the inhabitants of formerly colonized regions but the entire world (emphasized by the word "terre" in the title and an image of the Earth on the back cover). We might even treat this shift in Baruti's work, from the regional to the global, as participating in Bonnie Roos and Alex Hunt's assertion that "any postcolonial critique must be thoroughly ecocritical at the same time" (3) and also as anticipating the expansion from what Cajetan Iheka describes as first-wave ecocriticism, which "was complicit in colonial violence," to a form of decolonial environmentalism (2)—that is, a form of environmentalism that not only questions Western notions of progress and development but also challenges the Enlightenment bifurcation of humans and nature by repositioning humans within and as part of the environment.

Objectif terre! Les Aventures de Sako et Yannick, meant as a pedagogical tool, is set in Kinshasa and presents an (aspirationally) inclusive present that is equally informed by scientific and Indigenous forms of knowledge. Best friends Sako, a Black girl, and Yannick, a White boy, who share a love of nature, serve as proxies for the reader as they follow a teacher's suggestion to learn more about how integral the well-being of the natural world is to the well-being of humans. Through the characters' active and diverse learning experiences, Baruti transmits key information about the important balance maintained by natural environments and simultaneously critiques transcolonial ways of understanding and inhabiting the world. Just before the midpoint, he includes a page with three horizontal panels depicting waterfowl peacefully at rest, then taking to flight, and the reason for their fleeing: a man equipped for hunting and his dog. While the first two panels are wordless, Baruti adds voice-over from Sako's father that ironically contrasts with the image of the hunter: "There isn't man on one side and nature on the other; in exploiting his environment, man loses what he has that is most precious" (13).[8] At a later point, Sako and Yannick come across

---

7. "Pour la protection et l'amélioration du milieu naturel dans le tiers monde."

8. "Il n'y a pas d'un côté l'homme, de l'autre la nature; en abusant de son environnement, l'homme perd ce qu'il a de plus cher."

a parking lot full of run-down busses where the attendant energetically tells them not to forget that the North pollutes by its wealth and the South by its poverty. With these statements, Baruti acknowledges that blame for environmental harm is not restricted by geography, but he makes sure to underline how ongoing inequity between the Global North and the Global South and an artificial binary between humans and the environment influence individuals' actions. Most significantly, at the end of the two-page epilogue, Baruti delivers the most direct message of this manifesto, which he pairs with a small panel showing a close-up of Sako's eyes: "Development as we know it today is certainly not possible for the whole planet. This will most likely entail destructive revisions of the idea of Progress we make for ourselves. Ecology can be—must be—the motor for another development" (32).[9] His use of the plural "nous" (we) is unquestionably global. Like his presentation of blame, his presentation of responsibility is not restricted by geography. All are invited to actualize change. The corrective in the very last sentence, from "peut" (can) to "doit" (must), which suggests a hesitation or timidity, softens the outright challenge of Western notions of Progress central to change.

Equally central, for Baruti, is an environmentally driven artistic practice that challenges conventions from earlier mainstream *bandes dessinées*. In direct opposition to the *ligne claire* aesthetic, especially that of Hergé's *Tintin au Congo*, Baruti employs a rich verisimilitude much closer to painting. Whereas Hergé prioritized simplification to maximize legibility and, especially in the earlier albums, presented generalized settings as little more than backdrops for Tintin's adventures, Baruti refuses to treat setting as secondary to human protagonists. Rather, all environments, natural as well as urban, are foundational to his storytelling. However, the only splash page in *Objectif terre!*, what Silke Horstkotte would call a "memorable panel," is particularly central for Baruti's effort to reconfigure development as stemming from ecology (41). To accompany the teacher's explanation of how forests and national parks provide for and protect humans, Baruti presents a dense tropical scene with the sun's rays beaming through from on high (figure 4.1) (7). This moment of pause casts the forest as a spiritual place made up of multiple visible and possibly invisible layers all working together. Baruti recycles this "memorable panel" in the epilogue and also on the front cover. In the epilogue, the smaller reproduction reminds readers that we must live in harmony with nature. On the cover, Baruti presents the

---

9. "Le développement tel que nous le connaissons aujourd'hui, n'est certainement pas possible pour l'ensemble de la planète. Cela entrainera probablement des révisions déchirantes de l'idée que nous nous faisons du Progrès. L'écologie peut être—doit être—le moteur d'un autre développement."

FIGURE 4.1. A singular splash page exalting nature. *Objectif terre! Les aventures de Sako et Yannick*, AGCD, 1994.

forest image as an actual painting with a gilded frame hung in a museum behind a red rope. With this literal and figural reframing, Baruti presents his own work as high art and the natural environment as worthy of great esteem. When we recognize Baruti's *Objectif terre!* as a kind of decolonial ecological manifesto, we can consequently backdate his commitment to restorative memory work by nearly twenty years. Instead of seeing the 2014 album *Madame Livingstone: Congo, la Grande Guerre*, written by Christophe

Cassiau-Haurie and illustrated by Baruti, as the turning point in Baruti's "development of [a] new esthetics and oppositional perspective"—as Véronique Bragard argues—we can trace that turn to the much earlier environmental work (335).[10]

In many ways, Miagotar's *Cargaison mortelle à Abidjan* parallels Baruti's *Objectif terre!*, as it, too, critiques transcolonial inequity and advocates for a decolonial ecology, which necessarily involves the development of a countervisuality central to the text's restorative work. But Miagotar's narrative and artistic decisions emerge, most immediately, from the circumstances surrounding the 2006 Trafigura dumping rather than from a broad reflection on environmentalism.

Trafigura's Toxicity

On the night of August 19, 2006, when the *Probo Koala*'s crew unloaded its cargo of hazardous caustic washing by-product into the Ivorian port city, the event was just one episode in a pattern of toxic dumping orchestrated by the commodity trading company Trafigura.[11] When we trace the trajectory of the hazardous waste back to its origin as coker naphtha in Mexico, we see at every stage the profit-driven decisions of this multibillion-dollar multinational company, decisions that skirt—or in some cases violate outright—national and international laws and regulations meant to protect the environment, people, and also "countries with weak regulatory regimes" (MacManus 8). Because pipelines in the United States and Mexico only permit refined oil to be transmitted, the coker naptha that had accumulated throughout Mexico had to be trucked to the Port of Brownsville in Texas at the Mexico-US border (MacManus 15). There, from April to June, it was loaded onto three ships, one of them the *Probo Koala*. On board the cargo ship, flying under Panama's "flag of convenience" (convenient in delivering freedom from many regulations), the crew conducted the caustic washing on its way to Amsterdam (MacManus 15). At the start of July, once in port in Amsterdam, they unloaded the waste, which they claimed was common ship slop, a direct violation of European Union regulations; when the actual nature of the waste was identified, they were forced to reload it (MacManus 20). After traveling to Estonia the following week to sell the refined gasoline,

---

10. For more on how Baruti exposes and challenges the colonial gaze, see also Bumatay, "*Notre histoire.*"

11. For a detailed account, see MacManus, *State-Corporate Crime*.

the ship traveled to Lagos, Nigeria, where, at the start of August, the crew were unsuccessful in off-loading the waste. Directly following this failed attempt, Trafigura engaged Compagnie Tommy SARL, an ostensibly Ivorian waste management company whose licensing, initiated in late May, had been processed with unusual speed by the Ivorian government (MacManus 37). In August this new company, cooperating with the Abidjan port authority, dispersed the toxic waste throughout Abidjan. In a careful investigation of the wide-ranging corruption surrounding the initial dumping event and subsequent attempts to render justice, Thomas MacManus leaves no doubt that the operation and its subsequent cover-ups constitute a series of state-corporate crimes:

> deviant acts (or omissions) that cause human rights violations as a result of a mutually reinforcing interaction between (1) policies and/or practices in pursuit of the goals of one or more institutions of political governance and (2) policies and/or practices in pursuit of the goals of one or more institutions of economic production and distribution. (MacManus 4–5)

Dutch and Ivorian courts unsuccessfully brought criminal charges against Trafigura executives for illegally dumping toxic waste and then trying to cover it up—charges, that, ironically, Trafigura met by bringing a libel case against the BBC (British Broadcasting Corporation). The BBC settled out of court by withdrawing the statement that Trafigura was responsible for any deaths, but defiantly reported on Trafigura's £30 million payout to victims at the same time (Leigh). This payout was Trafigura's way of sidestepping justice: in 2009, around 30,000 victims sued Trafigura, the civil case "the largest personal injury claim ever filed with England and Wales Courts," but Trafigura chose to settle out of court for an estimated $1,000 per victim (MacManus 2). It was not until 2010, four years after the initial incident, that a Dutch court found Trafigura guilty for its environmental crime in Amsterdam (concealing the toxic nature of the ship's waste in an effort to off-load it, and therefore having to reload it) and forced the company to pay a fine of €1 million. In the interim, although Trafigura denied all liability, the company settled out of court with the Ivorian government for a sum of $198 million, supposedly earmarked for cleaning up the toxic waste (this has not happened). While Trafigura's employees were never convicted, the Ivorian subcontractors who dispersed the waste were tried in Abidjan and received sentences of up to twenty years in prison. The long legal battles around this incident, and evidence of the impunity with which Trafigura conducts business, have made the *Probo Koala* case a textbook example illustrating that existing governmental and regulatory bodies have little capacity to enforce international, and especially environmental, laws.[12]

Japhet Miagotar: Drafting a Manifesto

Even before the legal battles following the dumping came to their disappointing conclusions, though not directly affected, Cameroonian artist Japhet Miagotar decided to tell the story of the *Probo Koala* as a gross miscarriage of justice, considering the impunity enjoyed by those who benefited from the dumping to be just as toxic as the ship's waste. Choosing the popular medium of *bandes dessinées*, he hoped to bring this story to a broad readership, first in Africa and then worldwide. The creative challenge, then, as posed by Rob Nixon in *Slow Violence*, was "how to devise arresting stories, images, and symbols adequate to the pervasive but elusive violence of delayed effects" (3). Miagotar's successive iterations to respond to this challenge culminated in the album *Cargaison mortelle à Abidjan*, published by L'Harmattan BD in 2012. Previously, in 2009, Miagotar submitted *Trafigoura I*, material that would eventually become the first part of the album, to the Italian-based Africa e Mediterraneo's annual Africa Comics competition (see chapter 3). In 2010, he submitted *Trafigoura II* to the Algiers International Comics Festival and won the prize for best graphic style. While page layout and overall style remained the same between these early versions and the 2012 album, Miagotar's use of colors changed dramatically as he redeveloped the material for wide publication with L'Harmattan BD. While the initial versions feature a vibrant range of saturated digital colors, the album demonstrates more restraint; the range of colors is smaller, and the colors themselves are more muted. This change, as we will see, allows for important thematization. In addition, Miagotar originally planned to publish the album under the title *Peur sur Abidjan* (Fear in Abidjan), a choice that—in stark contrast to *Trafigoura* (a purposeful misspelling of the trading company, which remains in the album)—foregrounds the experiences of the Ivorians living in the port city (Cassiau-Haurie, "Je préfère"). Yet the Ivorians' fear in the face of the toxic waste is not what Miagotar's story is about. Rather, as signaled by the album's final title, *Cargaison mortelle à Abidjan*, Miagotar's allegorized story is about the multiple ways in which hold politics result in Black death and, at the same time, the possibilities for

---

12. For more on the legal context, see Archer, "*Trafigura* Actions"; Dezalay, "Building."

combating the anti-Black racism foundational to hold politics. Through the multipronged forms of symbolic justice at work in the album that punish those in the Global North responsible for the dumping and also restore Fang art to Africans, Miagotar, like Baruti, generates a manifesto that advocates for decolonial ways of seeing, representing, and being in the world.

Allegory, Renaming, and Figurative Shapes for Formless Threats

Among the increasing number of cultural productions seeking to make urgent the extended violence of environmental disaster, allegory has been an effective tool. Elizabeth DeLoughrey, in *Allegories of the Anthropocene* (2019), argues that allegory has become a key genre for postcolonial ecocriticism, in particular "due to its ability to represent both historical and scalar relations" (4–5). For DeLoughrey, allegory's usefulness derives from "its embeddedness in history (time), its construction of a world system (space), and its signification practices in which the particular figures for the general and the local for the global" (5). Furthermore, allegory is able to signal "an era of calamity and a way of responding, inadequately but necessarily, to crisis" (10). Miagotar zeroes in on the individuals responsible for planning and executing the dumping in his allegorical retelling of the 2006 scandal as a way of more broadly critiquing neocolonial and neoliberal power imbalances between those driven by profit and their victims. He not only organizes the plot around them, he also targets them linguistically and through page layout. As a response to the calamity of Trafigura's flagrant disregard for laws and life, Miagotar employs magical realism, which Ben Holgate cites as an effective tool for environmental discourse because of its ability to "disrupt perceived ideas about time and space," through the addition of an African woman character who is more than she seems and who carries a baby on her back (7). This new character, who appears to be in multiple places at once and visibly cares for Africans by physically carrying the next generation, metes out vengeance by methodically assassinating those responsible for the dumping and delivers a warning to anyone who would dare imitate Trafigura.

Associated with allegory in the project of redressing the postcolonial dimension of environmental disaster is a specific linguistic strategy: renaming. Observing common trends among postcolonial authors, DeLoughrey and coeditor George B. Handley explain that postcolonial authors' process of responding to the legacy of colonial taxonomy results in rendering "language more ironic, self-reflexive, and unstable" and leads to a "self-conscious process of renaming and revisioning" (11). Though the renaming in *Cargaison mortelle à Abidjan* does not extend to the vocabulary that describes nature or the environment, Miagotar's ironic strategy nevertheless critiques those in power. He targets his most prominent example right on the front cover. The album's all-black cover alludes to that of Hergé's *Coke en stock*, where the layout mimics a periscope's point of view, suggesting a targeted enemy (a crucial choice to which I return below). Miagotar centers his own periscopic view on the ship carrying the deadly cargo, and he sets his sights squarely on the multinational trading company by rebaptizing the *Probo Koala* the *Trafigoura*. The shift in focus, a minor respelling achieved by adding the letter *o* to the company's name, leaves no doubt as to who bears the most responsibility. It also skirts being targeted for libel by Trafigura. Miagotar carries this cheeky renaming tactic throughout the text, both to underscore the range of international actors involved and to provide satiric commentary. Captain Igor and first mate Aboussayev allude to the *Probo Koala*'s Ukrainian crew, while a later captain, Papadopoulos, refers to the Greek shipping company Prime Marine Management Inc., chartered by Trafigura. Moreover, in a two-page montage of international media coverage of the health crisis resulting from the dumping, Miagotar humorously renames world leaders from the time: "Kofi Nana," "Laurent Gbogba," "Niculae Sarkowsky," "Tony Black," and "Georgius Busher." In poking fun at these leaders, some of whose altered names evoke comedic characters such as Astérix and Obélix, Miagotar seems to suggest that no reader should take these figures or their empty promises seriously.

Miagotar's most evident narrative tactic is the introduction of the African woman character who transforms into a vengeful spirit. Representing her as an omnipresent entity capable of changing shape at will, he adds the urgency that Nixon seeks. In the revised color scheme of the album version, most colors throughout (apart from black and white) are cool and muted (grays, browns, blues); these color choices emphasize the industrial setting of the cargo ship and the masculine world of the nefarious plotting. Against these, Miagotar adopts a strongly thematized use of pinks and magenta. Though present from the second page as the outfit of the strange new African secretary of the Dutch CEO of Trafigoura, these colors emerge more prominently as the backdrop of panels depicting the victims and the discovery of the toxic waste as the source of the health crisis. These more feminine colors are thus thematically anchored in relation to the victims. The African secretary, adorned in the same colors, is thus visually linked with the victims through "braiding," as Thierry Groensteen calls it. When she reappears, just after the halfway point in the story, one of her hands, which she uses to assassinate the boat captain and the Dutch CEO, has

FIGURE 4.2. The African spirit's amorphous approach. *Cargaison mortelle à Abidjan*, L'Harmattan BD, 2012.

become a black and magenta symbol. In the last third of the story, Miagotar introduces an entirely new character—the professor. Announced by tans, oranges, and a chalkboard with detailed calculations, he arrives to help plan the next dumping scheme and moves the narrative forward by recognizing the woman's symbol. He explains to the new Greek captain and the intermediary who has been assisting the Dutch CEO that this powerful symbol is used in many regions of Africa, with its meaning depending in part on its orientation: vertically ascending, the symbol implores the heavens after a catastrophe; horizontal, it seals a reconciliation pact after war and is used in purification rituals; and vertically descending, the symbol declares war and distinguishes enemies as murderers (45). He tells his fellow schemers that they should not expect reason to help them understand the woman or the symbol. Instead, he explains, "It's a matter of an unpredictable and changing force, capable of taking whatever form" (46).[13] The professor's characterization of the spirit's formlessness seems like a mirror image of Nixon's explanation that confronting "slow violence requires . . . that we plot and give figurative shape to formless threats whose fatal repercussions are dispersed across space and time" (Nixon, *Slow Violence*, 10). In the face of the shapeless urgent threat that emanated from the Trafigoura's hold, Miagotar creates an equally formless entity to threaten those who would mete out environmental harm and subsequent Black death.

Miagotar thus imbues the spirit with dramatic elasticity that dominates the last five pages. Up to this point, all the panels are rectilinear, primarily structured in a grid pattern, and all the characters and objects are represented by geometric shapes. In contrast, the culmination of the spirit's revenge drastically disrupts the contours of the diegesis. As a function of her actions, the spirit easily transforms from an intimidating amorphous specter to her human form and back again. She seeps in as a haunting vapor, her irregularly curved contours visibly swarming around the more geometric characters who are in the midst of planning the next scheme (figure 4.2). Her vengeful anger shapes the world around her as the frames expand and contract as a function of her presence. On the penultimate double-page spread, Miagotar even locates the avenging spirit outside the frame: her figure dominates more than half of the right-hand page, which attests to her supernatural powers that supersede the diegesis. The unique layouts of the album's last pages, and the spirit's overbearing and malleable form, emphasize the dramatic urgency of preventing further dumping. In the final

---

13. "Il s'agit d'une force imprévisible, changeante, capable de prendre n'importe quelle forme."

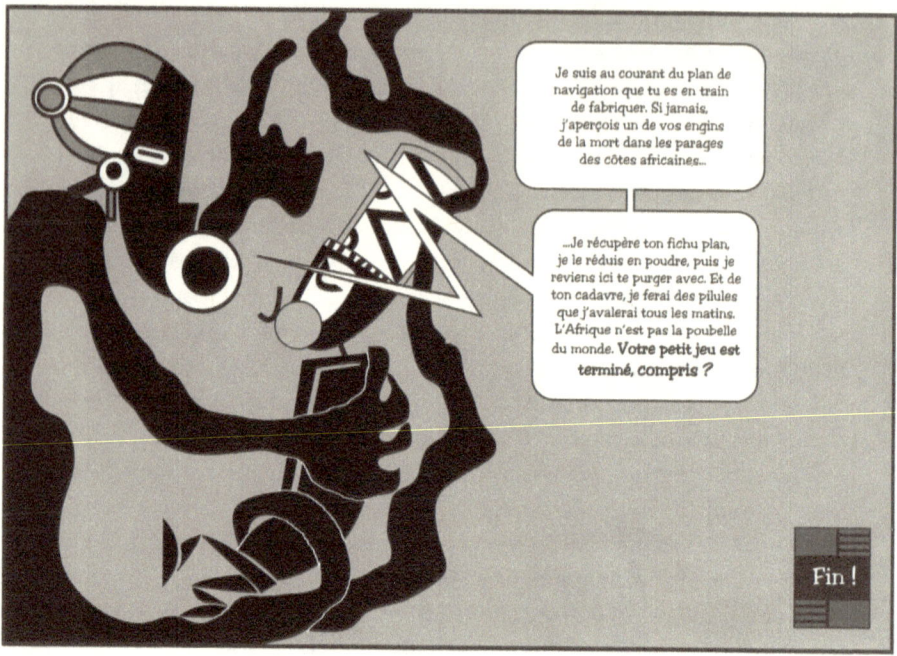

FIGURE 4.3. The African spirit's final warning. *Cargaison mortelle à Abidjan*, L'Harmattan BD, 2012.

panel, Miagotar draws her clutching the professor (a proxy for all would-be polluters) as she declares such flagrant machinations at an end: contrary to Larry Summer's memo, Africa is not "under-polluted," and it is not the world's trash can (figure 4.3). As a final note, Miagotar adds a small inlay in the bottom right-hand corner, an emphatic "Fin!" that punctuates both the album and the spirit's claim (52). Sandwiching it above and below this last word, Miagotar presents the spirit's symbol horizontally, the position that, according to the professor's earlier explanation, indicates purification and solidifies a reconciliation pact. Miagotar's pairing of the threatening more-than-human retribution in the form of the all-knowing spirit with this last symbolic gesture of reconciliation and purification suggests a powerful if speculative truce.

Through allegory and the introduction of the vengeful spirit, Miagotar simultaneously raises awareness about the 2006 dumping, generates symbolic justice on behalf of the victims, and, to prevent such crises in the future, renders urgent the need for responses to the slow violence of the scandal. Through an artistic practice that purposefully walks the line between familiar and uncanny, he also posits the dumping's violence and harm as the flip side of the Global North's broader legacy of extraction. Likewise, just as Miagotar's African spirit offers symbolic justice to Trafigura's real victims, his artistic practice based on Fang art both exposes the toxic waste of anti-Black racism and symbolically restores African cultural objects to African artists.

3D to 2D: Virtually Restoring Fang Art

Miagotar's specific choice of Fang masks and statues is not at all arbitrary. Many art historians cite the arrival in France of traditional artwork from L'Afrique française occidentale et équatoriale (French West and Equatorial Africa) at the end of the nineteenth century and the beginning of the twentieth century—what British anthropologist Dan Hicks calls "World War Zero"—as a critical turning point for avant-garde movements.[14] Highly esteemed Fang ancestral sculpture was shipped to Europe, often arriving in the same vessels that carried extracted raw materials.[15] Many cultural objects, after initially being wrenched from their cultural contexts, often underwent further violence. They might be physically mutilated (with statuary detached from other objects, as happened with Fang reliquary boxes) and symbolically stripped of their significance and artistry.[16] African art historian Simon Gikandi cites Picasso's process for works such as *Les Demoiselles d'Avignon* as emblematic of this symbolic stripping, noting that for Picasso, turning African art into high art entailed "a meticulous attempt to separate the African's art from his or her body, to abstract ... [and] evacuate" (456–57). This exploitative use of the so-called Primitive by practitioners of modernism such as Picasso, Gikandi argues, demonstrates European "modernism's relationship to its Other," which sought to contain the Other's culture while evacuating any trace of the Other from the process and the end result (457). The colonial ideology of European modernism thus denied the African artists their humanity through abstraction, and this continues to be the case. Fang artwork, intimately linked with European modernism—due in large part to significant museum exhibitions in the Global North highlighting this relationship, dating from 1939 to the present day—remains highly

---

14. See Hicks, *Brutish Museums*, chapter 5.
15. See Kaehr et al., "Masterwork"; Grunne, "Fang Statuary."
16. For a detailed account, see Martinez, "Ephemeral Fang Reliquaries."

sought after.[17] Pieces of Fang artwork have recently sold for huge sums: one mask sold for €5.9 million in 2006, and several since have fetched upward of €2 million.[18] Moreover, as a form of figurative toxic dumping, while the original African artists' names were stripped away almost immediately, the Global North provenance of Fang art—the fact that Picasso or Matisse or previous prominent collectors had possessed the object—supplants cultural meaning and material artistry with symbolic capital restricted to wealth's propagation.[19]

In choosing Fang art then, Miagotar targets a primary pillar of Western modernity to expose the toxicity and violence of colonialism's practices and to restore African art to Africans, if only virtually. Remarking on his practice in 2019, he explains that his characters "translate a reappropriation, an aesthetic claim on African art that had been dispossessed, confiscated, and stripped of contextualization" (Bulling and Miagotar). Initially, he began this practice in 2002 while at art school, and in 2013, following the publication of *Cargaison mortelle à Abidjan*, he authored an article that advocates for more artists drawing from African cultures. In "L'Anthropologie au cœur de la bande dessinée: Pertinence d'une bande dessinée africaine avec des personnages issus de la statuaire africaine" ("Anthropology at the heart of *bande dessinée*: The relevance of an African *bande dessinée* with characters derived from African statuary"), Miagotar describes his process for rendering three-dimensional Fang art into two-dimensional characters by asking:

> How do we transform atypical proportions, masses that are both elongated and stocky, volumes, in short, figural values into comics characters? How do we articulate rigid parts, torsos and legs of geometric shapes derived from cylinders and cones, arms and calves made of concentric cones? How do we integrate characters with faces that are concave, convex, overly con-

---

17. It is worth highlighting that the two main institutions for historically important exhibitions on Primitivism and Modernism—the Museum of Modern Art in New York City and the Musée du Quai Branly in Paris—are, according to Dan Hicks in *The Brutish Museums*, some of the only museums in the Global North who have not issued a statement about the colonial origins of their collections following the 2018 Sarr-Savoy Report. For more on the numerous exhibitions on Primitivism and Modernism, see Blier, *Picasso's Demoiselles*.

18. For more, see Monroe, *Metropolitan Fetish African Sculpture*; and Christie's Auction House website (www.christies.com).

19. For an uncritical appreciation of such Global North provenance, see Scheller, "Genesis."

cave and overly convex or rectangular yet oval heads with faces hedging on spherical into a real environment? (Miagotar, "L'Anthropologie")[20]

Immediately evident in this anaphora of questions is Miagotar's formal analysis of Fang sculpture in all its complexity. However, since the majority of the physical objects remain in the Global North, Miagotar relied heavily on art history and anthropological books written by Western researchers (qtd. in Cassiau-Haurie, "Je préfère"). In many ways, Miagotar's process echoes that of Picasso in spite of the fact that Picasso had physical access to Fang art. In her scrupulous remapping of *Les Démoiselles d'Avignon*, art historian Suzanne Preston Blier disrupts an older consensus and convincingly argues that Picasso's study of Fang art was heavily mediated through anthropological books rather than emerging from direct study of the physical objects themselves (118). Thus, while many calls for restitution of African cultural objects continue to go unanswered, Miagotar's practice, in light of Blier's work, demonstrates that there are productive alternatives to physical restoration.

To transform what he learned, Miagotar developed an intricate process, which he calls "SVA" (simplification, variation, animation). He begins by capturing the main shape of a three-dimensional object and simplifying it. The subsequent steps, variation and animation, Miagotar describes as the most crucial, for it is in these that the artist's innovation is realized. Reading through *Cargaison mortelle à Abidjan*, one recognizes the extraordinary expressiveness and dynamism of the characters. From the first page, Miagotar introduces readers to the visual logic through repetition and variation, as the same characters are presented straight on, in profile, and from behind (figure 4.4). He conveys characters' emotions through body language, facial expressions, framing, and transitions and extrapolates the SVA rendering process to nonhuman objects such as food, furniture, and phones. However, because this extrapolation relies on simplification, it also produces an eerie effect in which the specificity of Fang art risks being read as little more than a generalized Africanization of the *ligne claire* style.

---

20. "Comment transformer les proportions atypiques, les masses à la fois longiformes et trapues, les volumes, bref les valeurs plastiques des œuvres en personnages de bande dessinée? Comment faire marcher ces parties rigides, ces troncs et jambes traités en volumes géométriques simples dérivés du cylindre et du cône, ces bras et mollets constitués de volumes biconiques? Comment intégrer des personnages au visage concave, sur-concave, convexe, sous-convexe ou rectiligne à la tête ovoïde avec un front tendant vers la sphère dans un environnement réel?"

FIGURE 4.4. Stylized phone conversation. *Cargaison mortelle à Abidjan*, L'Harmattan BD, 2012.

Black Death in the Ship's Hold

Since Miagotar never mentions Fang art in the album, the lack of shading in conjunction with the somewhat static nature of the statue-inspired characters and the direct allusion to the cover of Hergé's *Coke en stock* might suggest little more than an exoticized imitation of Hergé's work. Indeed, many reviews of *Cargaison mortelle à Abidjan* point to the visual affinity with Hergé's *Coke en stock* but quickly dispel any suggestion that Miagotar's album mimics Hergé's, instead foregrounding Miagotar's innovative practice.[21]

---

21. See, for example, the entry on the website of Takamtiknou (Takamtiknou.bnf.fr)— an official branch of the French National Library dedicated to reviews of international books for children (Camara, "Review"). Reviewer Fatou Camara observes the cover's resemblance to Hergé's *Coke en stock* but argues that Miagotar's style has no relationship at all to Hergé's *ligne claire* aesthetic. Similarly, Alain Brezault acknowledges the cover's *clin d'œil* to *Coke en stock*, but his passing comment that the ship in Hergé's album also carries "a strange cargo" fails to clarify the important constant between the two: each ship carries Black death in its hold (Brezault).

However, the reviewers' anxiety around possible overlap with Hergé's album forecloses an examination of more significant similarities between the two, such as plot, page layout, and narrative tropes. Reading *Cargaison mortelle à Abidjan* as in dialogue with *Coke en stock* exposes how Miagotar draws attention to the ship's hold and therefore hold politics. By linking his album to Hergé's older album, Miagotar advocates for Ferdinand's proposed decolonial ecology by exposing and challenging colonial epistemologies. Miagotar not only encourages readers to compare toxic dumping with slavery but also invites them to interrogate the complex ways in which neoliberalism has changed international calls for justice, as in the case of Hergé's *Coke en stock*, into short-circuited calls for support, as in the case of *Cargaison mortelle à Abidjan*.

Hergé drew inspiration for his work from a magazine article about Arab smugglers enslaving African pilgrims on their hajj to Mecca in the 1950s. As Tintin explains toward the end of the story, the title for the action-packed *Coke en stock*—known in English as *The Red Sea Sharks* and originally published from 1956 to 1958—is a code the smugglers use to tell other ships their hold is full of human beings. The euphemism linguistically supplants coke—a dark-colored solid fuel derived from coal—for Black people held in captivity. And yet, since the paradigm of anti-Black racism foundational to slavery seeks to dehumanize Black people, the coded phrase functions more as a synonym than a euphemism. In both cases, the "stock" is a source of energy; as a synonym rather than a euphemism, however, the term evacuates the captive peoples' humanity. Ironically, though Hergé's visual depictions of the African Muslim captives in this album are more nuanced than the racist stereotypes of his 1931 album, *Tintin au Congo,* his use of so-called *petit-n***e* or *français tirailleur,* a pidgin form of French used by the French colonial armed forces in the early twentieth century and forever linked with racist stereotypes as a result of Banania's marketing, was condemned by Belgian journalist Gabrielle Rolin as racist in her 1962 *Jeune Afrique* article, which lambasted Hergé's self-declared turn away from such gross stereotypes (Delisle, *Tintin* 16). In response, Hergé changed the captives' speech to standard French but left Captain Haddock's use of *petit-n***e* when speaking with them for the 1967 edition of the album (Peeters 107). While Hergé biographer Benoît Peeters considers this alteration not only amusing but also evidence of Hergé's self-criticism, its textual effect, as well as Peeters's defense of Hergé, further promotes colonialism's paternalist ideology (107).[22] Indeed, in *Black Skin, White Masks* (1952), originally published in

---

22. Peeters characterizes Rolin's critique of *Coke en stock* as "extremely unfair" and altogether omits her name, citing only that the critique was published in *Jeune Afrique* (Peeters 107).

French four years before *Coke en stock* and over thirty years before Peeters's biography, Frantz Fanon explained that "to speak gobbledygook to a black man is insulting, for it means his is the gook. Yet, we'll be told, there is no intention to willfully give offense. OK, but it is precisely this absence of will—this offhand manner; this *casualness*; and the ease with which they classify him, imprison him at an uncivilized and primitive level—that is insulting" (15; emphasis added). Thus, though Hergé represents Tintin and Captain Haddock as White saviors who (easily) condemn Arabs' enslavement of Black Africans, by upholding what Philippe Delisle calls a "Belgian ideal of 'moral' imperialism," he maintains the dehumanization of the album's title (Delisle, "Le Reporter" 281).

Miagotar's deliberate allusion to Hergé's album—most explicitly obvious from, but not limited to, the two covers—exposes the specter of neocolonial anti-Black ideology at work in both cases and, more importantly, exposes its mutated contemporary form. The cover of *Coke en stock* features an all-black background and a large circular periscopic view of the protagonists in need of rescue. The point of view suggested is in fact that of the villain, Roberto Rastapopoulos, who, far from wanting to rescue them, is the one targeting them so that he may continue to profit from slavery. In accordance with the moral logic of Hergé's universe, this framing casts the protagonists as victims, thus displacing Europeans' colonizing role with White saviorism. Miagotar uses a similar composition, yet his framing centers and targets colonialism's legacy. The circular periscopic framing on the cover of *Cargaison mortelle à Abidjan* targets, as explained above, Trafig(o)ura. Through braiding, Miagotar suggests a link between Hergé's White saviors and the trading company. He thus highlights how Hergé's moral indignation in the face of modern-day slavery fails to extend to other related forms of Black death.

In both albums, we necessarily see the international community as the audience: the international perspective is implied in the always transnational reality of cargo ships and emerges more directly in the form of public scrutiny when the cargo of the offending ships is metaphorically unloaded into the light of day. In Hergé's story, Cold War alliances dominate the ethical impetus. While Tintin and a reluctant Captain Haddock are the obvious heroes and White saviors of the West African pilgrims, their international allies are also cast as morally good; collectively they stand in easy and direct opposition to the greedy and power-hungry villains (exemplified by Roberto Rastapopoulos and his seedy network), ready to exploit any and all at every moment. Hergé turns to his usual newspaper clippings at the end of *Coke en stock* to tie up narrative loose ends and mete out justice—all the while bolstering the importance of the media in reporting stories like these to influence public opinion, values, and emotions. Miagotar likewise includes collages of international media coverage of the 2006 scandal. But while the headlines at the end of *Coke en stock* generate a sense of community and shared values that coalesce into justice being served, Miagotar's images represent televised statements by mockingly renamed world leaders that ring hollow and ultimately prove ineffective. This seemingly innocuous difference demonstrates important shifts in mainstream media since Hergé's time. Whereas Hergé's panel implied a community of newspaper readers and Tintin followers, Miagotar's representation of the international media does not. His world leaders' condemnations of the dumping and pledges to act in support of the Ivorian people connote a world in which a small handful of powerful leaders pay lip service to victims and to justice, but those leaders are far removed from the general public. In Miagotar's world, there is neither a sense of community nor an adequate international framework for justice. In place of recognizable reporters uncovering nefarious plots, others, like *bande dessinée* artists, must take up the work of exposing state-corporate crimes in the hope that public opinion might engender change.

Conclusion

Though the *Probo Koala*'s brief docking in Abidjan is coterminous with the publication of the early volumes of Marguerite Abouet and Clément Oubrerie's hit series *Aya de Yopougon*, the tragic state-corporate crime instigated by Trafigura and the resulting health crisis for the local Ivorian population are a far cry from Aya's vibrant neighborhood (a suburb of the port city) of the late 1970s and early 1980s (see chapter 2). Miagotar seems to highlight this discrepancy with the very first panel of *Cargaison mortelle à Abidjan*, which can be read as a visual citation of the opening of *Aya de Yopougon*. Miagotar's opening panel is a close-up of a ringing telephone with a green oval behind it that emphasizes the ringing (figure 4.4). Originally, in the 2009 version *Trafigoura I*, the ringing telephone is brown and lacks a background. With the addition of the green oval, Miagotar alludes to the final panel of *Aya de Yopougon*'s opening sequence, which equally features a ringing telephone with a green background (figure 4.5). Oubrerie's cross-hatching, like Miagotar's oval shape, visually highlights the ringing telephone. In both Black *bandes dessinées*, the ringing Ivorian telephone sparks the plot's action. Aya's narration that the call was when things figuratively started to spoil playfully introduces the social lives of the protagonist and her girlfriends. In

FIGURE 4.5. Phone call that initiates the plot. *Aya de Yopougon*, vol. 1, Gallimard Jeunesse, 2005.

sharp contrast, the call between the Dutch CEO and his intermediary in Abidjan confirms the logistical details of dumping, or put another way, confirms when things literally started to spoil. Miagotar's *clin d'œil* to *Aya de Yopougon* draws attention to the socioeconomic reality of the Ivory Coast at the time, a reality that Abouet often obscures through her deliberate timelessness (see chapter 2). However, Miagotar's goal is not to focus on or perpetuate negative images of Africa. Rather, in representing real events of the twenty-first century in Abidjan, he seeks to reveal colonialism's ongoing legacy in an attempt to challenge it.

In the allegorical *Cargaison mortelle à Abidjan*, Miagotar calls attention to the interconnectedness of environmental state-corporate crimes and transcolonial forms of extraction. Through intertextual allusions to Hergé's *Coke en stock*, he targets the ship's hold as a devastating site of Black death, thus suggesting that the slave trade (as it takes place at any time, or in any body of water) and toxic dumping are really two sides of the same coin, both stemming from hold politics, an argument Ferdinand advances to account for the relationship between "loss of body and loss of Earth" stemming from the Global North's institutionalization of racism as "a way of inhabiting the Earth" (178). To counteract racism's multivalent harmful fallout in his decolonial ecological Black *bande dessinée*, Miagotar turns to African sources. By combining the virtual restoration of Fang art through his artistic practice with an omniscient more-than-human African spirit who symbolically avenges the real Ivorian victims in the face of Trafigura's impunity, Miagotar offers new ways of seeing the world and humans' position within it, thus gesturing toward decolonial ways of being in it.

As a kind of decolonial ecological manifesto, *Cargaison mortelle à Abidjan* serves as a critical intermediary between Baruti's *Objectif terre!* and more recent environmentally centered nonfiction Black *bandes dessinées* that unambiguously expose the consequences of colonial ways of inhabiting the Earth so as to challenge them. Two recent examples are worth mentioning for their use of expanded reality and their deep dive into the devastating consequences of extreme ecological injustice: *Tropiques toxiques* (2020), about the ongoing Chlordecone scandal in the French overseas departments of Guadeloupe and Martinique, by Jessica Oublié, Nicola Gobbi, and Vinciane Lebrun, and *A House without Windows* (2021), which links the fate of street children in the Central African Republic with political instability and diamond mining, by Marc Ellison and Didier Kassaï. In *Tropiques toxiques*, Oublié includes a QR code that readers can scan to access a range of various forms of extended reality such as digital animations augmenting certain pages, links to bibliographic sources, and further information. Conversely, *A House without Windows*, which alternates between Ellison's photographs of fieldwork, the making of the text, and Kassaï's artwork, is promoted as the first graphic novel to use 360-degree video. Via a link provided just after the preface, readers can access a fourteen-minute 360-degree video on YouTube that allows them to experience the limbo of life in the Central African Republic by placing them virtually in the physical spaces that make up the children's world (refugee camps for internally displaced people, diamond mines, schools, and hospitals), where they can look around while learning about the situation. Through this use of extended reality, readers get a sense of the grueling and dangerous physical work of diamond mining, the often crowded and underfunded camps and schools, and the devastating and wide-reaching impacts of political instability. Like *Objectif terre!* and *Cargaison mortelle à Abidjan*, these recent Black *bandes dessinées* function as a call to action, but in a much more overt manner.

CODA

Black *Bandes Dessinées* and Beyond

The exposition Kubuni, les Bandes Dessinées d'Afrique.s was originally slotted to premiere in 2020 at the Cité International de la Bande Dessinée et de l'Image in Angoulême as a flagship event sitting at the intersection of two major top-down initiatives from President Emmanuel Macron: Saison Africa 2020 and BD 20–21. Due to the global coronavirus pandemic, both yearlong series of events had to be pushed back but were nevertheless heavily promoted with eye-catching professional branding that thematized punchy juxtapositions of vibrant colors, not unlike the packaging of Marguerite Abouet's *Akissi* series. Though Macron jumped on the rising trend of spicing up French with English words to boost his image as a market-savvy cosmopolitan open to diversity in contrast to French presidents before him, Saison Africa 2020 and even its use of English feel like echoes of the yearlong events planned in 2010 by then president Sarkozy under the guidance of Jacques Toubon, supposedly commemorating the fiftieth anniversary of African independences. In both 2010 and 2020, the French state attempted to reinscribe its ties to Africa under the guise of celebrating diversity. However, there was more acceptance of diversity in 2021 than during the 2010 events. We might perhaps chalk some of this up to a newfound sense of shared values in the face of the global coronavirus pandemic, but many of the events had been in planning for years in advance in the wake of Macron's

November 28, 2017, speech in Ouagadougou, the capital of Burkina Faso, in which he declared that he was of a new generation that "doesn't come to tell Africans what to do" ("Macron"). To assure everyone that his speech was not just lip service, Macron commissioned a report on the restitution of African cultural objects, and almost exactly a year later, in November 2018, Felwine Sarr and Bénédicte Savoy delivered *Report on the Restitution of African Cultural Heritage: Toward a New Relational Ethics,* which has since dramatically changed discourse around European colonialism and ongoing imperial formations (see chapter 4). Saison Africa 2020 was a logical next step, and, given Fleur Pellerin's declaration in the wake of the Charlie Hebdo attack in January 2015, it was also logical that France would mobilize all means, including the Ninth Art, as part of the display of its soft power.

It is interesting then, that the promotional materials for Kubuni, les Bandes Dessinées d'Afrique.s and the related fifth Festival International de la Bande Dessinée du Congo, both organized by Joëlle Epée Mandengue (Elyon's), would be supplied by Juni Ba, a France-based Senegalese artist who publishes comics almost exclusively in English and produces artwork for anglophone comics groups in the United Kingdom and the United States. Should we consider his work part of Black *bandes dessinées* even though his work is aimed at anglophone audiences? The simple answer is yes. Many of the artists explored in each of this book's chapters work in multiple languages or at the very least include other languages and context-specific slang in their work. The simple answer is also yes in part because of Ba's reasons for publishing in English. In a tweet posted on March 1, 2021, Ba, who is very active on various social media platforms and encourages interactions and community building, explains in English: "An exercise I find interesting is writing down how you got to where you are in your career. Just the list of events. I'm doing this to try to properly answer the questions of why I don't work with French people more. And the answer is mundane: I followed opportunities as they came" (Ba). In responses to his own tweet, he elaborates that it was not a conscious decision, that he had just been going with the flow, but it was not until he started to write down what he had done that this realization became glaringly obvious. Through his energetic and impressively innovative graphic novels from the American independent publisher TKO Studios, Ba has rightfully garnered acclaim and much attention, which has resulted in more public appearances and signings in France. Nevertheless, it remains to be seen if any mainstream French or Belgian publishers will want to work with him. At the same time, Ba, like many Black francophone artists before him, has not let the conservative mainstream market in Europe stop him from producing *bandes dessinées*.

The colonial heritage of Franco-Belgian *bandes dessinées* and the ongoing forms of imperialism (including visual and material imperialism) since the formal end of colonization are important factors for the development of Black *bandes dessinées*; nevertheless, the effects they have on artists and their work varies from individual to individual and from one project to another. This book insists on the necessity of paying close attention to context to better grasp artists' many strategies for leveraging *bandes dessinées* as a restorative practice. In chapter 1, focusing on the specific context of Kinshasa from the late 1960s to the 1990s revealed how material and textual practices are linked to aesthetic and narrative ones and that self-fashioning is a crucial component of local and global Black cultures. Similarly, chapter 2 looked exclusively at Marguerite Abouet to analyze how she leans on the marketing of the postcolonial exotic through an elusive approach based on the novelty of timelessness to weigh in on multiple belongings throughout West Africa and the African diaspora, but also to advocate, through queer futurity, a new inclusive understanding of universalism that demands a reworking of notions of gender, race, and power. In chapter 3, comparing a wide range of Black *bandes dessinées* about northward migration, I argued that artists have been using *bandes dessinées* to theorize the compounded ruinous effects of increasing borderization for decades. Through a chronological approach, I demonstrated that the *bandes dessinées* expose intolerable truths about borderization, that it is neither recent nor ahistorical, and that it transforms people into specters, just as it dehumanizes border agents and transforms more-than-human entities such as the environment into agents of death. One of the crucial conclusions of a chronological approach is that while it seems that nothing has changed since the turn of the twenty-first century, in actuality, what has changed is the scale of suffering, of brutalization, of impunity, and of indifference. Lastly, chapter 4 turned to the more-than-human and considered certain edutainment Black *bandes dessinées* about the environment to be declarations in favor of what Malcom Ferdinand terms decolonial ecology. Linking extractive practices from the colonial era to the slow violence of toxic dumping in the postcolonial era and investigating the potential relationship between Western art, Franco-Belgian *bandes dessinées*, and Black *bandes dessinées*, I demonstrated how artists' textual, aesthetic, and narrative practices constitute important symbolic forms of restitution and, at the same time, models for new ways of seeing, representing, and being in the world that are decolonial.

Obviously, *On Black* Bandes Dessinées *and Transcolonial Power* is not an exhaustive study, as the artists and texts analyzed represent but a small fraction of what exists. More research is greatly needed to help fill in the global map and timeline of Black *bandes dessinées*. Until recently, scholarship has been constrained by limits on access to primary sources and by the sparseness of secondary sources (in French and even more so in other languages). Those conditions are changing. First, besides Abouet's various series, other key Black *bandes dessinées* have been translated into other languages, though much more translation is needed. Second, the simultaneous release of new *bandes dessinées* as physical books and digital texts has improved accessibility. Third, the digitization of older Black *bandes dessinées* offers new access to previously elusive archives. Additionally, moving forward, it is imperative that scholars attend to the specific context of each artist and text and that they draw from multiple disciplines to decolonize our understanding and appreciation of artists' impressive range of practices and the significance of their work.

WORKS CITED

Aboa, Ange, and Loucoumane Coulibaly. "Former Ivory Coast President Gbagbo Returns Home after Decade of Exile." *Reuters*, 18 June 2021.

Abouet, Marguerite. "Ce festival crée des passions et des métiers." *Le Journal de Cocobulles*, vol. 4, 2017, p. 7.

Abouet, Marguerite, Charli Beleteau, and Christian de Metter. *Terre gâtée: Ange, le migrant*. Rue de Sèvres, 2018.

Abouet, Marguerite, and Donatien Mary. *Commissaire Kouamé: Un homme tome avec son ombre*. Gallimard Bande Dessinée, 2021.

———. *Commissaire Kouamé: Un si joli jardin*. Gallimard Bande Dessinée, 2017.

Abouet, Marguerite, and Agnès Maupré. *Délices d'Afrique*. Editions Alternatives, 2012.

Abouet, Marguerite, and Clément Oubrerie. *Aya*. Translated by Helge Dascher, Drawn & Quarterly, 2007.

———. *Aya: Life in Yop City*. Translated by Helge Dascher, Drawn & Quarterly, 2012.

———. *Aya: Love in Yop City*. Translated by Helge Dascher, Drawn & Quarterly, 2013.

———. *Aya de Yopougon*. Vol. 1, Gallimard Jeunesse, 2005.

———. *Aya de Yopougon*. Vol. 2, Gallimard Jeunesse, 2006.

———. *Aya de Yopougon*. Vol. 3, Gallimard Jeunesse, 2007.

———. *Aya de Yopougon*. Vol. 4, Gallimard Jeunesse, 2008.

———. *Aya de Yopougon*. Vol. 5, Gallimard Jeunesse, 2009.

———. *Aya de Yopougon*. Vol. 6, Gallimard Jeunesse, 2010.

———. *Aya de Yopougon*. Vol. 7, Gallimard Bande Dessinée, 2022.

———. *Aya de Yopougon*. Vol. 8, Gallimard Bande Dessinée, 2023.

———, directors. *Aya de Yopougon*. Kino Lorber, 2013.

Abouet, Marguerite, Clément Oubrerie, and Jean-Claude Loiseau. *Aya de Yopougon: Ambiance le cinéma!* Gallimard, 2013.

Abouet, Marguerite, and Mathieu Sapin. *Akissi: Attaque de chats*. Vol. 1, Gallimard Jeunesse, 2010.

———. *Akissi: Super-héros en plâtre*. Vol. 2, Gallimard Jeunesse, 2011.

———. *Akissi: Vacances dangereuses*. Vol. 3, Gallimard Jeunesse, 2012.

———. *Akissi: Rentrée musclée*. Vol. 4, Gallimard Jeunesse, 2013.

———. *Akissi: Mixture magique*. Vol. 5, Gallimard Jeunesse, 2014.

———. *Akissi: Sans amis*. Vol. 6, Gallimard Jeunesse, 2015.

———. *Akissi: Faux Départ*. Vol. 7, Gallimard Bande Dessinée, 2016.

———. *Akissi: Mission pas possible*. Vol. 8, Gallimard Jeunesse, 2018.

———. *Akissi: Aller-retour*. Vol. 9, Gallimard Jeunesse, 2019.

———. *Akissi: Enfermés dedans*. Vol. 10, Gallimard Jeunesse, 2020.

———. *Akissi: Paix temporaire*. Vol. 11, Gallimard Jeunesse, 2024.

Abouet, Marguerite, and Sigeon. *Bienvenue*. Vols. 1–3, Gallimard Jeunesse, 2010–14.

Achille, Etienne. "A l'approche des cent ans de *Banania*, le retour du tirailleur." *Contemporary French Civilization*, vol. 38, no. 2, 2013, pp. 201–16.

Agnessan, Alain. "'Je suis fier d'amener 'mon soleil' dans la BD universelle': Entretien avec Barly Baruti." *Mouvances Francophones*, vol. 2, no. 1, 2017, pp. 1–4.

Archer, Simon. "The *Trafigura* Actions as Problems of Transnational Law." *Global Private International Law: Adjudication without Frontiers*, edited by Horatia Muir Witt, Lucia Bíziková, Agatha Brandão de Oliveira, and Diego P. Fernández Arroyo, Edward Elgar Publishing, 2019, pp. 102–16.

Assanvo-Kadjo, Rosemonde. "Marguerite Abouet: Une (im)posture dans la bande dessinée africaine francophone." *Mouvances Francophones*, vol. 2, no. 1, 2017, pp. 1–8.

Ba, Juni [@juni_ba]. "An exercise I find interesting is writing down how you got to where you are in your career. Just the list of events. I'm doing this to try to properly answer the question of why I don't work with French people more. And the answer is mundane: I followed opportunities as they came." *X*, 1 Mar. 2021, 7:45 p.m., https://twitter.com/juni_ba/status/1366550100621877249.

Balibar, Étienne. "Le Droit de cité ou apartheid." *Sans-papiers: l'archaïme fatal*, edited by Étienne Balibar, Monique Chemillier-Grendreau, Jacqueline Vosta-Lascoux, and Emmanuel Terray, La Découverte, 1999, pp. 89–116.

———. *We, the People of Europe? Reflections on Transnational Citizenship*. Translated by James Swenson, Princeton UP, 2004.

Bamba, Abou B. *African Miracle, African Mirage: Transnational Politics and the Paradox of Modernization in Ivory Coast*. Ohio UP, 2016.

Bancel, Nicolas, Pascal Blanchard, and Gilles Boëtsch. *Zoos humains: XIXe et XXe siècles*. Éditions La Découverte, 2002.

Bancel, Nicolas, Pascal Blanchard, and Laurent Gervereau, editors. *Images et colonies: Iconographie et propagande coloniale sur l'Afrique française de 1880 à 1962*. Bibliothèque de documentation internationale contemporaine / Association connaissance de l'histoire de l'Afrique contemporaine, 1993.

Bancel, Nicolas, Pascal Blanchard, and Dominic Thomas, editors. *The Colonial Legacy in France: Fracture, Rupture, and Apartheid*. Indiana UP, 2017.

Bandibanga, Célestin, Jaspe S. Mfumu'eto, and Stéphanie Suffren. *Papa Mfumu'eto 1er: Peintre*. Editions de l'oeil, 2003.

Barber, Karin, editor. *Readings in Africa Popular Culture*. Indiana UP, 1997.

Baruti, Barly. *Objectif terre! Les aventures de Sako et Yannick*. AGCD, 1994.

———. *Papa Wemba: Viva la musica!* Afrique Éditions, 1987.

Bathy, Asimba. *Apolosa: Un patrimoine en perdition*. Les éditions du Crayon Noir, 2020.

Bauman, Zygmunt. *Wasted Lives: Modernity and Its Outcasts*. Wiley, 2003.

Beaty, Bart. *Unpopular Culture: Transforming the European Comic Book in the 1990s*. U of Toronto P, 2007.

Becker, Romain. "How a German Publisher Appropriates Comics It Did Not Originally Publish." *Comics and Agency*, edited by Vanessa Ossa, Jan-Noël Thon, and Lukas R. A. Wilde, De Gruyter, 2022, pp. 59–79.

Bedecarré, Madeline. "Prizing Francophonie into Existence: The Usurpation of World Literature by the Prix des Cinq Continents." *Journal of World Literature*, vol. 5, 2020, pp. 298–319.

Bessora and Barroux. *Alpha: Abidjan–Gare du Nord*. Gallimard, 2014.

Bigelow, Benjamin, and Rüdiger Singer. "Introduction: Migration in Twenty-First-Century Documentary Comics." *Inks: The Journal of the Comics Studies Society*, vol. 5, no. 1, 2021, pp. 1–17.

Blanchard, Pascal, Nicolas Bancel, and Sandrine Lemaire, editors. *Culture post-coloniale, 1961–2006: Traces et mémoires coloniales en France*. Autrement, 2006.

———. *La Fracture coloniale: La Société française au prisme de l'héritage colonial*. Éditions La Découverte, 2005.

Blanchard, Pascal, and Gilles Boëtsch, editors. *Le Racisme en images: Déconstruire ensemble*. Éditions de La Martinière, 2021.

Blanchard, Pascal, Gilles Boëtsch, Nanette Snoep, and Lilian Thuram, editors. *Human Zoos. The Invention of the Savage*. Actes Sud, 2011.

Blanchard, Pascal, and Armelle Chatelier, editors. *Images et colonies. Nature, discours et influence de l'iconographie coloniale*. Éditions Syros, 1993.

Blier, Suzanne Preston. *Picasso's* Demoiselles: *The Untold Origins of a Modern Masterpiece*. Duke UP, 2019.

Boone, Catherine. "Commerce in Côte d'Ivoire: Ivoirianisation without Ivoirian Traders." *Journal of Modern African Studies*, vol. 31, no. 1, 1993, pp. 67–92.

Booty, Natasha. "Congolese rumba wins UNESCO protected status." *BBC*, 14 Dec. 2021.

Boukala, Mouloud. "Autoreprésentation et hétérostigmatisation en bandes dessinées. *La Vie de Pahé* de Bitam à Paname." *Ethnologies*, no. 31, vol. 2, 2009, pp. 219–39.

Bragard, Véronique. "Belgo-Congolese Transnational Comics Esthetics: Transcolonial Labor from Mongo Sisé's *Bingo en Belgique* to Cassiau-Haurie and Baruti's *Madame Livingstone: Congo, la Grande Guerre* (2014)." *Literature Compass*, vol. 13, no. 5, 2016, pp. 332–40.

Brezault, Alain. "Deux nouveaux albums dans la collection L'Harmattan BD." *Africultures*, 25 Nov. 2012, https://africultures.com/php/index.php?nav=article&no=11152.

Brouillette, Sarah. *Postcolonial Writers in the Global Literary Marketplace.* Pargrave Macmillan, 2011.

Brouillette, Sarah, and David Thomas. "First Responses." *Comparative Literature Studies,* vol. 53, no. 3, 2016, pp. 503–34.

Brown, Jeffrey. *Black Superheroes, Milestone Comics, and Their Fans.* UP of Mississippi, 2001.

Browne, Simone. *Dark Matters: On the Surveillance of Blackness.* Duke UP, 2015.

Bulling, Paula, and Japhet Miagotar. "From Berlin to Dschang—A Conversation in Images." *Schlosspost: Membrane,* 2019, https://schloss-post.com/from-berlint-to-dschang.

Bumatay, Michelle. "African *Bande Dessinée* Festivals and Competitions: Participation, Patronage, and Performance." *Research in African Literatures,* vol. 50, no. 2, 2019, pp. 35–48.

———. "The Feminine Plural in Africa and the Diaspora: Quartets of Women in *Aya de Yopougon* and *La vie d'Ébène Duta.*" *Drawing (in) the Feminine: Bande Dessinée and Women,* edited by Margaret C. Flinn, The Ohio State UP, 2024, pp. 124–41.

———. "Humor as a Way to Re-Image and Re-Imagine Gabon and France in *La Vie de Pahé* and *Dipoula.*" *European Comic Art,* vol. 5, no. 2, 2012, pp. 44–66.

———. "*Notre histoire* and *Madame Livingstone*: Travels in Time." *Contemporary French Civilization,* vol. 42, no. 2, 2017, pp. 141–69.

———. "Picturing the (Silent) History of Immigration in France and in French *Bandes Dessinées.*" *Immigrants and Comics: Graphic Spaces of Remembrance, Transaction, and Mimesis,* edited by Nhora Serrano, Routledge, 2021, pp. 149–61.

———. "Plural Pathways, Plural Identities: Jean Phillipe Stassen's 'Les Visiteurs de Gibralter.'" *Postcolonial Comics: Texts, Events, Identities,* edited by Binita Mehta and Pia Mukherji, Routledge, 2015, pp. 29–43.

Bush, Ruth. "'Mesdames, il faut lire!': Material Contexts and Representational Strategies in Early Francophone African Women's Magazines." *Francosphères,* vol. 5, no. 2, 2016, pp. 213–36.

———. *Publishing Africa in French: Literary Institutions and Decolonization 1945–1967.* Liverpool UP, 2016.

Bush, Ruth, and Claire Ducournau. "Francophone African Literary Prizes and the 'Empire of the French Language.'" *The Book in African: Critical Debates,* edited by Caroline Davis and David Johnsond, Palgrave Macmillan, 2014, pp. 201–22.

Camara, Fatou. "Review: *Cargaison mortelle à Abidjan.*" *Takamtikou,* 24 May 2013, https://takamtikou.bnf.fr/bibliographies/notices/afrique/cargaison-mortelle-abidjan.

carrington, andre m. "Minor Miracles: Toward a Theory of Novelty in *Aya of Yopougon.*" *Lateral: Journal of the Cultural Studies Association,* vol. 6, no. 1, 2017, pp. 1–21.

Cassiau-Haurie, Christophe. *La Caricature et le dessin de presse en Afrique.* L'Harmattan, 2009.

———. *Comment peut-on faire de la BD en Afrique?* L'Harmattan, 2011.

———. *Dictionnaire de la bande dessinée d'Afrique francophone.* L'Harmattan, 2013.

———. *Histoire de la BD congolaise.* L'Harmattan, 2010.

———. "'Je préfère parler d'innovation . . .': Entretien de Christophe Cassiau-Haurie avec Japhet Miagotar." *Africultures,* 20 Apr. 2012.

———. "Lépa Mabila Saye: 'Je vais mourir mais mes histoires continueront à me survivre dans la tête des lecteurs.'" *Africultures*, 29 Nov. 2018.

———. "Littérature en RDC: La Traversé du désert." *Africultures*, 3 Oct. 2007.

———. *Quand la BD d'Afrique s'invite en Europe.* L'Harmattan, 2012.

Cazenave, Odile, and Patricia Célérier. *Contemporary Francophone African Writers and the Burden of Commitment.* U of West Virginia P, 2011.

Césaire, Aimé. *Discourse on Colonialism.* Translated by Joan Pinkham, Monthly Review Press, 2000.

Chanson, Jean-François, and Gildas Gamy. "Un Congolais au Maroc." *Nouvelles d'Afrique*, edited by Christophe Cassiau-Haurie, L'Harmattan BD, 2014, pp. 24–31.

Chanson, Jean-François, and Koffi Roger N'Guessan. "Le Voyage de Bouna." *Nouvelles d'Afrique*, edited by Christophe Cassiau-Haurie, L'Harmattan BD, 2014, pp. 50–58.

Chute, Hillary. *Disaster Drawn: Visual Witness, Comics, and Documentary Form.* Belknap Press of Harvard UP, 2016.

Conklin, Alice. *A Mission to Civilize: The Republican Idea of Empire in France and West Africa, 1895–1930.* Stanford UP, 1997.

Dabley, Olvis, Venance Konan, Lassance Zohoré, and Patrick Chappatte. *Côte d'Ivoire, On va où là? 1993–2006.* Olvis Dabley Agency, 2007.

Dadié, Bernard. *An African in Paris.* Translated by Karen C. Hatch, U of Illinois P, 1994.

Danewid, Ida. "White Innocence in the Black Mediterranean: Hospitality and the Erasure of History." *Third World Quarterly*, vol. 38, no. 7, 2017, pp. 1674–89.

Davies, Dominic. "Intolerable Fictions: Composing Refugee Realities in Comics." *Comics and Migration: Representation and Other Practices*, edited by Ralf Kauranen, Olli Löytty, Aura Nikkilä, and Anna Vuorine, Taylor and Francis, 2023, pp. 257–70.

Delisle, Philippe. *Bande dessinée franco-belge et imaginaire colonial: Des années 1930 aux années 1980.* Karthala, 2016.

———. "'Le Reporter, le missionnaire et l'homme-léopard': Réflexions sur les stéréoetypes coloniaux dans l'oeuvre d'Hergé." *Outre-Mers: Revue d'histoire*, vol. 96, nos. 362–63, 2009, pp. 267–81.

———. *Tintin et Spirou contre les négriers: La BD franco-belge; Une littérature antiesclavagiste?* Karthala, 2013.

DeLoughrey, Elizabeth M. *Allegories of the Anthropocene.* Duke UP, 2019.

DeLoughrey, Elizabeth, and George B. Handley. "Introduction: Toward an Aesthetics of the Earth." *Postcolonial Ecologies: Literatures of the Environment*, edited by Elizabeth DeLoughrey and George B. Handley, Oxford UP, 2011, pp. 3–39.

Dezalay, Sara. "Building an Environmental and Human Disaster into a Transnational Case: A Socio-Political Perspective." *Global Private International Law: Adjudication without Frontiers*, edited by Horatia Muir Witt, Lucia Bíziková, Agatha Brandão de Oliveira, and Diego P. Fernández Arroyo, Edward Elgar Publishing, 2019, pp. 93–102.

Diallo, Tiémoko. "Félix Houphouë-Boigny, le 'Big Boss' de la Françafrique." *Cahiers d'histoire: Revue d'histoire critique*, vol. 157, 2023, pp. 23–41.

Diop, Boubacar Boris. "Françafrique: A Brief History of a Scandalous Word." *New African*, 23 Mar. 2018.

Djungu-Simba, Charles. "Le fonds littéraire médiaspaul (RD Congo) entre la spiritualité et la littérarité." *Colori dello spirito*, vol. 25, 2001, pp. 1–17.

Donadey, Anne. "'Y' a bon Banania': Ethics and Cultural Criticism in the Colonial Context." *French Cultural Studies*, vol. 11, no. 1, 2000, pp. 9–29.

Dubois, Laurent. "Translator's Introduction." *Critique of Black Reason*, by Achille Mbembe, Duke UP, 2017, pp. ix–xv.

Ducournau, Claire. *La Fabrique des classiques africains: Écrivains d'Afrique subsaharienne francophone*. CNRS Éditions, 2017.

Edimo, Christophe, and Simon Pierre Mbumbo. *Malamine, un africain à Paris*. Les Enfants rouges, 2009.

Ellison, Marc, and Didier Kassaï. *A House without Windows*. Humanoids, 2021.

Fagiolo, Nicolette, director. *Résistants du 9ème Art*. L'Harmattan, 2009.

Fanon, Frantz. *Black Skin, White Masks*. Translated by Richard Philcox, Grove Press, 2008.

———. *The Wretched of the Earth*. Translated by Richard Philcox, Grove Press, 2004.

Federici, Sandra. *L'Entrance des auteurs africains dans le champ de la bande dessinée européenne de langue française (1978–2016)*. L'Harmattan, 2019.

———. *'Je ne voulais pas d'histoires-calebasses': Entretiens avec les bédéistes africains*. Éditions Sépia, 2022.

Ferdinand, Malcom. *Decolonial Ecology: Thinking from the Caribbean World*. Translated by Anthony Paul Smith, Polity, 2022.

"Festival d'Angoulême: Fleur Pellerin veut aider les auteurs de BD." *RTL.fr*, 1 Feb. 2015.

Freeman, Jane. "The French 'Sans-Papiers' Movement: An Unfinished Struggle." *Migration and Activism in Europe since 1945*, edited by Wendy Pojmann, Palgrave Macmillan, 2008, 81–96.

Gandoulou, Justin-Daniel. *Au cœur de la sape: Mœurs et aventures de Congolais à Paris*. L'Harmattan, 1989.

———. *Dandies à Bacongo: Le Culte de l'élégance dans la société congolaise contemporaine*. L'Harmattan, 1989.

Gateward, Frances K., and John Jennings, editors. *The Blacker the Ink: Constructions of Black Identity in Comics and Sequential Art*. Rutgers UP, 2015.

Gikandi, Simon. "Picasso, Africa, and the Schemata of Difference." *Modernism/Modernity*, vol. 10, no. 3, 2003, pp. 455–80.

Gondola, Charles Didier. "Tropical Cowboys: Westerns, Violence, and Masculinity among the Young Bills of Kinshasa." *Afrique et Histoires*, vol. 7, no. 1, 2009, pp. 75–98.

Groensteen, Thierry. *The System of Comics*. Translated by Bart Beaty and Nick Nguyen, UP of Mississippi, 2007.

Grossi, Alessandra. "Marguerite Abouet, Clément Oubrerie, *Aya de Yopougon* (1)." *Altre Modernità*, vol. 2, 2011, pp. 281–83.

Grove, Laurence. *Comics in French: The European Bande Dessinée in Context*. Berghahn Books, 2010.

Grunne, Bernard de. "Fang Statuary: From Classic to Iconic." *Embodiments: Masterworks of African Figurative Sculpture*, edited by Christina Hellmich, Manuel Jordán, and Robert A. Kato, Delmonico Books / Prestel, 2015, pp. 25–31.

Hargreaves, Alec G., Charles Forsdick, and David Murphy, editors. *Transnational French Studies: Postcolonialism and Littérature-Monde*. Liverpool UP, 2010.

Hargreaves, Alec G., and Mark Mckinney, editors. *Post-Colonial Cultures in France*. Routledge, 1997.

Hergé. *Les Aventures de Tintin: Coke en stock*. Casterman, 1986.

———. *Tintin au Congo*. Éditions Casterman, 1974.

Hitchcott, Nicki, and Dominic Thomas, editors. *Francophone Afropean Literatures*. Liverpool UP, 2014.

Hicks, Dan. *The Brutish Museums: The Benin Bronzes, Colonial Violence and Cultural Restitution*. Pluto Press, 2020.

Hine, Darlene Clark, Tricia Danielle Keaton, and Stephen Small, editors. *Black Europe and the African Diaspora*. U of Illinois P, 2009.

Hochschild, Adam. *King Leopold's Ghost: A Story of Greed, Terror and Heroism in Colonial Africa*. Mariner Books, 1998.

Holgate, Ben. *Climate Crises: Magical Realism as Environmental Discourse*. Routledge, 2019.

Horstkotte, Silke. "Zooming In and Out: Panels, Frames, Sequences, and the Building of Graphic Storyworlds." *From Comic Strips to Graphic Novels: Contributions to the Theory and History of Graphic Narrative*, edited by Daniel Stein and Jan-Noël Thon, Walter de Gruyter, 2015, pp. 27–48.

Howard, Sheena C., and Ronald L. Jackson, editors. *Black Comics: Politics of Race and Representation*. Bloomsbury Academic, 2013.

Huggan, Graham. *The Postcolonial Exotic: Marketing the Margins*, Routledge, 2001.

Hunt, Nancy Rose. "Papa Mfumu'eto 1er, star de la bande dessinée kinoise." *Beauté Congo: 1926–2015: Congo Kitoko; Exposition, Paris, Fondation Cartier pour l'art contemporain, du 11 juillet au 15 novembre 2015*, edited by André Magnin, Fondation Cartier pour l'art contemporain, 2015, pp. 266–69.

———. "Tintin and the Interruptions of Congolese Comics." *Images and Empires: Visuality in Colonial and Postcolonial Africa*, edited by Paul Stuart Landau and Deborah D. Kaspin, U of California P, 2002, pp. 90–123.

Iheka, Cajetan. "Introduction." *Teaching Postcolonial Environmental Literature and Media*, edited by Cajetan Iheka, Modern Language Association of America, 2022, pp. 1–20.

Kaehr, Roland, Louis Perrois, Marc Ghysels, and Rachel Pearlman. "A Masterwork That Sheds Tears . . . and Light: A Complementary Study of a Fang Ancestral Head." *African Arts* vol. 40, no. 4, 2007, pp. 44–57.

Kauranen, Ralf, Olli Löytty, Aura Nikkilä, and Anna Vuorine, editors. *Comics and Migration: Representation and Other Practices*. Taylor and Francis, 2023.

Keaton, Trica Danielle, T. Denean Sharpley-Whiting, and Tyler Stovall, editors. *Black France / France Noire: The History and Politics of Blackness*. Duke University Press, 2012.

Kleppinger, Kathryn. "What's Wrong with the Littérature-Monde Manifesto?" *Contemporary French and Francophone Studies*, vol. 14, no. 1, 2010, pp. 77–84.

Kouassi, Abraham. "Gbagbo Acquittal: '3,000 Dead, and No One Guilty!'" *Justice Info*, 1 Apr. 2021.

Kümmerling-Meibauer, Bettina. "Seriality in Children's Literature." *The Edinburgh Companion to Children's Literature*, edited by Clémentine Beauvais and Maria Nikolajeva, Edinburgh UP, 2017, pp. 167–78.

Landau, Paul S., and Deborah D. Kaspin, editors. *Images and Empires: Visuality in Colonial and Postcolonial Africa*. U of California P, 2002.

Langevin, Sébastien. "Bande dessinée: l'Afrique doit construire son marché." *Africultures*, 31 Mar. 2006.

Langevin, Sébastien, and Jacques Tramson. "Cinquante titres de bande dessinée." *Notre Librairie: Revue des littératures du Sud*, vol. 145, 2001, pp. 108–17.

Le Bris, Michel, and Jean Rouaud, editors. *Pour une Littérature-Monde*. Gallimard, 2007.

"Le Dessinateur gabonais Pahé arrêté 36 heures pour une caricature de gendarmes." *Africultures*, Sept. 2009.

Leigh, David. "BBC settles Trafigura libel case." *The Guardian*, 17 Dec. 2009.

Lemaire, Sandrine, et al. *Colonisation and propagande: Le Pouvoir et l'image*. Le Cherche Midi, 2022.

Lent, John A. "African Cartooning: An Overview of Historical and Contemporary Issues." *Cartooning in Africa*, edited by John A. Lent, Hampton Press, 2009, pp. 1–38.

———, editor. *Cartooning in Africa*. Hampton Press, 2009.

Leroy, Fabrice. *Sfar So Far: Identity, History, Fantasy, and Mimesis in Joann Sfar's Graphic Novels*. Leuven UP, 2014.

Lesage, Sylvain. *L'Effet livre: Métamorphose de la bande dessinée*. PU François Rabelais, 2019.

———. *Ninth Art: Bandes dessinées, Books and the Gentrification of Mass Culture, 1964–1975*. Palgrave MacMillan, 2023.

Liking, Werewere. *Elle sera de jaspe et de corail*. L'Harmattan, 1983.

Limb, Peter, and Tejumola Olaniyan, editors. *Taking African Cartoons Seriously: Politics, Satire, and Culture*. Michigan State UP, 2018.

Lumbala, Hilaire Mbiye. *Cases et bulles africaines: Introduction à la bande dessinée africaine francophone*. Éditions Dalimen, 2009.

Mabanckou, Alain. "Preface." *La France noire: Trois siècles de presences des Afriques, des Caraïbes, de l'océan Indien, et d'Océanie*, edited by Pascal Blacnchard, Sylvie Chalaye, Eric Deroo, Dominic Thomas, and Mahamet Timera, La Découverte, 2011, pp. 6–7.

Mabanckou, Alain, and Dominic Thomas, editors. "Francophone Sub-Saharan African Literature in Global Contexts." *Yale French Studies*, vol. 120, 2011.

Maclean, Ruth. "Ex–Ivory Coast President Laurent Gbagbo acquitted at ICC." *The Guardian*, 15 Jan. 2019.

MacManus, Thomas. *State-Corporate Crime and the Commodification of Victimhood: The Toxic Legacy of Trafigura's Ship of Death*. Routledge, 2018.

"Macron: 'I Am of a Generation That Doesn't Tell Africans What to Do.'" *France 24*, 28 Nov. 2017.

Marie, Vincent, and Gillies Olivier, editors. *Albums: Des histoires dessinées entre ici et ailleurs; Bande dessinée et immigration 1913–2013*. Futuropolis, 2014.

Marker, Emily. "Obscuring Race: Franco-African Conversations about Colonial Reform and Racism after World War II and the Making of a Colorblind France, 1945–1950." *French Politics, Culture and Society*, vol. 33, no. 3, 2015, pp. 1–23.

Martinez, Jessica Levin. "Ephemeral Fang Reliquaries: A Post-History." *African Arts*, vol. 43, no. 1, 2010, pp. 28–43.

Maurin Abomo, Marie-Rose. "Tintin au Congo, ou La Nègrerie en clichés." *Images de l'Afrique et du Congo/Zaïre dans les lettres Belges de langue française et alentour*, edited by Pierre Halen and János Riesz, Textyles-Éditions, 1993, pp. 151–62.

Mbembe, Achille. *Critique of Black Reason*. Translated by Laurent Dubois, Duke UP, 2017.

———. "Necropolitics." Translated by Libby Meintjes. *Public Culture*, vol. 15, no. 1, 2003, pp. 11–40.

———. *Necropolitics*. Translated by Steven Corcoran, Duke UP, 2019.

———. *On the Postcolony*. U of California P, 2001.

McKinney, Mark. *The Colonial Heritage of French Comics*. Liverpool UP, 2011.

———. *Postcolonialism and Migration in French Comics*. Leuven UP, 2021.

———. *Redrawing French Empire in Comics*. The Ohio State UP, 2013.

Mehta, Binita. "A Reluctant Migrant in Paris: *Malamine, un Africain à Paris*." *Metropolitan Mosaics and Melting Pots: Paris and Montreal in Francophone Literatures*, edited by Pascale De Souza and H. Adlai Murdoch, Cambridge Scholars Publishing, 2013, pp. 156–81.

———. "Visualizing Postcolonial Africa in *La Vie de Pahé*." *Postcolonial Comics: Texts, Events, Identities*, edited by Binitia Mehta and Pia Mukherji, Routledge, 2015, pp. 111–28.

Memmi, Albert. *The Colonizer and the Colonized*. Translated by Howard Greenfeld, Beacon Press, 1991.

Miagotar, Japhet. "L'Anthropologie au cœur de la bande dessinée: Pertinence d'une bande dessinée africaine avec des personnages issus de la statuaire africaine." *Toom-Comics*, 18 Nov. 2013, http://www.toom-comics.com/lanthropologie-au-coeur-de-la-bande-dessinee/.

———. *Cargaison mortelle à Abidjan*. L'Harmattan BD, 2012.

Michel, Nicolas. "Simon Pierre Mbumbo, un dessein africain." *Jeune Afrique*, 24 Oct. 2015.

Mickwitz, Nina. *Documentary Comics: Graphic Truth-Telling in a Skeptical Age*. Palgrave MacMillan, 2015.

Miller, Ann. *Reading Bandes Dessinées: Critical Approaches to French-Language Comic Strip*. Intellect Ltd., 2007.

Miller, Christopher L. *Black Darkness: Africanist Discourse in French*. U of Chicago P, 1985.

Mirzoeff, Nicholas. *The Right to Look: A Counterhistory of Visuality*. Duke UP, 2011.

Monroe, John Warne. *Metropolitan Fetish African Sculpture and the Imperial French Invention of Primitive Art*. Cornell UP, 2019.

Morand, Catherine. "Marguerite Abouet, conteuse, universelle." *Tribune de Genève*, 11 Dec. 2022.

Muñoz, José Esteban. *Cruising Utopia: The There and Then of Queer Futurity*. New York UP, 2009.

Nama, Adilifu. *Super Black: American Pop Culture and Black Superheroes*. U of Texas P, 2014.

Nasr, Nahed. "Congolese Filmmaker Mweze Ngangura on Different Sides of African Solidarity." *Ahram Online*, 28 June 2019.

Naudillon, Françoise. "Popular Art Forms in the DRC: Practices and Peripheries." *Journal of World Literature*, vol. 6, 2021, pp. 197–215.

Newns, Lucinda. "Necropolitical Ecologies: Creative Articulations of Nature's Death-Work in the Borderzone." *Interventions: International Journal of Postcolonial Studies*, 2023, pp. 1–16.

Nganguè, Eyoum, and Faustin Titi. *An Eternity in Tangiers*. Translated by André Naffis-Sahely, Phoneme Media, 2017.

———. *Une éternité à Tanger*. Edizioni Lai-Momo, 2004.

Ngassu, Daniel Severin. "Entre la vie et la mort." *Africa Comics 2005–2006*, edited by Sandra Federici and Andrea Marchesini Reggiani, Africa e Mediterraneo, Lai-momo, 2006, pp. 62–65.

Nixon, Rob. *Slow Violence and the Environmentalism of the Poor*. Harvard UP, 2011.

Nzila, Valéry Badika. "Si la Mer Méditerranée pouvait parler . . ." *Africa Comics 2005–2006*, edited by Sandra Federici and Andrea Marchesini Reggiani, Africa e Mediterraneo, Lai-momo, 2006, pp. 106–7.

Olivier, Gilles. "Marguerite Abouet: Innocent d'*Aya de Yopougon*, c'est moi." *Albums: Des histoires dessinées entre ici et ailleurs; Bande dessinée et immigration 1913–2013*, edited by Vincent Marie and Gilles Olivier, Futuropolis, 2014, pp. 148–51.

Oublié, Jessica, Nicola Gobbi, and Vinciane Lebrun. *Tropiques toxiques: Le Scandale du chlordécone*. Les Escales, 2020.

Pahé. *Les Choses du pays*. Editions Raponda-Walker, 2008.

———. *Gabonaises . . . Gabonais . . .* Papa-Maurice Entreprises, 2006.

———. "Missié Tintin ? Moi yen a . . . ," *Le Blog de Pahé*, 5 Dec. 2010, https://pahebd.blogspot.com/2010/12/missie-tintin.html.

———. "Pahé: Comment j'ai obtenu d'Ali Bongo qu'il préface mon album." *JeuneAfrique.com*. 8 Feb. 2012.

———. *La Vie de Pahé: Bitam*. Editions Paquet, 2006.

———. *La Vie de Pahé: Paname*. Editions Paquet, 2008.

Patel, Samir S., editor. *Africa Comics*. Studio Museum in Harlem, 2006.

Peabody, Susan, Steven Nelson, and Dominic Thomas, editors. *Visualizing Empire: Africa, Europe, and the Politics of Representation*. Getty Research Institute, 2021.

Peltier, Elian. "A Graphic Novel Finds a Relatable Hero in a Modern African Woman." *New York Times*, 10 Feb. 2024.

Peeters, Benoît. *Tintin and the World of Hergé: An Illustrated History*. Translated by Michael Farr, Bulfinch Press, 1988.

Pieterse, Jan Nederveen. "Fictions of Europe." *Race and Class*, vol. 32, no. 3, 1991, pp. 1–10.

———. *White on Black: Images of Africa and Blacks in Western Popular Culture*. Yale University Press, 1992.

Pietromarchi, Virginia. "'The Soul of the Congolese': Rumba added to UNESCO heritage list." *Al Jazeera*, 15 Dec. 2021.

Polak, Kate. *Ethics in the Gutter: Empathy and Historical Fiction in Comics*. The Ohio State UP, 2017.

Ponzanesi, Sandra. *The Postcolonial Cultural Industry: Icons, Markets, Mythologies*. Palgrave Macmillan, 2014.

Powell, Richard J. *Going There: Black Visual Satire.* Yale UP, 2020.

Ptiluc. "Sur la piste des bulles." *Ptiluc présente BD Africa: Les Africains dessinent l'Afrique,* edited by Ptiluc, Albin Michel, 2005, pp. 1–2.

Repetti, Massimo. "African 'Ligne Claire': The Comics of Francophone Africa." *International Journal of Comic Art,* vol. 9, no. 1, 2007, pp. 515–41.

———. "African Wave: Specificity and Cosmopolitanism in African Comics." *African Arts,* vol. 40, no. 2, 2007, pp. 16–35.

———. "New Comics from Africa." *Africa Comics,* edited by Samir S. Patel, Studio Museum in Harlem, New York, 2006, pp. 241–50.

Roos, Bonnie, and Alex Hunt. "Introduction: Narratives of Survival, Sustainability, and Justice." *Postcolonial Green: Environmental Politics and World Narratives,* edited by Bonnie Roos and Alex Hunt, U of Virginia P, 2010, pp. 1–13.

Ross, Kristin. *Fast Cars, Clean Bodies: Decolonization and the Reordering of French Culture.* MIT Press, 1996.

Salomone, Rosemary. *The Rise of English: Global Politics and the Power of Language.* Oxford UP, 2022.

Sapiro, Gisèle. "Translation and Symbolic Capital in the Era of Globalization: French Literature in the United States." *Cultural Sociology,* vol. 9, no. 3, 2015, pp. 320–46.

Sarr, Felwine, and Bénédicte Savoy. *Report on the Restitution of African Cultural Heritage: Toward a New Relational Ethics.* Translated by Drew S. Burk, Ministère de la Culture of France, Nov. 2018, http://restitutionreport2018.com/sarr_savoy_en.pdf.

Schaffauser, Agnès. "The Wretched of the Sea: Clandestine Immigration and Graphic Artistry in Bessora and Barroux's *Alpha: Abidjan to Gare du Nord.*" *Inks: The Journal of the Comics Studies Society,* vol. 5, no. 1, 2021, pp. 100–118.

Scheller, Richard. "The Genesis of an African Art Collection." *Embodiments: Masterworks of African Figurative Sculpture,* edited by Christina Hellmich, Manuel Jordán, and Robert A. Kato, Delmonico Books / Prestel, 2015, pp. 9–14.

Scott, Joan Wallach. *The Politics of the Veil.* Princeton University Press, 2007.

Serrano, Nhora Lucía, editor. *Immigrants and Comics: Graphic Spaces of Remembrance, Transaction, and Mimesis.* Taylor and Francis, 2021.

Severin, Lucie. "Bayou: Les dix ans d'un concept." *Neuvièmre Art,* no date. https://www.citebd.org/neuvieme-art/bayou-les-dix-ans-dun-concept.

Shepard, Todd. *The Invention of Decolonization: The Algerian War and the Remaking of France.* Cornell UP, 2006.

Spear, Thomas C. "(R)Evolutions," *Transnational French Studies: Postcolonialism and Littérature-Monde,* edited by Alec Hargreaves, Charles Forsdick, and David Murphy, Liverpool University Press, 2010, pp. 164–77.

Stewart, Gary. *Rumba on the River: A History of the Popular Music of the Two Congos.* Verso, 2000.

Stoler, Ann. "Introduction: 'The Rot Remains'; From Ruins to Ruination." *Imperial Debris: On Ruins and Ruination,* edited by Ann Stoler, Duke UP, 2013, pp. 1–35.

Strömberg, Fredrik. *Black Images in the Comics: A Visual History.* Fantagraphics Books, 2003.

Taylor, Ian. "France à fric: The CFA Zone in Africa and Neocolonialism." *Third World Quarterly,* vol. 40, no. 6, 2019, pp. 1064–88.

Thierry, Raphaël. "Francophone African Publishing and the Misconceptions of World Literature." *Francophone Literature as World Literature,* edited by Christian Moraru, Nicole Simek, and Bertrand Westphal, Bloomsbury Academic, 2020, pp. 66–82.

Thomas, Dominic. *Africa and France: Postcolonial Cultures, Migration, and Racism.* Indiana UP, 2013.

———. *Black France: Colonialism, Immigration, and Transnationalism.* Indiana UP, 2007.

———. "Introduction: Afroeuropean Cartographies." *Afroeuropean Cartographies,* edited by Dominic Thomas, Cambridge Scholars Publishing, 2014, pp. 1–15.

Tiquet, Romain. "Marguerite Abouet, Donatien Mary: *Commissaire Kouamé; Un si joli jardin.*" *Afrique Contemporaine,* vols. 236–64, nos. 3-4, 2017, pp. 417–19.

Trapido, Joe. *Breaking Rocks: Music, Ideology and Economic Collapse, from Paris to Kinshasa.* Berghahn Books, 2017.

Versaci, Rocco. *The Book Contains Graphic Language: Comics at Literature.* Bloomsbury Academic, 2007.

Verschave, Xavier. *La Françafrique: Le plus long scandale de la République.* Stock, 1999.

Vessels, Joel E. *Drawing France: French Comics and the Republic.* UP of Mississippi, 2010.

Viodé, Didier. "Vise rejeté." *Africa Comics 2005–2006,* edited by Sandra Federici and Andrea Marchesini Reggiani, Africa e Mediterraneo, Lai-momo, 2006, pp. 54–57.

———. *Vive la corruption.* L'Harmattan BD, 2011.

———. *Yao visa refusé.* L'Harmattan BD, 2019.

Wanzo, Rebecca. *The Content of Our Caricature: African American Comic Art and Political Belonging.* New York UP, 2020.

Watts, Richard. *Packaging Post/Coloniality: The Manufacture of Literary Identity in the Francophone World.* Lexington Books, 2005.

Whaley, Deborah Elizabeth. *Black Women in Sequence: Re-Inking Comics, Graphic Novels, and Anime.* U of Washington P, 2016.

White, Bob W. *Rumba Rules: The Politics of Dance Music in Mobutu's Zaire.* Duke UP, 2008.

Whitted, Quiana. *EC Comics: Race, Shock and Social Protest.* Rutgers UP, 2019.

Winter, Bronwyn. *Hijab and the Republic: Uncovering the French Headscarf Debate.* Syracuse UP, 2009.

Wynter, Sylvia. "Towards the Sociogenic Principle: Fanon, the Puzzle of Conscious Experience of 'Identity' and What It's Like to Be 'Black.'" *National Identities and Sociopolitical Changes in Latin America,* edited by Antonio Gomez-Moriana and Mercedes Duran-Cogan, Routledge, 2001, pp. 30–66.

INDEX

Note: Page numbers in italics indicate figures.

Abidjan, Ivory Coast, 44, 53, 69, 104, 105, 111–12, 125

Abouet, Marguerite, 26, 41–71, 70n43, 130, 131; *Akissi* series, 3, 45, 53, 55, 55n31, 56, 57–58, 59, 60, 61, 65, 69, 128; *Aya de Youpougon*, 3, 9, 13, 16, 44–47, 48, 51–53, 53n26, 54–60, 60–69, 92, 125–26, 126; *bande dessinée* cookbook, 56; *Bienvenue*, 3, 45, 55, 55n31; branding and, 16–17, 54–67; *C'est la vie* telenovela series, 60; *Commissaire Kouamé* series, 58, 60, 61–62, 63, 64, 69; *Délices d'Afrique* (African delights), 55n31, 56n33, 57; gendered dimension of work, 16; on immigrants' rights, 65–66; narrative choices of, 61, 66–67; (re)packaging and, 53, 55, 57; political engagement of, 64–65; portraits of, 70; promotion of, 52–53, 56–57, 56n32, 57n34; strategic practices of, 53; success of, 47–48, 92; *Terre gâtée*, 52, 64, 75n6; translations and, 53, 53n26; treatment of migration, 64–65

abstraction, 79

Africa, 6–7, 15, 17. *See also specific locations*

Africa Comics 2005–2006, 84–92, *86, 88, 90*

Africa Comics competition, 17, 53n26

Africa Comics exposition, 91n15

Africa e Mediterraneo, 17, 75, 80, 84, 113

African art, 120. *See also* Fang art

African *bande dessinée* magazines. *See specific titles*

African francophone artists and European artists, 16–17

African francophone novel, 50

African independences, 128

"African wave," 6–7

L'Afrique française occidentale et équatoriale (French West and Equatorial Africa), 119

Agency for Cultural and Technical Cooperation, 49

Akligo, Joseph, *Sokrou, ou Les Méfaits des sacs plastiques* (Sokrou, or The dangers of plastic bags), 107

Alagbé, Yvan, 9, 48

Albums (Vincent and Olivier), 56

Algeria, 9

Algiers International Comics Festival, 113

allegory, 114–19

Al'Mata, *Les Tribulations d'Alphonse Madiba dit Daudet*, 75n6

American TKO Studios, 129

Amok, 9, 48

Amsterdam, Netherlands, 111

anglophone audiences, 129

Angoulême, France, 5, 25, 44, 68

Angoulême Cité International de la Bande Dessinée et de l'Image, 68

Angoulême International Comics Festival, 44

anthologies, 33–34; *Africa Comics 2005–2006*, 75, 75n6, 84–92, 86, 88, 90; *Côte d'Ivoire, on va où là?* (Ivory Coast, where are we going?), 43, 44, 70; *Nouvelles d'Afrique*, 75, 75n6, 92, 93–95, 102. See also specific anthologies

anti-Black racism, 4, 77, 80, 95, 123; borderization and, 18, 87–88, 91–92; "hold politics" and, 113–14; necropolitics and, 87–88, 98–99

Antilles, 7

anti-racism, 7

Arab Spring, 92

Assanvo-Kadjo, Rosemonde, 45

L'Association, 51

asylum seekers, 92

Atélier de creation, recherche et initiation à l'art (ACRIA), 33

"authenticité," 20

AWA: La revue de la femme noire (women's magazine), 55

"Aya effect," 45, 46; (Black) *bandes dessinées* and, 67–69; branding and, 54–67

Ba, Juni, 129–30

Badik'art (Valéry Bakida Nzila), "Si la Mer Méditerranée pouvait parler....," 86–89, *88*

Balibar, Étienne, 17, 74n2, 78

Banania, 10n16, 123

Bancel, Nicolas, 10n15

bandes dessinées, 2, 20–22, 46, 47–48, 129–30, 131; adopting/adapting imperially introduced medium, 23–24; African, 20–21, 45–46 (*see also specific writers and artists*); "Aya effect" and, 67–69; Black, 17–24, 46–53, 53n26, 67–69, 92–93, 104, 106–11, 129–31 (*see also specific writers and artists*); collections of, 47 (*see also* anthologies; *and specific collections*); critique of northward migration and, 17–18; decolonial ecocriticism and, 18–19, 104; as digital texts/digitization of, 131; environmentalism and, 106–11; feminization of, 17, 67–68, 92–93; festivals, 33; Franco-Belgian, 6, 10, 16–17, 23–24, 25, 34, 45, 48, 58, 130; history of, 32–33; industry, 50–51; legitimization of, 69; and/as literature, 48–53, 52n24; magazines, 58; market for, 67–68; northward migration and, 17–18; as physical books, 131; professionalization of, 17, 67–68; serialized, 12; translations and, 131; translations of, 53, 53n26; use of term, 4–5, 14–15

Banza, Waderi, 32–33

Barroux (Stéphane), 75n5, 106; *Alpha: Abidjan–Gare du Nord*, 17, 68, 75, 92, 95–102, 97n20, *100–101*; translations and, 92n16

Baruti, Barly, 12, 15, 16, 18, 19, 24, 25–30, 32–33, 34, 52, 53n26, 114; L'Espace à suivre workshop, 33; *Éva K*, 3; *Jeunes pour jeunes* (Young for youth) and, 25, 25n9; *Madame Livingstone*, 110–11; *Mandrill*, 3; mise-en-abyme strategies of, 27, 29; *Objectif Terre!* (Goal, Earth!), 18, 107–11, *110*, 127; *Papa Wemba: Viva la musica!*, 24, 25, 26–27, *27*, *28*, *29*; playful approach to layout, 27, 29; as "star of African *bande dessinée*," 25; *Temps d'agir!* (Time to act!), 18, 107–8

Bathy, Asimba, *Kin label*, 39

BBC (British Broadcasting Corporation), 112

BD 20–21, 128

Beaty, Bart, 51

Bedecarré, Madeline, 50

bédéistes, 32–33, 34n20, 37, 39, 45
Bédié, Henri Konan, 42
Belgian colonialism, 4, 15, 22–23, 24
Belgian Congo, 22
Belgian postcolonialism, 4
Belgian publishers, 129. *See also specific publishers*
Belgium, 10
Bessora (Bessora Nan Nguema): *Alpha: Abidjan–Gare du Nord*, 17, 68, 75, 92, 92–93, 95–102, 97n20, 100–101; translations and, 92n16
Bills, 21, 26
"Black," use of term, 4–5, 4n7, 6
Black Americans, representation of, 9
Black *bandes dessinées*, 20–22, 46, 47–48, 129–30, 131; adopting/adapting imperially introduced medium, 23–24; "Aya effect" and, 67–69; critique of northward migration and, 17–18; decolonial ecocriticism and, 18–19, 104; digitization of, 131; environmentalism and, 106–11; feminization of, 17, 67–68, 92–93; legitimization of, 69; and/as literature, 48–53; market for, 67–68; northward migration and, 17–18; professionalization of, 17, 67–68; translations and, 131; translations of, 53, 53n26. *See also specific writers and artists*
Black colonial enslavement and environmental changes, 106
Black comics studies, 9
Black death, 106, 113–14, 122n21, 126–27
Black diaspora, 73n1, 130
Black francophone artists, 2, 69
Black francophone identities, 69
Black Frenchness, 69
Black Panther (film), 14
Black satire, 2
Blackness, 4, 7
Blanchard, Pascal, 10n15
Blier, Suzanne Preston, 121
Blondy, Alpha, 43
borderization, 74–75, 75n4, 81–82, 84–92, 93, 96–97, 98, 130; anti-Black racism and, 18, 87–88, 91–92; historicization of, 102; mechanisms of, 17, 102; normalization of, 91–92

branding, 16–17, 47, 54, 70; "Aya effect" and, 54–67; importance of, 69
Brezault, Alain, 7, 122n21
Brouillette, Sarah, 47
Brownsville, Texas, 111
Brunhoff, Jean de, *Histoire de Babar*, 23n6
Brussels, Belgium, 25
Burkina Faso, 129
Bush, George W., 76n8
Bush, Ruth, 50, 55

Camara, Fatou, 122n21
Cameroon, 33, 39, 40
Canada, 15
cancel culture, 2
Caraïbéditions, 7
Caribbean, 8, 15
caricature, 12–13, 43n6, 89; as predecessor to *bandes dessinées*, 12; of racialized bodies, 10; racist, 2
cartooning, 70. *See also* caricature
Cartooning for Peace, 70, 70n43
Cassiau-Haurie, Christophe, 3, 7, 44–45, 55, 68; *Madame Livingstone*, 110–11; *Quand la BD d'Afrique s'invite en Europe*, 8
Casterman, 2
categorization, 45, 47, 51
Catholic Church, 23, 29
Catholicism, dissemination of, 22
Cazenave, Odile, 45, 46
Célérier, Patricia, 45, 46
Césaire, Aimé, 41, 98, 98n21
Chamoiseau, Patrick, 51
Chanson, Jean-François: "Un Congolais au Maroc," 92; "Le voyage de Bouna," 92, 93–94, 94
La Chanson illustrée, 21
Chappatte, Patrick, 43n6
Charleroi School, 12
Charlie Hebdo attack, 5, 129
children's series, 57, 58
Chirac, Jacques, 49, 49n15, 49n16
Chlordecone scandal, 127
Cissé, Samba Ndar, *Oulaï*, 46
Cité International de la Bande Dessinée et de l'Image, Angoulême, 128

climate justice, 105
Coco Bulles festival, 43, 69–70, 70n43
Coco et Didi, 21
Code Noir, 8
coker naptha, 104, 111–12
Cold War, 18, 124
collaborative projects, 16–17
colonialism, 4, 18, 72–73, 78, 79, 82, 104–5, 120, 123–24, 129, 130; Belgian, 4, 15, 22–23, 24; challenges to, 107–8; colonial epistemologies, 123; colonial taxonomy, 114–15; expungement of, 20; French, 4, 15, 22–23, 23n6, 24, 41–42, 67, 72–73, 104–5; modernism and, 119; unrest and, 49n15
colonization, 73n1, 82, 130
Columbo, 61
"comics," 5
comics: "creolization of," 13; as Ninth Art, 4, 5, 32, 39, 52n24, 129. See also *bandes dessinées*
Compagnie Tommy SARL, 112
Congo. See Congo Free State; Democratic Republic of the Congo (DRC)
Congo Free State, 22. See also Democratic Republic of the Congo (DRC)
Congolese culture, 30
Congolese musicians, 32, 35, 38–39. See also specific musicians
Congolese rumba, 15–16, 25–30
context, understanding of, 15
coronavirus pandemic, 128
Cosigny, Kim, 68
Côte d'Ivoire, on va où là? (Ivory Coast, where are we going?), 43, 44, 70
countervisuality, 13, 18, 111
Le Cri du Margouillat, 9
Cubism, 104–5
cultural hegemony, 5–6, 50
cultural superiority, myth of, 72

Dabley, Olvis, 43; *Côte d'Ivoire, on va où là?* (Ivory Coast, where are we going?), 43, 44, 70
Dadié, Bernard, *Un Nègre à Paris* (*An African in Paris*), 72, 73–74
Dallas, 44

Les damnés de la terre, la mer, et l'air, 92–102
Danewid, Ida, 77–78, 91
Danngar, Adjim, 3
Davies, Dominic, 17–18, 76–77
De Gaulle, Charles, 49
De Moor, Bob, 25
débrouilliards, 39
decolonial ecocriticism, 104
decolonial ecology, 18, 107, 123, 130
decolonial environmentalism, 108
decolonial representation, 114
decolonial ways of seeing, 6, 114
decolonization, 9, 14, 18–19, 49, 73n1, 131
dehumanization, 80, 97, 98–99, 106, 123, 124
Delisle, Philippe, 23, 124
DeLoughrey, Elizabeth, 114
Democratic Republic of the Congo (DRC), 7, 12, 25, 39. See also specific locations
"depersonalization," 76
detention, 78, 80, 81–82, 91, 102
development, 108, 109
developmental aid, 49
Devi, Ananda, 51
Diabaté, Nandy, 40
Diallo, Rokhaya, *Pari(s) d'amies*, 68
Diantantu, Serge, 7; *Mémoire de l'esclavage*, 7
diegesis, 99, 117, 130
dispossession, 79
doublespeak, 36
Drawn & Quarterly, 53
Dro, Edwige-Renée, 45
Ducournau, Claire, 50, 51
Dufaux, Jean, 3
Durango, 21
Dysart, Joshua, *Unknown Soldier*, 34n20

ecocriticism: decolonization and, 18–19; first-wave, 108
Edimo, Christophe: *Les Tribulations d'Alphonse Madiba dit Daudet*, 75n6; *Malamine, un africain à Paris*, 45–46, 72–74, 73n1
Éditions Médiaspaul, 22

Éditions Paquet, 2, 3
Éditions Rue de Sèvres, 52
Éditions Saint-Paul, 22
Éditions Soleil, 3
Edizioni Lai-Momo, 17
edutainment, 25; environmental, 18–19, 25, 107
Ekunde, Kabos, 32–33
Ellison, Marc, *A House without Windows*, 127
Elyon's (Joëlle Epée Mandengue), 68n41, 129; *La vie d'Ébène Duta*, 67–68
English-language publishers, 53
Enlightenment, 108
environmental changes and Black colonial enslavement, 106
environmental disaster, postcolonial dimension of, 114–15
environmental edutainment, 18–19, 25, 107
environmental laws, 112–13
environmental state-corporate crimes, 126
environmentalism, 106–11, 108; decolonial, 108; postcolonialism and, 106–7
"L'esprit de famille" (Kangol Ledroïd and Christophe Cassiau-Haurie), 93
Essono, Patrick (Pahé), 1–2. *See also* Pahé (Patrick Essono)
Estonia, 111–12
Eternity in Tangiers, An, 77–84
Europe, 15; borderization of, 17; migration and, 75–76, 76n8
European artists and African francophone artists, 16–17
European Border and Coast Guard Agency (Frontex), 78
European Union, 102, 111. *See also specific countries*
exoticism, postcolonial, 14
exploitation, politics of, 106

Fagiola, Nicoletta, 43n5
Falk, Peter, 61
Fang art, 104–5, 106, 114, 119–21, 127
Fang reliquaries, 19

Fanon, Frantz, 95; *Black Skin, White Masks*, 123–24; *The Wretched of the Earth*, 102
fashion, 24
Federici, Sandra, 7, 45
Ferdinand, Malcolm, 106, 107, 123, 127, 130; *Decolonial Ecology*, 18
Festival International de la Bande Dessinée du Congo, 129
festivals, 24, 33
figuration, 114–19
film, 21, 22, 24, 25, 26, 27, 30
filmmaking, 30
filtering systems, 78–79, 80, 102
First Ivorian Civil War, 44, 104
first-wave ecocriticism, 108
Foccart, Jacques, 42
Fochivé, Saïd, 40
Fons, T. T. (Alphonse Mendy), 12; *Goorgoorlou*, 40, 45, 46
Fortress Europe, 75–76, 76n8, 81, 92, 102
"Françafrique," 42, 42n2, 43
France, 10, 57; appeal of Satrapi's *Persepolis* in, 48–49; civilizing mission of Third Republic, 22–23; diversification of, 48, 49, 128; immigration and, 72–103, 74n2; modernization of, 49; postwar, 49; state sponsorship of *Aya de Yopougon*, 53
France-Afrique, 41–42, 42n2
Franco-Belgian *bandes dessinées*, 6, 10, 16–17, 23–24, 25, 34, 45, 48, 58, 130
francophone literature, 49–50
La Francophonie, 16, 50
Franquin, André, 12, 89; *Gaston*, 12; *Spirou*, 12
Franquin, Jijé, 12; *Gaston*, 12; *Spirou*, 12
French Antilles, 7
French Caribbean, 8
French Colonial Exposition, 23n6
French colonialism, 4, 15, 22–23, 23n6, 24, 41–42, 67, 72–73, 104–5
French cultural hegemony, 5–6, 50
French Indochina, 9
French language, 13, 21, 38, 46–47, 49, 50
French Ministry of Foreign and European Affairs, 53
French postcolonialism, 4

French print culture, 16–17
French public, diversification of, 16
French publishers, 46, 50–51, 52, 92, 129. *See also specific publishers*
French school system, 23
French universalism, 6, 16, 49, 74
French-language literature, 49–50
Fréon, 48
"Frère Jacques," 29
Le Front National, 74

Gabon, 33, 39, 40
"Galligrasseuil," 50
Gallimard, 3, 9, 14, 16, 47, 48, 50, 53, 56n33, 57, 75, 92–93; Bayou collection, 47, 48, 51, 52, 54, 55, 56, 58, 59, 69; Continents Noirs (Black Continents) series, 51; Gallimard Bande Dessinée, 52, 55; Gallimard Jeunesse, 55
Galvada, 52
Gamy, Gildas, 15; "Un Congolais au Maroc," 92, 94–95
gatekeepers, 24; decentering of, 14
Gateward, Frances, 9
Gavalda, Anna, 44
Gbagbo, Laurent, 42, 43–44, 43n6, 53
Gbich!, 13, 40, 43, 43n5
genre mixing, 47
Gikandi, Simon, 119
Giroud, Frank: *Éva K*, 3, 52; *Mandrill*, 3, 52
Glénat, 3
Global North, 4, 6, 13–14, 17–18, 46, 51, 69, 77, 105–7, 109, 114, 119–21. *See also specific countries*
Global South, 6, 104, 109. *See also specific countries*
"Global War on Terrorism," 76n8, 80
globalization, 78
Gobbi, Nicola, 68; *Tropiques toxiques*, 68, 127
Gombo, Cauphy, 40
Grand-Bassam, Ivory Coast, 69; terrorist attack in, 60–61
graphic novels, 5
Grasset, 50
Greder, Armin, *Mediterraneo*, 87n13

Groensteen, Thierry, 115
Guadeloupe, 7
Guéï, Robert, 42

hajj, 106, 123
Handley, George B., 114–15
Harel, Xavier, *L'Argent fou de la Françafrique*, 69
"headscarf affairs," 49
health crises, 125
Hergé (Georges Prosper Remi), 2, 10, 10n17, 32–33, 34, 94, 94n17, 95, 122–25; *Coke en stock*, 18, 106, 115, 122–25, 122n21, 123n22, 126; *ligne claire* style of, 23; *Tintin au Congo*, 2, 10n17, 11, 12, 18, 23, 23n6, 34, 94, 94n17, 95, 109, 123, 124–25
Hicks, Dan, 119, 120n17
Hindoubill, 21
"hold politics," 18, 106, 113–14
Holgate, Ben, 114
Hollande, François, 5
Horstkotte, Silke, 109
Houphouët-Boigny, Félix, 41, 42, 42n2, 43
Howard, Sheena C., 9
Huggan, Graham, 47
human trafficking, 123–25. *See also* slave trade
humanism, critique of, 99
humanity, 91
Hunt, Alex, 108
Hunt, Nancy Rose, 32
hybridity, 22, 23–24

Iheka, Cajetan, 108
imperialism, 12, 14, 74, 96, 102, 124, 129, 130; popular culture and, 14; visual, 2, 9
Indian Ocean, 8, 15
inequality, 91
inequity, transcolonial, 111
Institut français, 53
International Comics Festival, 5
International Criminal Court (ICC), 44
International Organization of La Francophonie (OIF; Organisation Interna-

tionale de la Francophonie), 49; Prix des Cinq Continents, 50
Islamic State, 92
"Ivoirité," 42, 43
Ivorian Miracle, era of, 60
Ivory Coast, 41–42, 43, 43n6, 45, 53, 54, 56–57, 70, 104–5, 112, 125. *See also* specific locations

Jackson, Ronald L., II, 9
Jennings, John, 9
Jeunes pour jeunes (Young for youth), 12, 15, 20–22, 23, 25, 35; as African *bande dessinée*, 22; diversity and plurality of, 24
journalism, 22
JunioR, 35

Kake (*L'Éclair*, "Lightning"), 20
Kassaï, Didier, *A House without Windows*, 127
Kassaï, Florent, *Destination le Tchad*, 75n6
Keïta, Modibo, 41
Kiala, Aundu, 32–33
Klesse, 32–33
Kikumba, Jules Shungu Wembadio Pene, 26. *See also* Papa Wemba (Jules Shungu Wembadio Pene Kikumba)
Kin label, 39
Kinois, 26
Kinshasa, Democratic Republic of the Congo, 15–16, 20, 35, 130
Kisangani, Democratic Republic of the Congo, 25
knowledge, schemas of, 79. *See also* categorization
Konan, Venance, 43n6
Kouachi, Chérif, 5
Kouachi, Saïd, 5
Kubuni, les Bandes Dessinées d'Afrique.s, 68, 128, 129

La Fontaine, Jean de, "The Laborer and His Children," 30
La Sape, 16, 26, 27, 29, 30
Lagos, Nigeria, 112
laïcité, 49n16

Lai-momo, 75, 80
Lamy, Benoît, 25
Le Pen, Jean-Marie, 74
Le Seuil, 50, 53
Lebrun, Vinciane, 68; *Tropiques toxiques*, 68, 127
Leopold II, King, 22
Lepas (Lepa Mabila), 32–33, 34; *JunioR*, 35, 38
L'Harmattan BD, 17, 69, 75, 85, 89, 92, 113
libanga, 32, 38, 39
ligne claire style, 25, 84, 109, 121
Liking, Werewere, 62n37; *Elle sera de jaspe et corail*, 62
Lingala, 13, 21, 30, 35, 38
linguistic strategies, 35
literary prizes, 46, 50–51, 58–59
literary success, 46
literature, 22
Louis XIV (king), 8
Loyongo, Denis Boyau, 32–33; *Apolosa*, 21
Lumbala, Hilaire Mbiye, 7, 36n28
Ly-Bek: *La merveilleuse aventure de João* (João's marvelous adventure), 107; *Défense d'ivoire* (Ivory tusk), 107; *L'empreinte de la tortue* (The turtle's footprint), 107

Mabanckou, Alain, 51, 52, 73n1; *Black Bazar*, 73n1
Mabila, Lepa. *See* Lepas (Lepa Mabila)
MacManus, Thomas, 112
Macron, Emmanuel, 105, 128–29
magical realism, 114
Malraux, André, 49
manga, 40
Manifesto of the 44, 50
Marboeuf, Olivier, 9, 48
marketing, 54–55, 130
Martinique, 7
Mary, Donatien, 58
Masioni, Pat, 3, 12, 32–33, 34, 34n20, 45
Mata, Al, 32–33
materiality, 13
Matisse, Henri, 120

Maupré, Agnès, 56
M'Ba, Léon, 41
Mbembe, Achille, 17, 74–75, 78, 82, 84, 84n11
Mbumbo, Simon Pierre, 45, 72–73; on hyperpopularity of *Aya de Yopougon*, 47; *Malamine, un africain à Paris*, 45–46, 80
McKinney, Mark, 9, 10
Mehta, Binita, 72–73
Memmi, Albert, 76
Mendy, Alphonse, 45. See also Fons, T. T. (Alphonse Mendy)
Meralli, Swann, *L'association des femmes africaines*, 69
Mexico-US border, 111
Miagotar, Japhet, 13, 18, 19, 113–14, 125–27; "L'Anthropologie au coeur de la bande dessinée" ("Anthropology at the heart of *bande dessinée*"), 120–21; *Cargaison mortelle à Abidjan* (Deadly cargo in Abidjan), 18, 105, 106–7, 115, *116*, 117–18, *118*, 120, 121, 122–25, 122n21, 126–27; *Trafigoura I*, 113, 125; *Trafigoura II*, 113
migrants: dehumanization of, 76, 77, 91–92, 97; empathy for, 102, 103; fictions about, 77–78; humanization of, 76–77, 92; imperialism and, 102; liminal status of, 85–86; stereotypes about, 95
migration, 17–18, 64–65, 75n4, 130; ahistoricity and, 77–78, 84, 130; borderization and, 84–92; fictions about, 77–78, 84, 103; history of twenty-first-century, 77, 130; "migrant crisis," 76; northward, 17–18; postcolonial, 72–103; reframing, 72–103
Le Militant parle, 21
Miller, Ann, 6
Mirzoeff, Nicholas, 6
Mobutu Sese Seko, 15, 20, 22, 36
modernism, 119, 120, 120n17
modernity, 120
modernization, 49
Le Monde, 50
Morocco, 15
Mukuna, Fifi, 32–33
Mulongo, Freddy, 20–21
multiculturalism, 56

multinational corporations, 111
Musée de l'Histoire de l'Immigration, Paris, 56, 57, 57n34, 65
Musée du Quai Branly, Paris, 120n17
Museum of Modern Art, New York, 120n17
music, 21, 24, 25–30; Congolese, 15–16, 25–30, 32, 35, 38–39 (*see also specific musicians*); Western, 29
Muslims, 106, 123
Le Mystère du tombeau de Kalina, 21

Napoléon Bonaparte, 8
Narinto, 40
Ndiaye, Marie, 51
necropolitics, 78, 82, 84, 84n11, 94n17, 97, 99, 102; anti-Black racism and, 87–88, 98–99; "necropolitical ecology," 87
"Négrologie," 89
neocolonialism, 6, 12, 107
neoliberalism, 107, 123
Newns, Lucinda, 87
Nganguè, Eyoum: *Une Éternité à Tanger* (An Eternity in Tangiers), 17, 75, 77–84, 80n10, *83*, 85, 86, 93, 94; "Le Flic de Gnasville," 80n10
Ngangura, Mwezé, 25
Ngassu, Daniel Severin, 106; "Entre la vie et la mort," 85–86, *86*
Ngoye, Achille Flor, 20–21
Nguema, Bessora Nan, 75n5. See also Bessora (Bessora Nan Nguema)
N'Guessan, Koffi Roger, "Le voyage de Bouna," 92
Ninth Art, comics as, 4, 5, 32, 39, 52n24, 129
Nixon, Rob, 106n5, 113, 115, 117
Nora, Pierre, 32
North Africa, 15
Nouchi, 13, 54
Nouvelles d'Afrique, 17, 75, 75n6, 92, 93–95, 102

oral storytelling, 22
Otherness, 54–55
Ouattara, Alassane, 42, 43–44, 58

Oublié, Jessica: *Peyi an nou*, 68; *Tropiques toxiques*, 68, 127
Oubrerie, Clément, 13, 16, 44, 46, 47, 54, 58, 60, 65, 69; *Aya de Youpougon*, 3, 9, 13, 16, 44–47, 48, 51–53, 53n26, 54–60, 60–69, 92, 125–26, 126
Ouedraogo, Roukiata, *Ouagadougou pressé*, 68

packaging, 68, 69
Pahé (Patrick Essono), 1–2, 12–13, 89; *Dipoula*, 3; homage to Papa Mfumu'Eto, 39; *La Vie de Pahé* (Pahé's life), 2, 3, 39, 75n6; *Le Monde de Pahé*, 3
Panama, 111
Papa Mfumu'Eto (Jaspe-Saphir Nkou-Ntoula), 13, 15, 24, 25, 36n28; as *bédéiste*, 32; *bédéistes préférés* list and, 32–33, 34, 39; engagement with history of *bandes dessinées*, 32–33; fan base and, 38–39; influence of, 39; leveraging of Ninth Art as part of his "égo-histoire," 32; Pahé and, 39; playful approach to layout, 27, 31–32, 36–37; posturing of, 32; *Revue Mfumu'eto*, 16, 26, 30, 31–40; self-promotion and, 31, 37–38
Papa Wemba (Jules Shungu Wembadio Pene Kikumba), 15–16, 25, 26–27, 27, 28, 29, 32; *Papa Wemba: Viva la musica!*, 15–16, 26
paratexts, 52–53
Patel, Samir, 6
Peeters, Benoît, 123, 123n22, 124
Pellerin, Fleur, 5, 129
Le Petit Vingtième, 10n17
photography, 24
Picasso, Pablo, 104–5, 120; *Les Demoiselles d'Avignon*, 19, 104–5, 119, 121
Pieterse, Jan Nederveen, 9, 75
Pilote, 34, 58
"Place Charlie," 5
Plantu (Jean Plantureaux), 70, 70n43
Polak, Kate, 76
Ponzanesi, Sandra, 47, 51, 53
popular culture, 2, 14, 22, 23–24
popular music, 35, 38–39
postcolonial authors, 16–17, 47, 50–51, 53

postcolonial ecocriticism and allegory, 114
postcolonial francophone literature, 16–17, 50–51
postcolonialism, 4, 6, 9, 12, 14, 46–47, 74, 114–15, 130; environmentalism and, 106–7; everyday, 20; and postcolonial ecocriticism, 114; postcolonial exotic, 67, 69, 130; and postcolonial (im)migration, 72–103
Powell, Richard J., 2, 9–10
Premier Salon des Auteurs Africains de Bande Dessinée (First Salon of African Comics Authors), 1, 2–3, 3n6
Primitivism, 120n17
print culture, French, 16–17
Prix SNCF, 58
Probo Koala case, 18, 104, 111–13, 115, 118–19, 125
progress, 108, 109
Ptiluc, *BD Africa*, 52
P'tit Luc (Ptiluc), 32–33; *Ptiluc présente BD Africa* (Ptiluc presents BD Africa), 33–34, 33n16
publishers: Belgium- and France-based, 22; English-language, 53; French, 46, 51, 52, 92, 129. *See also specific publishers*

queer futurity, 62, 130

race, 4, 8
racialization, 4, 8, 78, 82, 84, 91
racism, 2, 9, 78, 123; anti-Black, 4, 77, 80, 95, 113–14, 123; combatting, through education, 7; institutionalization of, 127; systemic, 73; visual language of, 12
radio, 21
Raives, Guy, 3
Rancière, Jacques, 77
realism, 34
refugees, 92
Remi, Georges Prosper. *See* Hergé (Georges Prosper Remi)
renaming, 114–19
repetition, 58
Repetti, Massimo, 6–7, 12, 13

Report on the Restitution of African Cultural Heritage, 19
resource extraction, 82, 107, 119, 126
restitution, 18, 19, 78, 105, 121, 129, 130
restorative practice, 9, 130
Réunion, 8
Revue Mfumu'eto, 16, 26, 30, 31–40; *Ba latisi ngalula masque po abala te / Masque de vieillesse* (Masque of old age), 31–32, 37, 38
Rizzo, Clément, *L'association des femmes africaines*, 69
Rock Against the Police (RAP), 66
Rolin, Gabrielle, 123
Roos, Bonnie, 108
Rousseau, Marie-Ange, 68
ruination, process of, 93
rumba, 15–16

Saint-Ogan, Alain, 10, 10n17
Saison Africa 2020, 128
Samba, Chéri, 36n28
Sapin, Mathieu, 55n31, 58
Sapin, Singeon, 55n31
Sarkozy, Nicolas, 3, 128
Sarr, Felwine, *Report on the Restitution of African Cultural Heritage*, 105, 129
"satiracy," 2
Satrapi, Marjane, *Persepolis*, 48–49
Savoy, Bénédicte, *Report on the Restitution of African Cultural Heritage*, 105, 129
Schaffauser, Agnès, 97–98, 99
Schengen Agreement of 1985, 75
Second Ivorian Civil War, 44
securitization, 102
segregation, 78
self-fashioning, postcolonial, 47
self-promotion, 30, 31
self-styling, 24
Senghor, Léopold, 41
Seraphine, 3
Sfar, Joann, 47, 51–52; *The Rabbi's Cat*, 56
Sinatra, 21
Sinda, César, 20–21
Sisé, Mongo, *Bingo* series, 107
slave trade, 106, 126–27

slavery, 8
small-press movement, 48, 50–51
Smith, Stephen, 89
soft power, 49, 71, 129
Sontag, Susan, 77
Spielberg, Steven, 98
Spirou, 34, 58
Stasi Commission, 49n16
Stassen, Jean-Philippe, 3
stereotypes, 11, 81, 95, 123; racialized, 9; racist, 2, 10, 10n16 (*see also* racism)
Sti, *Dipoula*, 3
Stoler, Ann, 17, 74, 77
Strömberg, Fredrick, 9
Studio Museum, Harlem, 6
Studios Hergé, 25
Summers, Lawrence, 106n5, 118
surveillance state, 80
"SVA" (simplification, variation, animation), 121
Syrian Civil War, 92

Tâche d'encre group, 70
Tehem, *Report on the Restitution of African Cultural Heritage*, 75n6
Thomas, Dominic, 51
Thuram, Lilian, 7, 8; *Mes étoiles noires*, 7–8; *Notre Histoire*, 7, 75n6
timelessness, 60–67, 130
Titi, Faustin, 17; *Une Éternité à Tanger* (An Eternity in Tangiers), 75, 77–84, 80n10, 83, 85, 86, 93, 94; "Le Flic de Gnasville," 80n10
Top Music, 21
Toubon, Jacques, 3, 128
Touré, Sékou, 41
toxic dumping, 104, 105, 106, 111–14, 118–19, 120, 123, 127, 130
Trafigoura. *See* Trafigura
Trafigura, 104, 111–13, 115, 118–19, 125, 127
transcolonial power dynamics, 24, 106, 126
translations, 47, 53, 53n26, 92n16, 131
transmedia storytelling, 47
transnational networks, 24
Les Trente Glorieuses, 49

"underpollution," 106, 106n5, 118
UNESCO, 25, 29
Universal Declaration of Human Rights, 102
universal humanism, critique of, 99
universalism, 6, 16, 49, 74, 91, 99, 130
urban painting, 22
US American visual imperialism, 10

La Vie est belle, 15, 25, 27, 30
Vieux pour vieux, 21
vignettes, 17, 33, 46, 57–58, 65, 68, 75, 92–94, 93, 102
Viodé, Didier, 17, 68, 84–85; *Africa Comics 2005–2006*, 75, 75n6; *Étrangers sans rendez-vous*, 89n14; "Visa Rejeté," 85, 89, 90, 91, 91n15; *Vive la corruption*, 85, 89, 91; *Yao visa refusé*, 85, 89, 91
violence, 18
visual imperialism, 2, 9
Viva la musica, 26

Wanzo, Rebecca, 2, 9–10
Warnauts, Éric, 3
Watts, Richard, 52

Western visual imperialism, 2, 8–9
White, Bob W., 35
white supremacy, 78
Wolinski, Georges, 89
world literature, in French, 50
"World War Zero," 119

Le XXe Siècle, 10n17

Yopougon, Ivory Coast, 44, 45

Zaïko Langa Langa, 26
Zaire, 15
Zaïre (magazine), 23
Zairianization campaign, 20
Zekid, Willy (Willy Mouélé), 3, 7
Zohoré, Lassane, 7, 43, 43n5; *Côte d'Ivoire, on va où là?* (Ivory Coast, where are we going?), 43, 44, 70

STUDIES IN COMICS AND CARTOONS
Charles Hatfield and Rebecca Wanzo, Series Editors
Lucy Shelton Caswell and Jared Gardner, Founding Editors Emeriti

Books published in Studies in Comics and Cartoons focus exclusively on comics and graphic literature, highlighting their relation to literary studies. The series includes monographs and edited collections that cover the history of comics and cartoons from the editorial cartoon and early sequential comics of the nineteenth century through webcomics of the twenty-first. Studies that focus on international comics are also considered.

On Black Bandes Dessinées *and Transcolonial Power*
   MICHELLE BUMATAY

Petrochemical Fantasies: The Art and Energy of American Comics
   DANIEL WORDEN

Drawing (in) the Feminine: Bande Dessinée *and Women*
   EDITED BY MARGARET C. FLINN

Lost Literacies: Experiments in the Nineteenth-Century US Comic Strip
   ALEX BERINGER

Growing Up Graphic: The Comics of Children in Crisis
   ALISON HALSALL

Muslim Comics and Warscape Witnessing
   ESRA MIRZE SANTESSO

Beyond the Icon: Asian American Graphic Narratives
   EDITED BY ELEANOR TY

Comics and Nation: Power, Pop Culture, and Political Transformation in Poland
   EWA STAŃCZYK

How Comics Travel: Publication, Translation, Radical Literacies
   KATHERINE KELP-STEBBINS

Resurrection: Comics in Post-Soviet Russia
   JOSÉ ALANIZ

Authorizing Superhero Comics: On the Evolution of a Popular Serial Genre
   DANIEL STEIN

Typical Girls: The Rhetoric of Womanhood in Comic Strips
   SUSAN E. KIRTLEY

Comics and the Body: Drawing, Reading, and Vulnerability
   ESZTER SZÉP

Producing Mass Entertainment: The Serial Life of the Yellow Kid
   CHRISTINA MEYER

The Goat-Getters: Jack Johnson, the Fight of the Century, and How a Bunch of Raucous Cartoonists Reinvented Comics
   EDDIE CAMPBELL

Between Pen and Pixel: Comics, Materiality, and the Book of the Future
  AARON KASHTAN

Ethics in the Gutter: Empathy and Historical Fiction in Comics
  KATE POLAK

Drawing the Line: Comics Studies and INKS, 1994–1997
  EDITED BY LUCY SHELTON CASWELL AND JARED GARDNER

The Humours of Parliament: Harry Furniss's View of Late-Victorian Political Culture
  EDITED AND WITH AN INTRODUCTION BY GARETH CORDERY AND JOSEPH S. MEISEL

Redrawing French Empire in Comics
  MARK MCKINNEY

www.ingramcontent.com/pod-product-compliance
Lightning Source LLC
Chambersburg PA
CBHW030139240426
43672CB00005B/197